Bill 'Swampy' Marsh—Chris Carter

Bill 'Swampy' Marsh is an award-winning writer/performer of stories, songs and plays. He spent most of his youth in rural south-western New South Wales. Bill was forced to give up any idea he had of a 'career' as a cricketer when a stint at agricultural college was curtailed because of illness, and so began his hobby of writing. After backpacking through three continents and working in the wine industry, his writing hobby blossomed into a career.

His first collection of short stories, *Beckom Pop. 64*, was published in 1988, his second, *Old Yanconian Daze*, in 1995 and his third, *Looking for Dad*, in 1998. During 1999 Bill released *Australia*, a CD of songs and stories. That was followed in 2002 by *A Drover's Wife* and *Glory, Glory—A Tribute to the Royal Flying Doctor Service*, in 2008. He has written soundtrack songs and music for the television documentaries *The Last Mail from Birdsville—The Story of Tom Kruse, Source to Sea—The Story of the Murray Riverboats* and the German travel documentary *Traumzeit auf dem Stuart Highway*.

Bill runs writing workshops in schools and communities and is employed part-time in the Adelaide Institute of TAFE's Professional Writing Unit. He has won and judged many nationwide short story writing and songwriting competitions and short film awards.

Great Australian Stories — Outback Towns and Pubs is a follow on from *Goldie* (2008) and is part of the very successful 'Great Australian' series: *More Great Australian Flying Doctor Stories* (2007), *Great Australian Railway Stories* (2005), *Great Australian Droving Stories* (2003), *Great Australian Shearing Stories* (2001) and *Great Australian Flying Doctor Stories* (1999).

More information about the author can be found at www.billswampymarsh.com

Great Australian Stories

OUTBACK TOWNS AND PUBS

Bill 'Swampy' Marsh

ABC
Books

The ABC 'Wave' device is a trademark of the
Australian Broadcasting Corporation and is used
under licence by HarperCollins*Publishers* Australia.

First published in Australia in 2009
by HarperCollins*Publishers* Australia Pty Limited
ABN 36 009 913 517
www.harpercollins.com.au

HarperCollins*Publishers*
Level 13, 201 Elizabeth Street, Sydney NSW 2000, Australia
Unit D1, 63 Apollo Drive, Rosedale, Auckland 0632, New Zealand
A 53, Sector 57, Noida, UP, India
1 London Bridge Street, London SE1 9GF, United Kingdom
2 Bloor Street East, 20th floor, Toronto, Ontario M4W 1A8, Canada
195 Broadway, New York NY 10007, USA

National Library of Australia Cataloguing-in-Publication data:

Marsh, Bill, 1950–
    Great Australian stories – outback towns and pubs / Bill 'Swampy' Marsh.
    ISBN: 978 0 7333 2452 9 (pbk.)
    Series: Great Australian stories.
    Country life – Australia – Anecdotes.
    Australia – Social life and customs.
305.9630994

Cover designed by Design by Committee
Typeset in 10/15pt Bookman by Kirby Jones
Printed and bound in Australia by McPhersons Printing Group
The papers used by HarperCollins in the manufacture of this book are a natural, recyclable
product made from wood grown in sustainable plantation forests. The fibre source and
manufacturing processes meet recognised international environmental standards, and carry
certification

Dedicated to—Richard Keith Norris
'There's a bridle hanging on the wall ...'

Contents

Acknowledgements

In memory of: George Bell, Ivan Boucher, Joe Connell, Delphine Elwin, Terry Golden, Rita Gorton, Gerd Janssen, Joan Langley, Fred Loveday, Len Opie, Norma Shelton, Keith 'Sooty' Johnson and Jan White.

Special thanks to: Jeff Richardson, Serpil Senelmis and the crew at Summer all Over 2007/8, Angie Nelson (Program Director, ABC Networked Local Radio), Nola and Mick Gallagher, Bruce Campbell AM MBE (Chairman—Australian Outback Development Consortium Ltd), Phil O'Brien (NT), Frank Partington (NSW), Ian Parkes and Graham and Val Cowell (WA), Dave Burge—Back of Beyond Tours (SA), Kalyna Micenko, Bob Daly, Neil McDougall (QLD) and Kevin 'Kev' Murphy—www.simpsondesert.fl.net.au

'Louth (NSW)' has been adapted from an interview by Jan Nary for Tradnow, (Dec '04) Publicist & Journalist for the National Folk Festival. Special thanks to Tonchi McIntosh and Bill Legg.

The story 'Tibooburra' has been adapted from the story 'Boots and Booze' in R. Paul Brady's book *Silver, Lead and Saltbush*.

The story 'Beckom—NSW' has been adapted from the story 'The Concert' which was published by Hudson Publishing in Bill 'Swampy' Marsh's first book, *Beckom Pop. 64*.

Contributors

Great Australian Stories—Outback Towns and Pubs is based on stories told to Bill Marsh by:

Bernard Arrantash

Garry & Barbara Barber

John Bartlett

R. Paul Brady

Dave Burge

Geoff Catterson

Tony Coen

Diane Cooper

Graham & Val Cowell

Bob Daly

Ian Doyle

Russ Elwin

Birdy & Gail Fahey

David Farquhar

Noel Fayers

Ted Gade

Nola & Mick Gallagher

Jack 'Goldie' Goldsmith

Bill 'Bones' Hanson

Tony Hayes

Dr Hans-U. Henschel

Stuart Johnson

Keith & Nancy Jubb

Jimmy Keyes

Ruth Ko

Susan Lang-Lemckert

Keith 'Bill' Langley

Bill Legg

Ian 'Mac'McKechnie

Cameron Marshall

Neil McDougall

John McInnis

Tonchi McIntosh

Noel McIntyre

Kalyna Micenko

Tony Misich

Bev Mizzen

Edna & Mick Monaghan

Kevin Murphy

Phil O'Brien

Ian Parkes

Frank Partington

Covey Penney

Fred Peter

Bruce & Bronwyn Power

Pol & Garry 'Gazza' Purcell

Bill Rawson

Paul & Ide Rush

Graeme Shelton

Frank Sontag

Doug Sprigg

Clyde Thomson

Graham Townsend

Arthur Webb

Graham Winterflood

Marjorie Woodhouse

... plus many, many more

Introduction

Over my lifetime I've lived and worked in many small towns. The dynamics are different to those of larger places. Everyone knows everyone and everyone knows what everyone's doing and, what's more, how they're doing it. To some, that may be a negative. To others it offers a network of support in times of need, on many levels. It also offers many stories—far too many to fit into one book. I remember, when I was a kid, one of the early television shows I used to watch was called *Naked City*, where the announcer started off by saying something like, 'There are eight million stories in the Naked City and this is just one of them'. Well, after spending the last couple of years visiting and contacting people in small towns across Australia the introduction to this book could well read 'There are ten people in this town and every one of them has eight million stories they could tell'.

So thanks to all those who offered to tell a story or two. I've also included a couple of favourites from my past books. Also, many thanks to those who have supported me along the way: my partner, Margaret Worth, who joined me on a trip from Adelaide to Wilcannia, up the Darling River, through Bourke, into south-western Queensland, via Hungerford (Pop. 6), then over into north-eastern South Australia and back down the Strezelecki Track, to Arkaroola, then home. For once, it was great to have someone come along who could help change flat tyres, drag dead snakes and kangaroos off the road and push the car out of bogs and ditches, as well as experience the wonderful characters, the beautiful Australian Outback landscapes and the heavenly starry nights. There's Chris Carter, photographer extraordinaire, the only person who manages to make me look half-intelligent; David Hanford who, at times, has kept the 'ship on the road'; David and

Christine Harris who, from my very first trip for my very first book, have always given me fifty dollars as a travelling emergency-relief fund. Many thanks, also, to those at ABC Books who have been such a great help throughout all my book adventures, in particular the amazingly supportive Brigitta Doyle. There's my family: my dear little mum, who has recently turned ninety-five and still has a far better memory than what I do, and my two sisters Barbara and Margaret who put me up and put up with me whenever I travel through their way.

A future venture is going to be a collection of outback school days stories. So, if you have a quirky, funny, sad, interesting, dramatic, entertaining story of your childhood school days in the bush, feel free to contact me via my website—www.billswampymarsh.com—before the cut-off date of June 2012. And please don't send any written material as the stories in my books are adapted from recorded interviews.

Anyhow, thanks for coming along on this journey of Great Australian Stories—Outback Towns and Pubs. Enjoy, and may there be many more.

The Beginning—Beckom—NSW

As a young kid I lived in a small town in the south-west of New South Wales called Beckom. Back then, Beckom only had a population of sixty-four. I know the exact number because whenever I had difficulty sleeping, instead of counting sheep, I'd systematically count the people in town. Of course, with so few of us, we didn't have a library and so books were hard to access. Instead, people told their stories. Some were true to life. Some were much larger than life. Still, tragic or humorous, tall or tender, it became the craft of the storyteller to try and make their tales as entertaining as possible. And that's how I grew up: sitting on the front step of the Beckom pub, waiting for Dad, and listening intently to those old masters, the likes of Bob O'Riley, Frank Langley, Terry Golden, Errol Foster and so forth, spin their yarns. So, I guess, my craft had its roots away back then. It's been my passion ever since, and I'm still learning.

To pick the moment when I came to realise this is hard to pinpoint. But, in a funny sort of way, I'd say it all began during a cold winter in about the late 1950s. Our school teacher was a man called Mr Donovan and so when Mum found out that amongst his wife's many fine qualities lurked a certified piano teacher, my fate was sealed. Week after week through black, frosted mornings I crunched my way to piano lessons—ears and fingers bitten from the savage cold—fumbling painfully for forgotten notes. Then, halfway through Lesson 10 of Practical Piano Grade 1, I was ordered to pull up my socks if I was going to play 'God Save the Queen' at the start of the town concert.

This was news to me.

Apparently a variety night was being organised to raise money to renovate Beckom's leaning corrugated-iron War Memorial Hall. All acts were invited to perform and one of Goodtime Charlie's singing mates, from his old 'Wild West' days, had agreed to be the star attraction. The star's name was Rocky Rivers. Rumour had it that someone had even heard him singing over the wireless on a Saturday Night Country and Western Show. So it was to be a big occasion. So big, in fact, that even our publican, Bluey Saunders, had agreed to close the pub for the night and set up a bar in the hall to ensure maximum attendance. Mrs Donovan was to be the MC as well as play a classical piano piece, sing an opera song and organise the yet non-existent school choir.

There were fifteen of us kids attending Beckom Public School, ranging from five to fourteen years old, all of us having been weathered by life's elements, even at our tender ages: washed by flood and rain, burnt by sun and bushfire, dried to the core by drought, frozen by frost, pitted in skin by dust and hail. But not a single one amongst us knew the first thing about the gentle art of song. Then, to make matters worse, Brownie, McCaughney and me bowed under pressure and agreed to perform the popular hit song of the day—'Donald, Where's Yer Trousers'.

Six weeks isn't a long time when even the basics have to be learned. The whole town suffered under a cloud of rehearsal fatigue. Sheep sales took a dive. The football team started its run of losses. Even the pub became a more contemplative place as men sipped on their schooners, their minds locked in silent rehearsal.

But above it all soared Mrs Donovan. She pranced and gesticulated, shouting advice and encouragement through her clattering false teeth at our retrogressive school choir. She galvanised the women of the area and had soon organised the printing and distribution of the advertising posters. She organised the cleaning, washing and decoration of the hall. She organised the mending and arrangement of the seating. She helped cook supper for the big night. Almost single-handedly she built the whole town up to fever pitch.

A certain quiet washed Beckom on the day of the concert. What wasn't learned by now would never be learned. All us 'entertainers' were in the hands of the unknown, treading on virgin ground. Butterflies fluttered within our stomachs, breeding rapidly as the day gathered pace. By tea time any desire for food had been replaced by a deep hollow feeling of tense sickness.

News spread that Rocky Rivers had arrived in town and was renewing his friendship with Goodtime Charlie over in the pub. Adults and school kids alike drifted in the vicinity, hoping to catch a glimpse of that star whose voice had floated over the airwaves. There was laughter from within the pub but no one dared enter, for we knew now, from personal experience, just how temperamental some entertainers could get before a big performance.

I stepped out onto the stage, mortified with panic, and sat at the piano. The hall was packed to the hilt with over sixty expectant people. The eyes of the world seemed upon me. Mrs Donovan stepped into the footlights and hushed the throng. 'I ask you all to be upstanding for "God Save the Queen". To lead you on piano we have Bill "Swampy" Marsh.'

I somehow managed the opening chord, then my fingers refused to move. They dangled over the piano as strung skeletons, mesmerised by the daunting task before them—ten complete strangers to my body. Mrs Donovan began singing. The audience followed suit. Then, mid-anthem, my fingers inexplicably reared and began to first trot, then to canter over the keyboard. Two-thirds through I'd caught up with the cacophony of voices surrounding me. But, by now, my momentum was such that I galloped past them as if they were standing still, leaving them in my dust. I'd finished playing, stood up, and was heading off stage even before the audience had entered the last line.

'And now the school choir to enchant you with "Greensleeves".

I felt safer in a crowd of my own kind. United against a common foe—the audience—we stumbled on stage to take up our appointed positions. Mrs Donovan signalled our start and we carried the song off, sounding more like a lost flock of Border Leicesters than an enchanting choral group.

But we survived.

'And to complete the school's performance for tonight we have the "Three Likely Lads" with their rendition of "Donald, Where's Your Trousers".'

The instant we walked out on stage we knew it was a mistake. Dressed in mock kilts that'd been shaped from older sisters' skirts, and with sporrans semi-fashioned from recently caught rabbits' pelts, the wolf whistles and crude remarks echoed the tin hall. Brownie wet himself. McCaughney opened his mouth but not a word came out. So it was left to me, the veteran of 'God Save the Queen' and 'Greensleeves', and I fled through the song like a chipmunk on fire before diving for the security of back stage, leaving my mates, wet and wordless, to sort out their own fates.

It was then Mum's turn to grace the footlights. Mum'd dreamed of being a great performer all her life; reading all the entertainment magazines and singing along with the tunes on the wireless. But, unfortunately, the transition from kitchen to stage proved too difficult a hurdle for that lady of dreams, upon that icy winter's night, and she fainted in front of a packed house.

Things started to improve after Mum was aided off stage, as each performer learned the necessary survival skills from the previous act's mistakes. Porky Squealer gave us a grand performance of pig impersonations. From Landrace sow through to Wessex Saddleback boar he had their 'oinking' sounds down to perfection. Big Red Brewster stepped up and gave an unbelievable darts display whereupon, landing his first dart in the bullseye, his second and third darts lodged themselves tight beside the first. And all from a distance of five paces.

At Doctor Granger's command, Buster, the town's adopted dog, twice entered the audience to return on stage carrying a shoe between his teeth. The third time into the hall, Buster returned with a pair of lady's knickers. This brought the house down and sent eyes darting in all directions in search of the owner. Bluey Saunders took time off from behind the bar to give a rousing rendition of 'The Man from Beckom'. He'd changed the town's

The Belles of Beckom—The Marsh Collection

name from 'Ironbark' which did nothing for the rhyming of the poem but the sentiment remained.

Following Bluey came Mrs Donovan. She broached the piano like she was stalking a stray wether. She sat, raised her hands ready for attack, then crashed, banged and walloped her way through a frenzied piano piece written by a German named Beethoven. She followed that up with a song from an Italian opera. No one understood the words but, still, she was given a standing ovation and we suffered through the encore, knowing that this night wouldn't have happened but for her efforts. She deserved all our applause, and more.

Mrs McCaughney then appeared, unannounced, to perform a version of the 'Dance of the Seven Veils'. As the women muttered their misgivings, the cheering and foot-stamping from around the bar raised such a dust storm that I remained only to dream of the nakedness I imagined behind those light, floating, coloured veils.

Amid this scene of careless profusion was helped the star of the show, Rocky Rivers. Dad propped the beer-sodden body upon a stool, guitar limply hanging in hand. Empty stool to his side. As we looked towards that derelict man—this star of wireless—our whole world stopped spinning. He lifted his head as if by winch, gazed at us as though we were miles away, somewhere over near Ariah Park. His bloodshot eyes rolled in their sockets. As we waited for his first utterance you could've heard a feather drop. We sat, frightened, quivering at this drunken star's mercy.

'Wheeeeersh ssme ol' mate ssCharlie?'

Dad rushed out the back to get Goodtime Charlie out of the dunny while Rocky Rivers struggled to get some focus on his audience. We, in turn, sat before him, mouths agape. Seconds passed like minutes until Dad and Bluey returned with Goodtime Charlie and helped him onto the vacant stool on stage. Rocky Rivers placed a loving arm around his mate and announced, 'Shemeee 'n' Charl' wou' like ter ssshing yer some sssshongs.'

Then he lifted his guitar. Started a slow strum. His mouth opened and out fell a pure velvet voice … 'There's a bridle hanging on the wall …'

Goodtime Charlie, as if called to heel by his mate's voice, raised his head. His ears pricked. His eyes began to sparkle. Then he smiled and he joined in as if singing a diamond hymn. Apprehension washed from our hearts. They sang songs of horses, which brought the smell of sweated flanks to the nostrils. Songs of flood and drought. Songs torn out of blistered and bloodied hands. Songs of the raw earth being cracked by disc-ploughs. Songs that'd erupted from deep within working-men's souls. They sang songs of love that made the men look down at their riding boots and the women fumble for their handkerchiefs.

To this glorious sound, my leaden eyes fell into slumber. I was lifted, carried, and placed onto the back seat of our chilly car. Tightly wrapped in a blanket, I dreamed I was a singer, a storyteller, travelling the country; bringing hope to the despairing, laughter to the sad, love to the lonely. Then I dreamed that I had to play 'God Save the Queen' before every performance.

Aramac—Qld

Aramac's about 100 miles north-east of Longreach; sort of in the south-west of Queensland, you could say. It was mentioned in your railway book, where the train from Aramac was so slow on its trip down the forty-odd mile of track to Barcaldine that, when the train driver stopped and asked a swaggie if he wanted a lift, the swaggie replied to the train driver, 'No thanks, mate, I'm in too much of a hurry.' So that's the sort of place it is. Nice and slow.

Mind you, Aramac was one of the first towns out this way. A feller called William Landsborough and another feller called Nat Buchanan came through here in the late 1850s, when they were trying to find the lost explorer Ludwig Leichhardt. Oh, he was always getting lost, was Leichhardt. As mad as a hatter. Used to go charging around the camp swishing an old army sabre, with his saddle on his head as a helmet and wearing his saddle bags as if they was armour. As blind as a bat too, they say, so no wonder he kept getting lost. Oh, and another interesting thing about Aramac, that most people wouldn't know, is how it got its name. See, initially, Landsborough named the local creek after the first Premier of Queensland, R.R. McKenzie. So it was known as the R.R. Mac Creek. Then, over time, with lazy speech and all that, it got turned into Aramac—a.r.a.m.a.c. Not too many people know that.

So there you go. I thought that might be of interest. Then, as time went by, Aramac turned into a big wool-producing area. There was a station about forty mile out of town, called Bowen Downs, and in its heyday they shore something like 360,000 sheep on the property. Actually, I believe it was the biggest station in the world, back in those days, and during the season it employed over 100 shearers; meaning it had about 100 stands. So, it was a pretty big operation.

But anyway, my story's got nothing to do with any of that because, see, in the 1950s people called Toby and Ruby Langdon kept the Marathon Hotel in Aramac. Then there was also a well-known local character who everyone knew as 'old Jack'. At that time, old Jack was looking after a small place about twenty mile from town and he had this old model car. Now, I'm not too sure what make the car was but every couple of weeks old Jack would drive this thing into Aramac to collect all the supplies and things he needed till the next time he came to town. Then after he'd done that he'd drive down to the Marathon Hotel for a few grogs before he headed off, back home. He enjoyed a drink.

So on this day, after collecting whatever stores he needed, old Jack drove his car down to the Marathon Hotel. It was about 3 o'clock in the afternoon and he pulled in, alongside the hotel, off the street, into the vacant area used for parking. He got out and he went into the pub for a few drinks. Toby was behind the bar this particular day. This is Toby Langdon.

'Give us a beer, Toby.'

'Yeah, Jack.'

Aramac's about a hundred miles north-east of Longreach
—The Hansford Collection

Toby poured a beer. 'Here yer go.'

'Thanks.'

'So how's things, Jack?'

'Not bad.'

And so, while old Jack downed a few ales, they started having a bit of a chat about this, that and the weather and how damn lucky they were to be living in a nice quiet place like Aramac, where everyone got along pretty well and there was none of that terrible crime you read about happening in so many other places. There was no disagreement over that and so old Jack decided to have a few more ales to confirm it. But after a couple more hours, Toby could see that if the old feller was going to get home that night he'd better not serve him any more grog.

'I reckon that's about enough, ay, Jack?'

'Yeah, okay then,' said old Jack. 'I gotta be goin' anyway.'

So Jack left the bar. By now he's pretty unsteady on his feet so, just in case, Toby followed the old feller out of the bar. Then as old Jack made his way to the side of the hotel, where he'd parked his car, Toby stood at the top of the steps, just to keep an eye on him.

'See yer later,' old Jack called out to Toby. 'I'll be okay from here.'

Then, to Toby's surprise, instead of getting in the front seat of the car to drive off, old Jack opened the back door and he climbed in there.

Wonder what's going on 'ere, thought Toby. Must be checkin' in the back of the car to make sure he's got everything he needs till he comes back into Aramac, again.

Anyhow, old Jack kept fumbling about in the back of the car, searching here, there and everywhere. Then, when he looked up and saw Toby still standing on the step of the pub, old Jack reached over and opened the car door and he called out, 'Hey, Toby, I thought we said that these Aramac people were supposed'ta be honest. Well they're bloody well not, 'cause some bugger's gone 'n' pinched me bloody steerin' wheel.'

Arkaroola Village—SA

We don't actually have a street address up here at Arkaroola Village. We're only a small place, in the far northern Flinders Ranges of South Australia, and, even though we're about 400 kilometres north of Port Augusta, that's where our post box is. And the mail still gets through most times, so it's not too bad.

Now, Arkaroola was taken up by the Greenwood family, back in 1937, as a sheep station. That was fairly late as far as this area goes, considering how the earliest station was taken up in 1856. But, because of its geological diversity, Sir Douglas Mawson, who you may have heard of, had been coming here since the very early 1900s and he always made a point of bringing his students along. So my father, Reg Sprigg, first came up here as a geology student under Mawson. Actually, it was within weeks of the station starting up.

But Arkaroola was never profitable as a sheep station. It was virtually 610 square kilometres of wilderness country and, with it being so rugged, they could never run more than 3000 head of sheep, which would hardly pay one person's wage. So it was only, at best, a subsistence sheep station. But because the area was so untouched and isolated, a certain climate vegetation group remained here, which doesn't really exist anywhere else; a vegetation group dating back to the Pleistocene era. Now, the Pleistocene era's an era that ended about 15,000 years ago, when we had a much wetter climate, probably in the order of about a metre of rain per year. To give you some idea, we now have an average rainfall of, supposedly, six inches or 150 millimetres, though, because we're in a ten-year drought, we don't even get that.

So there was this virtually untouched country, which wasn't much use to anyone other than geologists and botanists and so,

12

Doug Sprigg at Arkaroola Village—The Marsh Collection

when it came up on the market, Dad approached the South Australian government with the suggestion that Arkaroola should have a national park. They weren't too keen on that idea. But he kept persisting, so much so they finally said, 'Well if you feel so strongly about it, do it yourself.' So he did. Dad bought the property. I think it was supposed to be a Christmas present for my mother, Griselda, but he wasn't game enough to tell her— well, not for a couple of months at least. That was at the end of 1967 and the following year Arkaroola started up as a fauna and flora reserve, with the aim of tourism supplying the money to run the various environmental programs we have.

But before my parents moved up here permanently, in about 1980, Dad was still doing geophysical work for various companies, particularly Beach Petroleum, a company he started. Now, Dad believed very strongly that there were some places where you just didn't go looking for oil. The thinking behind that was: if you don't go looking, you don't find it and so you don't make a mess of it. With that philosophy in mind he started the

Australian Petroleum Exploration Association and, as head of that, he instigated a no-go zone for the Great Barrier Reef. Because, you know, if there was an oil spill on the Barrier Reef it'd be catastrophic. The same goes for Arkaroola; it's an area that's too diverse geologically and botanically to mess up with mining. It's that precious.

Well, for a start, Arkaroola Village itself is built on sedimentary sea beds. Then just to the east we've got glacial tillites, which are the remains from a global ice age dating back 650–700 million years. If you say it quickly you don't quite comprehend it, do you? A little further east we've got volcanic lavas, which were pushed up between Australia and Canada and North America in a continental break-up. That happened during a time that well preceded Gondwanaland, which we've only recently broken up from. When I say 'recently', I'm talking about 40,000 million years ago.

Then out to the north, about four kilometres, you go into the deep crustal granites and that's rock which is around 1600 million years old. It's granites that were formed about ten kilometres underground and when they were uplifted they pushed the sediments back, hence the rugged mountain landscape around us. Then you go out to the hot springs. They're still quite radioactive. Actually, on the Mawson Plateau, just north of the Ridge Top area, there's a big crust of young granites—only 440 million years old—which are also quite radioactive.

So that's a quick rundown on the landscapes of Arkaroola. Then I guess the indoors focal point might be the Pick and Shovel lounge-bar. You don't have to drink alcohol. There's also coffee and tea or whatever. But it's one of those places where people gather of an evening and trade experiences, not just about Arkaroola but about their travels in general. And we do have a wide variety of visitors. We get people coming from all over the world, both the older people and the young backpackers. Then there's the grey nomads, as they're called these days. We also have people like Ian Plimer, a professor of mining geology at

Adelaide University. Ian often holds, sort of, bar-room science classes, where he plays the devil's advocate, because his take on it is that science is a revolving dynamic and if you believe implicitly then it's not science. Ian comes up on a regular basis, along with some of his students, and he's a great character.

Dick Smith's also been here a few times and though he's not a drinker, he's certainly an incredibly social person who's always willing to throw in an opinion. He's great, and so passionate about Australia. Then you get the mining people who are exploring in the area. The Dog Fence contractors also come in and they're always ready to put another side to things. The Dog Fence is about fifty kilometres east of Arkaroola and it's an extremely difficult bit of the fence to maintain because it runs along the edge of Lake Frome and the salt rusts out the netting. The fence also runs through Lake Callabonna, which is at the centre of the diprotodon fossil discovery. The diprotodon were mega fauna, like giant emus and giant kangaroos but still from the same sort of families. They're so well preserved out there that I joke how, even though the diprotodons died when the lake dried up around 15,000 years ago they were so well preserved that they could tell they'd had their last meal at McDonalds. Only joking, of course, but some people fall for it.

So all sorts of stories get related in the Pick and Shovel, both big and small, serious and not so serious. And, with our tyranny of distance—where there's such long distances to travel—of course, the first place a weary traveller goes is to the nearest bar, or watering hole, as we Australians call it. It's a place to meet and interact with a variety of people who hold a variety of opinions, plus it's a place that breaks down barriers. And that's what it's all about.

Barton—SA

Now Barton's an interesting little place. Ever heard of it? Not many have. It's away out on the Nullarbor, in South Australia, at the start of the world's longest straight stretch of railway track, leading from there to eternity then further on to Kalgoorlie, in Western Australia. There's bugger-all there these days apart from flies and a fluctuating population of somewhere between one and ten, and that's counting the wild horses and stray camels. Even for the most imaginative of real estate agents the best that could be said about the place is that it's 'nestled comfortably among endless rolling red sandhills'. Beyond that, you'd be scratching.

Anyhow, back a few years the railways scaled down and there was an old German bloke, by the name of Ziggie, who worked as a fettler out there. With all the kerfuffle, Ziggie decided to chuck it in after thirty years on the job. But instead of retiring to the Big Smoke of Port Augusta, like the rest of the workers out that way tended to do, he thought, 'Vell, bugger it. I haft seven dogs, no-vere to go. Zo as-t long as-t zee Tea an' Sugar Train still delivers vater an' supplies, I'll stay in zee Barton.' Ziggie loved his dogs.

The trouble was that he and the dogs had been left with no place to live and so for the next couple of years he wandered up and down the track picking up the sleepers that had been cast aside during track maintenance. And out of those he built a huge three-roomed bunker, complete with a patio, where he and his dogs could sit and sip on their Milo and watch the sun set over the endlessly rolling sandhills. Now you may think that the mention of Ziggie sipping on Milo instead of a gin and tonic or a cold beer was a slip of the tongue. But it wasn't. Ziggie drank nothing but Milo. In actual fact, his staple diet was Milo, oranges, potatoes and, as the strong rumour had it, dog food. Yep, you heard it right ... Milo, oranges, potatoes and dog food for breakfast, dinner and tea, and a good brand it was too.

So Ziggie settled down to life at Barton and, believe me, he just happened to be one of the best informed individuals that you're ever likely to meet. As you might imagine, there wasn't too much else for him to do out there except listen to his short-wave radio. So Ziggie got to know more about the goings-on of the world than anyone I've known. What's more, he had an opinion on any subject, and if he didn't he'd soon make one up.

So it was a pretty solitary affair out at Barton which, in turn, caused the few Bartonites who also lived there to get extremely suspicious when a blow-in lobbed in town. Not that many did, mind you. Maybe one or two each decade or so. But that was just enough for the locals, including Ziggie, to have formed the solid opinion that the rest of the world was inhabited by weirdos. And so it was when one of the locals wandered out at the crack of dawn one day and discovered that some bloke, a blow-in, had appeared from God-knows-where in the middle of the night and had been bowled over by the Tea and Sugar Train as it was pulling into the siding. The evidence was right there for all to see. There was this complete stranger, sprawled under the front of the train, out to the world, comatose in fact, with his head split open, stinking of grog and looking at death's door.

'Typical, ay?' one Bartonite muttered, to which there was total agreement.

Of course, the train driver was upset. But as he said, 'How the hell could I have bowled someone over when the train only travels at snail's pace?' And there were those who understood what he was on about. See, it'd been rumoured that the driver of the Tea and Sugar Train was given a calendar, rather than a timetable, upon departure from Port Augusta because it could never be guaranteed as to what actual time of the day he arrived at Kalgoorlie, it was more like what month of the year it was.

Anyhow, naturally, not long after Ziggie and his dogs arrived upon the scene of the accident, Ziggie had come up with his own theory. He reckoned that the train hadn't hit the blow-in but that

The Tea and Sugar Train arrives—The Hansford Collection

the bloke had been so pissed, when he'd staggered out of the sandhills at some ungodly hour of the night, he'd inadvertently walked headlong into the stationary train. Crack! Split his head open and down he'd gone like a sack of spuds, right under the front wheels, and hadn't moved a muscle since.

But, theory or no theory, the bloke was in a bad way and so someone got in touch with the Flying Doctor Service at Port Augusta. 'We'll be there in an hour,' they said, and then, while they were waiting for the RFDS plane to arrive, a healthy discussion raged as to why the hell the blow-in had been wandering out in the desert in the first place. And that debate continued right up until the RFDS plane landed and a hold was put on proceedings while a ute was sent out to pick up the doctor and the nurse.

It was during this brief respite that Ziggie took on the responsibility of making a bush stretcher. The reasoning behind that was to save precious time so the blow-in could be placed into the back of the ute as soon as the doctor had checked him over. Ziggie slung a bit of canvas around a couple of bits of gidgee then rolled the unconscious blow-in onto the stretcher.

When the doctor arrived he went through the full medical procedure. 'This bloke's in an extremely critical condition,' he concluded. 'So fellers, when you pick up the stretcher, take it nice and easy.'

Now, constructing a house out of railway sleepers may have been one of Ziggie's fortes but making a bush stretcher out of a strip of canvas and a couple of bits of gidgee apparently wasn't. Because, when they lifted the stretcher, the canvas gave way and the blow-in fell straight through and hit his head on the railway track with an almighty thud.

'Holy Jesus,' someone said, 'we've killed him fer sure.'

But almost before those words had been spoken, the blow-in miraculously snapped back into consciousness. What's more, to everyone's surprise, particularly the doctor's, he sat bolt upright. He took one look at the menagerie of faces gawking down at him, then he had a quick glance out at the endlessly rolling red sandhills.

'Where the bloody hell am I?' he squawked.

'Barton,' came the reply, at which the blow-in got up, shook his head and staggered off down the track, leaving the doctor mystified and the locals only more reassured as to the weirdness of mankind in the outside world. Of course, that included Ziggie and his seven dogs who wandered back home to tuck into a nice hearty breakfast.

Beaudesert—Qld

I've never done anything like this before but I think that some of my stories should be told. That's the way it was in my family. Stories were always passed along. There's one I'm currently following up about my uncle who was a horse dealer and he used to catch a train up to Toowoomba where he'd buy fifty horses or so at the auctions there. And if there wasn't a broken-in horse in amongst them he'd break one in, on the spot, then he'd drive these fifty or so horses all the way back to Beaudesert on his own. *On his own.* So that's just one little story but I need to get a bit more information on that because I've often wondered how the hell he could've managed fifty horses, all by himself.

But this story's just a bit of a yarn about my brother and I. It happened out at a place called Beaudesert, which is in the hinterland, behind the Gold Coast. Beaudesert actually got its name from Beau Desert Station, which was established there back in the 1840s. It's a big farming region—dairy and beef, mainly, these days—set in the valley, near the Logan River. But our family had some property out that way. Now I'm talking back in the early 1950s, probably about '52 or '53. A long time ago when Beaudesert was a much smaller place than what it is now. Anyhow, the brother and I had been out to one of our family properties, a couple of hours out from Beaudesert, and we were heading home in an old Jeep. We're driving along and we come across this big carpet snake, stretched out across the road. Huge it was, absolutely huge.

'Here's a go,' says my brother and he jumped out and he caught the snake and he stuffed it into a hessian bag, then he threw it into the back of the Jeep and we continued on our way. When we arrived in Beaudesert we had to drive past the Logan-Albert Hotel. We were well known in the establishment so it was natural that we'd call in to have a couple of beers. You know, just to break the journey.

Anyhow, we walked into the pub. To set the scene, it was a Saturday afternoon and the place was absolutely chockers. A real hive of activity. There's SP bookies, the lot. Mind you, it was an illegal operation to run the SP back then. But they were there anyway and they're doing a roaring trade. Now, with the place being so packed, you virtually had to push and shove your way through the crowd just to get to order a drink. There were two or three barmaids working behind the bar. Not bad lookers either, I might add.

'This's no good,' I said to the brother.

'Hang on a tick,' he says, 'I'll sort this out,' and he disappeared.

Actually, I was hoping he wasn't going to do what I was thinking he was about to do. But, anyway, he did. He appeared back inside with the hessian bag. Now, you really need a cartoonist to draw this but, the instant someone shouted

'We came across this big carpet snake ... Huge it was; absolutely huge'
—The Hansford Collection

'Snake!', blokes scattered in all directions. Oh, there were blokes up on top of the bar, blokes up on top of the tables; on top of chairs. Blokes diving out windows. Blokes trying to scramble out the doors. 'Snake!' and blokes just went everywhere. Mind you, some of these fellers were real tough—as tough as nails—you know, men, some as large as brick shithouses. But it didn't matter. They scattered anyway.

'What's going on? What's going on?' the barmaids started calling out from behind the bar.

So my brother picked up the snake. 'Here,' he said, 'this's what's going on,' and he dropped it over their side of the bar.

Well, these barmaids almost shit themselves. They took off into the storeroom and you could've just about heard their screams over on the Gold Coast. The only trouble was that the snake must've been attracted by their high-pitched squeals because it took off after the barmaids. It followed them. Hot on their heels. By the time my brother had jumped over the bar, the snake was already three feet under the door of the storeroom. Anyhow, he managed to drag the thing back just before it completely disappeared in with the barmaids. So then he stuffed it back in the hessian bag, took it outside, and dumped it in the back of the Jeep.

The bar area was pretty clear by then. But we were none too popular. We'd upset the barmaids. The drinkers were peeved about having their Saturday afternoon, down the pub, disturbed. Then there was the bookies. They'd lost a lot of business because, by the time things had returned to normal, the race meeting at Eagle Farm was well and truly over. So, all in all, things weren't feeling that comfortable. In fact, I'm thinking now, it was just as well that everyone around the place knew that my brother was a Queensland amateur champion boxer or otherwise it could've easily turned nasty. So, yes, we weren't the most popular couple of blokes around Beaudesert there for a while.

Beltana—SA

Now I might've already told you this one. It's about Beltana. Beltana doesn't operate as an actual town these days, it's what's called a 'heritage town' now. It's a pretty place, right on the banks of the Warrioota Creek, in the Flinders Ranges area of South Australia. It was first surveyed way back in the early 1860s. Then in the mid-1860s Thomas Elder and Samuel Stuckey set up the Beltana Pastoral Company and they imported 100 camels, along with their Afghan drivers. They were unloaded here, at the wharf in Port Augusta, then they walked the 150 mile or so up to Beltana. And those Afghanis and their camels were used for many, many years as the main source of transporting supplies, food and passengers all throughout the Simpson Desert area.

Then in the late 1860s they discovered copper near Beltana and the population shot up to around 500. But like most of the copper mines in the Flinders, the seams were very narrow and vertical and in them days they didn't have the technology to drill vertically to any great depth. Plus, they struck water so then the whole mining thing collapsed. So it wasn't till they set up an operations centre for the Overland Telegraph Line that Beltana came back to life. Actually, the first telephone contact reached Beltana in 1874. Then in the early 1880s, the narrow gauge railway line followed the Overland Telegraph Line through and, during the war in particular, Beltana became a very busy place. In fact, at one stage there was up to sixty-four trains a week—mostly troop trains—going through from Adelaide, up to Alice Springs, then on to Darwin by road. Oh, and I must also add that, around the late 1800s or early 1900s, John Flynn set up a post for the Australian Inland Mission at Beltana and the building—the Smith of Dunesk

Mission—still exists today. So Beltana's got a decent amount of history behind it, which is why it's been designated as a 'heritage town'.

But through all its ups and downs, like many of these little places, Beltana still hung onto the usual establishments, like a bakery, a shop and a pub. Now the pub was called the Royal Victoria Hotel. It was quite a substantial, solid brick building and I suspect—though I can't be a hundred percent sure—it was built of the local stone from the Warrioota Creek. It was a beautiful old building, and in the early days it seemed that the proprietors would just stay for a year or two before they'd leave. Then in 1942 a feller called Lance Nicholls purchased the pub and he remained the publican till he closed it in 1958. Actually, Lance wasn't only just the publican at Beltana, he also took on a host of other jobs including that of the grave digger; you know, the undertaker. So old Lance was just about everything.

We lived at Quorn in them days. My father, Ted Gade, had transferred from BHP in Whyalla and he went to Quorn and got a job with the Commonwealth Railways and he eventually became a loco-engine driver. Now, fortunately, as part of my life as a young feller, at times I used to travel with my father on the old steam engines through to Alice Springs and back, which was absolutely illegal. And it was on one of these trips that we were coming south with a goods train. It was the Christmas Eve day of 1955 and I can't remember the exact course of things—possibly it was a washaway—but, whatever the problem was, it held the train up and Dad and his crew were told that they couldn't proceed from Beltana for at least a day-and-a-half or two days. Of course, the train crew was pretty upset about this because they all wanted to spend Christmas Eve and Christmas Day at home with their families.

Anyhow, Dad and one of the firemen, Laurie Payne, decided to go over to see if old Lance would put on a Christmas dinner for the train crew. So, with me tagging along, they went over to the Royal Victoria and Lance said, 'No, sorry. It's not worth puttin' on a dinner fer just a few people.'

So that was it. But then, just as we were about to leave, old Lance must've had second thoughts because he said, 'Look, hang on a bit. Tell yer what, if yer'd like ter do a little job for me, I'll do somethin' about puttin' on a Christmas dinner for the train crew.'

'Yeah, that's fine,' Dad said. 'What do yer want us to do?'

Lance said, 'I've got a kerosene fridge that needs movin'.'

Now, if you remember, those bloody kerosene fridges—say a Charles Hope for argument's sake—they were very, very heavy things. But, of course, with a Christmas dinner in the offing, Dad and Payney didn't even blink. 'Yeah,' they said, 'that'd be no problem, Lance, no problem at all.'

'Okay then,' says Lance, 'come over tomorra' mornin' 'n' we'll move this fridge then I'll sort yers all out with a nice Christmas dinner.'

So Dad, Payney and me, we turned up at the pub the following morning. I was only about thirteen back then so I was too small to help move this heavy fridge. I just hung around and watched. But unbeknown to both myself and Payney, old Lance happened to have had a wooden leg and a glass eye. Yes, both a wooden leg and a glass eye. Anyway, they've got this bloody fridge and they were moving it from one room to another. Then, at one point, someone moved the thing one way and the other feller moved it the other way and poor old Lance got jammed up in the doorway. 'Crunch.' And with the force of it, old Lance's glass eye shot out on the floor then, as he tried to reach down to pick it up, his wooden leg fell off.

Well I was stunned at the sight of all this and so must've been Payney because I remember him looking absolutely aghast and calling out to Dad. 'Jesus Christ, Ted,' he said, 'I've never seen a man fall to pieces so quick in all me life.'

Birdsville—Qld

The township of Birdsville, in the far south-west of Queensland, is on the edge of the Simpson Desert. The Diamantina River runs just to the east. Well, in actual fact, it hardly runs at all. It's usually dry. So it's a pretty remote sort of location. Even Charles Sturt, when he came through, back in the mid-1840s, described it as being, and I quote, 'a desperate region having no parallel on earth'.

It wasn't until the 1880s, when they began moving cattle through the Channel Country and down the Birdsville Track to the railhead at Marree, that Birdsville came to life. Being so close to the South Australian border the Queensland government set up a Customs House and pretty soon Birdsville had something like three pubs, a couple of general stores, a doctor, a bank, a police station; just about everything a town of around 3000 people and a few billions of flies could want for. But, after Federation, when interstate customs collection was abolished, just about everyone left, either through lack of work and/or the living conditions were too harsh.

My first contact with Birdsville was in 1963 when I ran the administration for the Compagnie Generale de Geophysique (CGG) during the construction of the French Line. The French Line was a rough sort of track that we built across the Simpson Desert, which was used for the seismic work we were doing. By then the population of Birdsville had shrunk to eight whites and sixty-three blacks. But, of course, a pub remained. Back then it just had a small bar. There was only one narrow entrance. The room to the right, as you went in the front door, was what's called the Drunk's Tank. I'll tell you more about that later. Out the back were six rooms for accommodation. The existing western verandah faced the airstrip and from the comfort of a chair, say, placed there for the purpose of a twilight drink, across the way was the combined post office and police station.

Now for a brief run-down of the police station because it's crucial to this story. Birdsville lockup consisted of only two cells, whose doors had been removed so that the occupants could come and go during their wait for the next visit of the circuit judge, which could be anything up to six weeks. You might think that's a bit lax but, considering how Birdsville's situated at the apex of the Simpson Desert and the Birdsville Track, even the dumbest of criminals would've realised that they'd reached the end of the line, in about every respect, and escape was out of the question.

So now may I introduce the leading character in this particular story—the legendary Police Sergeant Eric Sammon; also known as 'Lord of the Lockup', plus a few more colourfully descriptive titles, the vast majority of which aren't printable. Eric Sammon ran the one-man police station. His word was law in this, the second largest police district in Queensland. Eric was into everything that moved. Anyone with business in Birdsville had to deal with Eric at some stage or other because, other than being the local copper, he also held all the State and Federal government agencies like the post office and Customs as well as the fuel distributorship and the Trans-Australia Airlines agency.

In my capacity as Admin Officer for the CGG party, every time I came into the airstrip to load or offload gear, grog, mail and personnel, I had to deal with Eric. And as he would so proudly boast, 'I've got nineteen emoluments 'n' I earn more than Bischoff.' Bischoff being the Queensland Police Commissioner. Now, an emolument is a small government payment, or stipend, that's given out for doing certain things like being the Customs Officer. Then he'd receive an emolument for the post office. He also had one for being the jailer and probably one for airport fuel. I don't know what the others were. It'd be interesting to know. Oh, he probably looked after the cemetery as well. Though, and I must add that, to his credit, Eric also took on many honorary community jobs such as being an office-bearer for both the Birdsville and Bedourie Race Clubs. But who knows what went

The Birdsville Hotel—The Carter Collection

on with those. Not me. So these emoluments were government payments and no one had as many as Eric, not even his boss, Police Commissioner Bischoff, who, coincidentally, not only hired Sammon but was also responsible for hiring that fellow, Lewis, who, later on, got caught up in the Fitzgerald Inquiry into police corruption in Queensland.

But when I first came to Birdsville it was the advent of late-night closing in Queensland, which only allowed drinkers to stay on a licensed premises till 11 pm. And on this particular evening a bunch of us CGG fellows were enjoying a few quiet drinks in the bar. Other than us there was the publican, Norm Portch, and his wife, Elva, two other guests and Eric Sammon's wife, Joan. Then out of the blue, Eric arrives and issues a warning to just the two women: Elva and his own wife, Joan. 'If you two aren't out by eleven o'clock closing I'll come back 'n' arrest you.'

And he did. Come eleven o'clock, Eric returns and says to Elva and Joan, 'That's it. You two, you're off.'

Now, he didn't arrest the publican, Norm. He didn't arrest Norm's two guests. He didn't arrest us, maybe because whenever we were in town the local economy was given a huge boost. He only arrested the two women—Elva, Norm's wife, and his own wife, Joan. Naturally, I was horrified. So was everyone else, apart from Norm, that is, and the two women. The two women hardly seemed concerned at all. 'Okay,' they said and off they went.

I only found out later that this sort of thing happened on a regular basis and it all had to do with Eric lining his pockets through emoluments. See, to all intents and purposes—to the letter of the law—Eric had arrested two people, which allowed him to receive an emolument for having to look after the prisoners till the circuit judge came around. Seeing they were women, he may've even got a bit more. Meanwhile, he'd also get a payment for having to buy food for the two prisoners. But, without any doors on the cell, these women were free to come and go. In this case, one went back to work at the pub while the other one went back to her normal home duties, while she was also being paid to cook for two prisoners plus her husband, the policeman, who was being paid to guard them both. Six weeks later, along comes the circuit judge, they go up before him, they're let off with a warning or something, and Eric pockets all the dough.

So there you go, that's one story stemming from the Birdsville pub and I'm yet to meet anyone who'd disagree with anything I said about Eric Sammon. Then there's just another quick story. Now, remember when I mentioned that the Drunk's Tank was the room to the right as you went in the front door. Every outback pub had a Drunk's Tank. It was where the publican put the blokes after they'd blown their money. Like, take a shearer for example, he might've worked, like we did, for three months straight so he arrives in the pub with a significant cheque and, when he's done the lot on grog and food and can't afford the accommodation, the publican puts him in the Drunk's Tank, to sleep there. Then, when he's right in the morning, off he'll go back out to the next shed or wherever. So that's how it worked.

Anyhow, a bunch of us arrived in Birdsville. We'd been three months in the desert and we were due to catch the plane out to

Brisbane the next morning. So we were in transit. We'd had a few beers in the pub and Norm said, 'Look fellers, I'll just put you in the Drunk's Tank for the night so it won't cost you anything.'

Now, the Drunk's Tank at the Birdsville pub had about fifteen or so single beds, all lined up. Iron framed. Very simple, no sheets, just a single blanket and a very thin, ungenerous mattress. It would've been about September so it's around 35 degrees. Anyhow, it was 8 o'clock in the morning and we were still blissfully sleeping things off. And the funny thing about it was that none of us even heard the noise. But I clearly remember waking up and looking out through my toes and there's the entire population of Birdsville, sixty-three Aborigines and eight whites, looking in from the main street, sniggering at us. For a moment I wondered what the hell was going on, then I realised that the front wall of the pub had somehow fallen out into the street. And there we were, completely exposed. And no one had pushed it. No one did anything. The whole wall just fell outwards. Thankfully.

Blighty—NSW

The village of Blighty is located in the southern Riverina roughly halfway between Deniliquin and Finley. I'm not too sure of its exact history, but there used to be three old sheep stations in the area that were cut up for Soldier Settlement, after World War I. So I imagine that Blighty grew out of that. It only consisted of a general store, post office, a garage and a pub, though I do know— through extensive research—that the Blighty Hotel was made from local mud brick, around 1941/42. Then, as far as the store goes, by the time of this story, in the 1970s, it was owned and run by Gerald and Florence McMillan, or Gerry and Flow as they were better known.

Now, if you called in at the store, say, anytime after 2.30 pm, the first thing Gerry would say was, 'Are you goin' to the pub?'

Of course, the answer would be, 'Is the Pope a Catholic?'

Then he'd say, 'Well, set one up for me. I'll be over soon.'

So you'd go over to the pub and, not long after, Gerry would turn up, with a couple of his mates. So you'd all have a few drinks, with everyone taking turns for a shout, and then after about an hour—and more importantly, just after his shout— Gerry would say, 'Look, fellers, I've got some business to attend to over at the store. I'll be back, so don't leave me out of the shout.'

'Okay, see yer.'

Then, no sooner had Gerry returned to the store than, lo and behold, his wife, Flow, would rush out, over to the pub, to take over Gerry's stool and, more importantly, his turn in the shout. And they'd carry on like this, swapping between entertaining the clientele at the pub and minding the store, until around 5.30 pm, when they'd shut the shop and they'd both settle in at the pub. So that's the way it was in Blighty. You always got the best of both worlds—good service and friendly customer relations. Always.

Then, just up the road a bit is a place called Finley and one of the real characters of the area was a Scottish-born farmer by the name of Bill Bennett. I'd say Bill would've been about sixty-five years old, semi-retired, and he lived on his property at Mayrung. In fact, I think Bill's son managed the farm while Bill just helped out a bit by doing small transporting jobs he picked up around the place. He did this in an old 3-tonne Bedford truck. You know, if there was a bit of stock carting to be done, Bill was the man to see about it. Rice and wheat carting, the same. Really, he'd cart just about anything, just as long as it was small and easily loaded. As I said, he was getting on a bit so he didn't want to overdo things, neither for himself nor for his old Bedford truck.

Actually, many of us believed that there were only two reasons why Bill kept on working: one was to have an excuse for a little tipple and the other was to make enough money to ensure that he could afford his little tipple. Not much else mattered to old Bill. So, yes, the old Scot liked his grog, and he'd turn up at all the local clearing sales and stock sales and that, where he'd pick up small carting jobs which would, eventually, finish up with him in some pub or club at the end of the day, just 'to wash down the dust'. A very dusty place is the Riverina, and hot too.

Anyhow, this particular afternoon Bill had picked up about fifteen Border Leicester rams from the Deniliquin Sheep Market and he was heading back towards Finley. Now, as I said, Blighty's roughly halfway between Deniliquin and Finley and the Blighty pub was the only watering-hole along the way. The only difficulty was that Bill needed to do a small turn, off the main road, to get into Blighty.

Now I forgot to mention one important point: see, Bill's Bedford had no brakes. None at all. And, what's more, everyone in the district knew that its brakes were shot, so they'd keep a safe distance. It was just one of those things Bill always meant to get fixed but never seemed to find the time to get around to doing. So, with regard to a visit in to Blighty, Bill had it worked out that,

The dependable Bedford—The Hansford Collection

at a cruising speed of forty kilometres per hour—which was about the best the Bedford could do—all he had to do was to take his foot off the throttle at around the one-and-a-half kilometre mark from Blighty and coast the rest of the way. By doing that, he could easily manage the turn-off and still have enough momentum to roll right up to the door of the pub. Over time, this manoeuvre had virtually become second nature to both Bill and his Bedford. So much so that whenever the sales were on in Deniliquin, everyone at the Blighty pub would be waiting for him to turn up and have a round or two, along with Gerry and Flow, the aforementioned store owners.

So that was the plan and Bill was looking very much forward to catching up with everyone and having his tipple. But unbeknown to Bill, Joe Connell, a local Finley carrier, was also on the road, heading back to Finley. Now you could describe Joe as being a 'lubricant-type, who always liked a joke'. For example, it was he who once had a difference of opinion with one of the trees in the street of Finley and decided to settle the argument once and for all by setting three sticks of gelignite under the offending tree. Then after he'd lit the fuse he went home, changed into some night attire, and came back to join in with the onlookers as they gathered around discussing the terrible damage that had been inflicted upon the tree. 'Who did this?' 'Who'd do such a thing?'

'It's got me,' Joe joined in. And that was Joe's nature. 'Never take the credit or the blame for anything' was his motto.

Anyhow, so on this same particular day, Joe was driving back to Finley in his International 180 C-line semi. It was a pretty big rig, powered by a 160 Cummings Diesel. Big and powerful. And empty. He had no load on. So Joe was driving along in this thing when old Bill's Bedford appeared just up ahead. Then, when Joe noticed Bill's Bedford was starting to slow down, he realised that Bill was heading to the Blighty pub.

It was then that Joe decided on a little surprise. He drove right up behind old Bill and he gently rested the bull bar of the International 180 C-line against the back tray of the Bedford. Then, from a cruising speed of forty kilometres per hour, Joe pushed the speed up to fifty kilometres per hour. Then to sixty kilometres per hour. By seventy kilometres per hour old Bill could see that his plan of a nice tipple at the Blighty pub was evaporating rapidly so, in a vain attempt to rectify proceedings, he leaned out the driver's side window and commenced waving his fist and shouting all the profanities in the world at Joe—in Scottish, of course. But all Joe did was to reply in a friendly manner and crank his rig up to eighty-five kilometres per hour. The old Bedford had never gone so fast. Neither had old Bill. He was in a dead panic.

Then just before the turn-off to Blighty, Joe eased back on the power, and Bill and his Bedford sailed off into the distance, down the main road, like a shunted railway carriage on the loose, with no hope of pulling up for at least another four or five kilometres. Joe then veered off to the left and he pulled his rig up right in front of the Blighty Hotel.

Of course, everyone's there, expecting old Bill to turn up.

'Hey, Joe,' they said, 'yer haven't seen old Bill Bennett, have yer?'

'Well,' Joe said, 'in actual fact I just saw him out on the main road but he drove straight past the Blighty turn-off.'

'Geez,' they all chorused.

'Yeah,' replied Joe. 'He was really pushin' it, too. I'd say he was doin' at least eighty-five k's an hour.'

'Wow,' came the reply. 'Something really musta been the matter for him not to drop in for his usual drink, ay?'

Of course, Joe never let on the truth of it. I mean, as I said before, that was just his nature: 'Never take the credit or the blame for anything.'

Bogan Gate—NSW

Bogan Gate is in central-western New South Wales; about 400 kilometres from Sydney and thirty-five kilometres from Parkes. It was first settled back in the 1880s to cash in on the drovers and other travellers, like Cobb & Co., who were passing along the stock route that ran through the central part of New South Wales, up into Queensland.

Now I'm led to believe that the word 'Bogan' comes from the Aboriginal word meaning the 'birthplace of a notable headsman' and the 'Gate' part comes from the actual gate that stood between the two large sheep properties that led the stock to the nearby Bogan River; one being Gunningbland Station, which is to the east, the other, Burrawang Station, to the west, which was said to have had one of the largest shearing sheds in the state—about a hundred stands. Now, although that original gate's gone, a replica has been erected near the original spot and I was recently re-reading a booklet, 'Gateway to the Bogan', and in it there was a caption that read 'they will **never** shut the Gate'. So, even though the town's been in decline over a number of years now, we'll see. But it just shows you the resilient thinking of, in particular, the local farming community.

The original township of Bogan Gate started off about a mile from where the gate was with just a pub, some shanties and a few tents, then a saw mill was built because of a good supply of native pine. From what I can gather, the original pub was called the Bogan Gate Hotel and, in the early days, it was burnt down once or twice before the Selectors Arms was built on the same site. Actually, Bogan Gate seems to have a bit of a habit of having its pubs burn down because—even when they built two two-storey hotels over at the new township site—one, Schofields, which was where my mother worked for a short while before she was married, well, it burnt down. Then, when I was only a kid, I can remember the other one, the Railway Hotel on the corner, burning down. These days there's the new Railway Hotel-Motel, and it's still there. It hasn't burnt down, as yet.

Now, how the moving of the town came about was that the original Bogan Gate was built on quite a large flood plain. So then, in the late 1890s, when they put through the railway line, they decided to run it along higher ground, about a mile to the south. Naturally, because it was easier to build a town around a railway rather than having to cart everything from a railway out to the town, all the businesses and that gravitated to the new spot.

But like so many little communities, sport's played an integral part. Perhaps the most legendary sporting event held at Bogan Gate happened back in the late 1890s, with a polo match between Australia and Great Britain. One of the participating Poms, Will Ogilvy, even wrote a poem about it, 'The Polo Match at Bogan Gate'.

On Saturdays and Sundays many polo men of late
Have mustered up for practice near the pub at Bogan Gate

So a challenge was set up and, mind you, there were some pretty famous names included. In the Great Britain team there was, as I've already mentioned, Will Ogilvie, the Australian-Scottish poet. There was 'Breaker' Morant, the horse-breaker, stockman and poet, who was later executed during the Boer War for various monomanias—he was English—then there was Paddy Ryan and Eddie McDonald, both Irishmen. The Aussie team consisted of a fellow called Bert Balcombe, who owned a property nearby, Arthur Pike, an agent from Trundle, Victor Foy, who owned Mordialloc Station—actually, Victor Foy was the brother of Mark Foy of the big Sydney store, Mark Foy's—then there was Will Black who later became Black's Store in Bogan Gate. But, as it turned out, the Aussies didn't fare too well and they got done four goals to two.

> *Then the victors cheered and the vanquished and all gaily*
>   *sought the pub*
> *And drank the toast of polo and the Mordialloc Club*
> *To each Australian member and every British boy*
> *And filled a final bumper for the patron saint St. Foy*

Anyway, we eventually got a few back on the Poms when, later on in the early 1960s, a local lad, Ian Walsh, captained the international Kangaroo Rugby League team.

Anyhow, down through the years, there's been many achievements both on and off the sporting field and Bogan Gate was quite a lively town there for a good while, especially when the army set up a Central Ammunitions Depot. When I was a kid you could hear and feel the old explosives being detonated in the hills. But, unfortunately, as time's passed, the town's activities, along with its population, have fallen. There'd be less than a hundred people there, these days. The tennis club still struggles on and the CWA is still going strong. But the annual Debutante Ball and Spring Flower Show aren't held any more. The cricket club folded in the mid-1960s and the membership of the

The Guardians of Bogan Gate—The Marsh Collection

Toastmistress' Club fell below the required level in the mid-1980s. The Soccer Club only had a brief existence. The eighteen-hole Bogan Gate Army Golf Club had to be relocated when the Air Force replaced the Army and they requisitioned two of the fairways to be used for airstrips.

But, since the RAAF has now flown the coop, there's not too much left, not even in the main street. As you come into town, the old café's almost fallen over. The service station's closed. All the old shops, further up from the pub, have gone. Hitchick's garage is still there but it doesn't sell petrol anymore. It's just a mechanical place now and so, when everyone goes into Parkes to shop, like they all do, they fill up over there. Of course, the pub continues to thrive and also one event that really does unite the community is the ANZAC Day dawn service. That's a very moving occasion at which the local Troop of Light Horse is presented and through the early morning light you can hear the sounds of bugles and horses' hooves.

Still, as it is with most small towns these days, it's a struggle to survive. But, as I said, they're a resilient mob and with their motto being 'they will **never** shut the Gate' one never knows ... though, in the quiet of night after the pub's closed down and when the ghosts of a long lost polo match have evaporated, you can sometimes hear the Gate's hinges squeaking.

Bourke—NSW

Okay, so Bourke. I'd say that most people's image of Bourke would be of a dusty God-forgiven bloody hole, where there's always some trouble or other going on. But then, when they get here, they'll soon realise what's really happening. Though, to be honest, it's been pretty tough of late. What with the drought and all that, we've lost about 1000 people over the last seven years and that includes about 25 per cent of our Aboriginal population as well. Absolutely. And, mind you, when you lose someone, you don't just lose one person, you lose a whole family. Still, populations go and come as jobs go and come. Everything's relative. It's the glass half-full or the glass half-empty analogy. And to my mind, the glass is half-full.

See, we're a pretty tough lot out here. We've always survived; always will. History shows that. So I suppose, as far as white settlement, it all goes right back to 1828 when Charles Sturt came out here looking for the inland sea. He didn't find one, of course. Then a few years later Thomas Mitchell, the Surveyor-General, came looking for the missing explorer, Richard Cunningham. That even proved too difficult, even for Mitchell who was one of the real characters of the outback; a fellow who always dressed in military uniform, with the big plume in his hat which, I believe, is where the bird—the Major Mitchell—got its name from. Anyhow, seeing how, in those days, the Aboriginal people were pretty native, Mitchell built a stockade to protect his stores and he called it Fort Bourke Stockade, after the then Governor of New South Wales, Richard Bourke. That's why Bourke's named Bourke, with an 'o', unlike Burke, the explorer, who didn't have an 'o' in his name. So the name of the town's got nothing at all to do with Burke and Wills. Then, following on from Mitchell, Vincent Dowling arrived in the late 1850s to set up a property which he called Fort Bourke Station, and it's not too long after that the township of Bourke began to sprout up where it is now.

Our main produce, in those days, was wool and so the first paddle boats started to come up from river port towns on the Murray, like Echuca and Moama. The wool bales were then taken back down the Darling, into the Murray, and were eventually unloaded at places like Goolwa, at the mouth of the Murray River, in South Australia. So it would've been a hell of a trip. And it all had to be seasonal. See, the Darling River, in particular, comes up slowly but it drops very dramatically and so the paddle boats could easily get stuck. One paddle boat was grounded for three years. Of course, the men on board still had to fend for themselves. Most probably they did that by knocking off the cocky's sheep or maybe the cocky gave them some work and food to tide them over until the river began to flow again. It's an extraordinary story, really.

So it would've been an amazing town when Henry Lawson arrived in 1892. He was working for *The Bulletin* magazine, at the time. One rumour has it that they thought Bourke was so distant from anywhere that it'd be the last place on earth where he'd find a pub, so they sent him up here to dry out. Now, I don't know where they got their information from but it wasn't very reliable because, when Henry arrived, there were twenty-nine pubs in the area. North Bourke alone had eight pubs. In fact, many of his poems were written over in the Carriers Arms Inn. It's now a church, and I'm sure Henry would turn in his grave if he ever found out his favourite watering hole's now a church.

Other than another failed attempt to kick the demon drink, another rumour was that Lawson was pretty keen to prove himself to be the rightful Bard of the Bush. See, he had this ongoing thing with Banjo Paterson about which one of them deserved the title and because Banjo had a passion for the more central country, like Bathurst and all through there, Henry thought he'd really outdo him so it was a case of, 'Well get stuffed, Banjo, I'm off to Bourke.' Anyhow, whatever the reason, *The*

Bulletin gave Henry five quid and a train ticket and off he come to Bourke. And he didn't like the place at all. Actually, as he described in his poem 'Bourke'.

> *No sign that grass ever grew in scrubs that blazed beneath the*
> *   sun;*
> *the plains were dust in ninety-two, and as hard as bricks in*
> *   ninety-one.*
> *On glaring iron-roofs of Bourke the scorching, blinding*
> *   sandstorms blew,*
> *no hint of beauty lingered there in ninety-one and ninety-two.*

But as much as he mightn't have liked the environment, he certainly warmed to the rough and hardy characters of the area, like the shearers and the unionists. And it was he who basically declared Bourke to be 'mateship country'. So, to my mind, the town and its surrounding area was formed on the concept of mateship, where mates stick together and help each other. And that's what happens, here in Bourke. If anyone's going through a rough patch we all pitch in and help them out—Aboriginal or non-Aboriginal, it doesn't matter.

And even though we don't take claim to Henry, many people still come up here on poet treks, following the footsteps of Lawson, Will Ogilvy, Harry 'Breaker' Morant and the like. And when you think that, while he was here, Lawson worked out in Sir Samuel McCaughey's wool shed then, to actually go out there, almost 120 years later, and recite his poetry in the very same wool shed, well, for many it's an extremely emotional thing. Because, even though he may not have enjoyed it, the experiences of Lawson's short time in Bourke had a huge impact on his writing.

So, yes, it's hard to believe that a rough and tumble town like Bourke would actually tell its story through poetry. And poets like Lawson, Ogilvy and 'Breaker' Morant did bring out the folklore of the area. They really did. They made us what we are today. Even now, every Wednesday and Friday night, people go

'If you know Bourke you know Australia'—Henry Lawson
—The Marsh Collection

out in their droves to sit around a campfire, at the Kidman's Camp, and recite poetry. Just last Wednesday they had near on eighty people out there. So it's a wonderful thing to think that poetry's still alive and well out the 'back o' Bourke'. And so, to finish, here's a verse from Henry's poem 'The Roaring Days'.

> *The night trip too quickly passes and we are growing old*
> *so let us fill our glasses and toast the days of gold ...*
> *the rough bush roads re-echoed the bar-room's noisy din*
> *when troops of stalwart horsemen dismounted at the inn.*
> *And oft the hearty greetings and hearty clasp of hands*
> *Would tell of sudden meetings of friends from other lands.*

So come and visit us out here in mateship country. It's a place where you'll enjoy a poem, a yarn and a few drinks, with some real characters in the local pub because, as Henry Lawson so rightly wrote, 'If you know Bourke, you know Australia.'

Cape Crawford—NT

Yeah, Heartbreak Hotel in at Cape Crawford. But first, Cape Crawford's about 300 k out along the Carpentaria Highway, east of Daly Waters. I'm not sure how it got called Cape Crawford other than I think a feller named Crawford found the place. But as to the 'Cape' bit I wouldn't have a clue 'cause it's miles from the nearest sea. But Heartbreak Hotel's pretty much all that's there; just that, the campground, with a few roos—kangaroos—out the back and a little roadhouse part. It's sort of all in one block. Then there's a helicopter space. That's also out the back and they do trips out into the Abner Ranges, where there's all these fantastic rock formations—huge sandstone things like skyscrapers—out at a place called the Lost City. Yeah, that's about it really. So now do you want to hear about the kangaroo?

Well, like, it's real cattle country out there and I was on Macarthur River Station, about twenty or thirty k down the road from Cape Crawford. This's 'round 1999 or 2000 or something like that, and I was working for a contract musterer; a bloke named Ben Tapp. So we'd been, like, working out there for about two or three months without a break really and Ben decided to give us a night off. So probably about four of us, we went into Heartbreak Hotel in this old Toyota with a tray-top back on it.

But Ben had his two kids with him, so we had this governess out in the stock camp with us, teaching his kids every day. So she was out on the stock camp, too. Like, she wasn't that old; probably in her mid to late-twenties. Something like that. And she came along with us, into Cape Crawford. I mean, she was a nice enough girl. A little bit cranky. You know, a little bit moody and all that. Really, I didn't get on with her all that good 'cause, well, she was one of those people who sort of judges you all the time, like, as if you weren't up to scratch or something or not good enough.

Anyhow, there we were, we all arrived at Heartbreak Hotel at about sunset for this piss-up and, you know, if you haven't been drinking for a while it really knocks you. Then, like, there was never any set times as to when they shut the place down. They just shut when they felt like it. So you can imagine what we were like by about two or three in the morning.

Then, I must've just passed out, right, 'cause I got thrown in the back of the Toyota, face down, and the governess, she was in the back too. I just remember Ben's brother, Daniel, was driving and, anyhow, we took off back to the stock camp 'cause we were going back to work that day. The stock camp was around a place called Main Road Bore, and so we're heading out there and I'm just passed out in the back of the Toyota tray-top, face down, and the governess, she was in the back, there, too. And we're going along and I don't know how it happened but Daniel must've hit a kangaroo and, like, he had a few dogs back at the camp so he just threw this dead roo in the back; you know, as a bit of an easy feed for the dogs. So he chucked it in the back and he roared off.

Now, like, I must've been asleep when all that happened 'cause I didn't remember anything about it. So then I woke up, you know, face down and I felt this warm body pressed in against me back, and, like, when you're drunk, you know, you think all sorts of crazy things. Anyhow, I thought it was the governess. You know, I thought, Well, I know we don't get on that good but, like, she must've had a few drinks and she's loosened up and she's feeling a bit toey and romantic so she's decided to cuddle up against me.

I'm still face down at this stage, with me back turned away and so I thought I might try and encourage her a bit, you know, to keep her on the boil. So I reached around to give her a bit of a reassuring touch with my fingers and I felt this warm bit of fur. And, like, I'm still not thinking that straight, right, but the first thing that come into me head was, Gee, she's really come out of her shell. She's even got her strides off. Like, that's what I

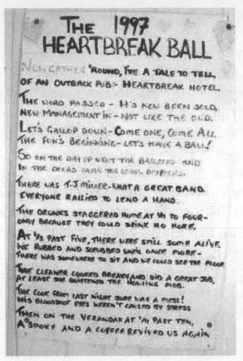

Many a heart has been broken—Phil O'Brien

thought. Then that got me going and so I decided to grab my chance while it was there for the easy taking. So I sort of pulled my strides down a bit. Then I rolled over, to get on top, and there's this dead kangaroo looking at me. So I spun off that pretty quick. But that's when I saw the governess on the other side of the tray-top. She'd been watching the whole thing unfold, you know, and by the look on her face I don't think it helped my credibility too much. So, yeah, that happened on our way back from Heartbreak Hotel at Cape Crawford.

Cato—NSW

Because my parents split up when I was young I was brought up by my grandparents. So I can only ever remember living with my grandfather and grandmother. But I never lacked for love or loving care or anything, and I just adored my grandfather. Grandfather's name was Charlie. He wasn't that tall but he was very stocky and, from my earliest time, I remember how, whenever any of his old mates from the bush or some relatives came down, they'd pat me on the head and say, 'You know, Fred, your grandfather's one of the greatest grass-fighters the back country's ever seen?'

Grass-fighting's different to in-the-ring-fighting in as much as, with in-the-ring-fighting, you wear boxing gloves. Grass-fighting's the bare-knuckled fighting that happens out the back of dance halls or out the back of pubs. It's the real fair-dinkum stuff. So it made me wonder how such a kind and gentle man, as Grandfather was, could even get involved in something like that. So much so that, in those very early days, I even thought that by 'grass-fighting' they meant that he'd lie down and punch hell out of the lawn or he'd roll around with a clump of saltbush or whatever because I just could not imagine him out the back of a pub having a bare-fist fight.

Anyway, I always wanted to work on the Broken Hill mine, with Grandfather. That never quite happened because he retired before I got a job there. Then, when I did, Grandfather always used to offer to drive me to work. And it didn't take long for me to find out that his kind offer was made because, if he did, then he also had to come and pick me up and, on the way home we'd just happen to pass a pub and he'd say, 'Do yer feel like a beer?'

'Yeah, I feel like a beer.'

And so we'd go into the pub. And, when we did, we'd always just happen to run into a few of Grandfather's grey-haired old mates or some old codgers that'd known him from somewhere and it was always a warm, 'G'day, Charlie. Want a drink?' Then, inevitably, at one stage or other, they'd say to me, 'Yer know, yer grandfather's one'a the greatest grass-fighters the outback's ever seen? Oh, yer just should'a seen 'im.'

So then, when we'd get home and we were having tea, I'd say, 'What's this about you being a great grass-fighter, Grandfather?'

And he'd say, 'Oh, it's nothing', and he'd leave it at that.

Anyway, this particular time, after work, Grandfather and I were in the pub and an old mate he hadn't seen for years come in for a drink and they were talking and going on and when Grandfather's mate was about to leave I said, 'Goodbye,' and this old green-eye said, 'Yer know yer grandfather's one'a the greatest grass-fighters the west's ever seen?'

I would've been about twenty-two or twenty-three by this stage and Grandfather would've been in his late sixties, say. So that night we were having tea and I insisted that I get the story. 'Come on,' I said, 'what's all this about you being a great grass-fighter?'

'It's nothing,' he said, and he just left it at that.

Anyhow, Grandmother's eyes used to twinkle when she was in a humorous mood and she said, 'Oh, go on, Charlie, tell him.'

And this's the story as I got it.

Apparently they were reasonably newly married. Grandmother was pregnant with my father and they took over the proprietorship of this hotel at Cato. Cato was up on a tributary of the Darling River system, out from Bourke somewhere. I saw it on an old map once, though I don't think the place exists anymore. But it was on a ford, which was where the bullock wagons and the stage coaches and that crossed the river. So, of course, all the old bullockers would stop there and the stage coach passengers used to stop there and all the shearers and itinerants would stop there on their way through. It was a real meeting point. Whenever anyone was going through that back country they had to go past Cato.

Anyway, so Grandfather's there with a pregnant wife and, as what happened in those days, whenever possible, pregnant ladies always had a female companion. So out from Sydney came Grandfather's sister, Alice. Alice was about seventeen at that time. Gorgeous looking too, as you can see in some of them old photos over there. So Alice came out to Cato to become Grandmother's companion. But, in doing so, she'd left her boyfriend behind in Sydney. They were later to marry. Fred Kerr was his name and, even by then, Fred and Grandfather were the greatest of mates; always ready to try and put one over, whenever an opportunity arose.

Now Fred had been a real Sydney street-kid. He'd learned to stick up for himself by the time he was five. He worked on the wharves and if there was anything he liked, it was a fight. Oh, he loved to fight. But the thing was, apart from the love of a good stoush, even though he was pretty much self-educated, he'd also developed a great love of the English language. He used to roll these beautiful and eloquent words around his tongue. He was like a gardener with a beautiful rose. He just had to use all this wonderful, flowery language and, what's more, he dressed to suit. To use the common word of the day, as tough as he was with his fists, he dressed like a true English 'dandy'. A back country shearer or a bullocker might come up with a more derogatory term, but we'll get to that.

But the story is, when Alice came out to be a companion to Grandmother, Fred missed her terribly. So he decides to come out to Cato. He arrives. He gets off the stage coach. And there he is, 'the essence of sartorial elegance', as he would put it, with his white boater hat, black and white striped blazer, a cravat with a pin through it, sparkling white-cream trousers, spats, shoes, and a little baton, with a jewel embedded in the end of it. Now, you might be able to imagine what sort of impression this made on the local clientele of bullockies, hard-bitten shearers, outback ruffians and the like. Anyhow, he gets off the stage coach and he walks into this rowdy bar. He raps his baton on the bar. Grandfather comes up. Fred gives him a bit of a wink and he announces in a loud voice, 'A modicum of your famous ale, please, publican.'

Grandfather goes and gets Fred a beer. He comes back. Fred says, 'Thank you, my fine gentleman,' and he takes a delicate and savoury sip.

As I said, the place is full of just about every sort of ruffian the back country could produce. Of course, they're all quite bemused by all this carry-on and so one of the roustabouts—a huge feller, he was, in a dirty blue singlet—he comes up and he starts feeling the material of Fred's blazer. 'Not bad stuff, mate,' he says, and he looks around to his mates who are smirking at the show. Then the rousie went one further and he tried to pull the pin out of Fred's cravat.

'Unhand me, sire,' says Fred, 'or I shall remonstrate with thee most severely.'

But, egged on by his mates, this bloke persisted. So Fred says, 'Desist at once, sire, or I shall be forced to handle you, physically.'

'Will yer,' says the roustabout.

'Yes I shall,' replies Fred.

The rousie says, 'So how's about we go outside 'n' settle it, then.'

So they go out the back of the pub to have this grass-fight. Everyone follows, even Grandfather. Then Grandfather described Fred taking off his boater; just like this—very showy—and he very carefully placed it on an old gum tree stump. Then he pulled off his gloves, fingers, one by one, neatly, and puts them down there, beside his boater. Takes off his blazer, folds it two or three times, and just puts it down there. Brushes a speck of dust off it. Rolls up his sleeves. 'Now, sire, are you ready for your lesson in the fine art of pugilism?', which brings smatterings of laughter all around.

Of course, this roustabout's half-full of beer and so he's pretty steamed up by now and so, when Fred finally shapes up, the bloke comes charging in at him, throwing hay-makers left, right and centre. Of course, Fred being a seasoned street fighter neatly ducks aside and 'bang', with a straight right, into the rousie's belly button, which takes the wind out of him, and then 'thwack',

Grass-fighting—The Hansford Collection

one to the jaw, to straighten him up, followed by two or three sharp jabs into the ribs for good measure and down goes this huge roustabout, like the proverbial sack of potatoes. He's out to it.

Well this feller's mates didn't like the outcome of that. It's, 'Hey, yer can't get away with that, yer bloody city slicker.' So in comes one of the rousie's mates and Fred goes 'bang!', straight into the mush and down the second feller goes; out cold. Then in comes another feller, 'bang!', the same thing. Followed by another feller, 'bang!'. And before long there's about ten or fifteen of them, all lying out cold, and Fred hasn't even got a scratch on him. So then all these outback ruffians decided that discretion's the better part of valour and so they all tumble back into the pub and they all want to buy Fred a drink. He's their hero now. He's their new best mate. 'We'll shout yer a drink,' they're all saying.

Then someone called out, 'Hey, mate, where did yer learn ter fight like that?'

And Fred pointed his baton at Grandfather and he said, 'That gentleman there, behind the bar, Charlie, he taught me everything I know about the art of pugilism.' And everybody looked over at Grandfather in awe. 'Yes,' Fred added, 'so don't ever pick on him.' Then he pushed back the hair on his forehead and he said, 'See that scar there.' Actually, he'd fallen down a hold in a ship somewhere and he'd had about eight stitches.

Everyone looked. 'Yeah,' they said.

Fred said, 'Charlie gave me that one when I forgot to duck one of his left hooks.' And he had another bit of a scar on his stomach and so he opened up his spotless shirt and he said, 'See that one there. That's where Charlie busted four of my ribs.'

And there was a stunned silence in the bar and Grandmother said, 'And, after that, if anyone was a bit noisy in the Cato pub, Grandfather would just bang the bar, with his hand, and say, "Righto, fellers, that's enough."'

And it was, 'Yes Charlie.' 'Alright Charlie.' 'Sorry about that Charlie.'

And that's how Grandfather became known as the best grass-fighter in the back country.

Clara Creek—Qld

You know how embarrassing things happen and they haunt you for the rest of your life? Like, years later, you're doing something that's got nothing to do with nothing and, right out of the blue, the incident comes back and you feel embarrassed, all over again, like it was only yesterday. Well, I've just remembered one of those times from when I was only about seventeen years old. I was out droving. Pretty new to the game, I was, back then. In fact, the fellers used to call me 'lad', which was a term that really got up my nose. But, anyhow, we were camped just out of a little place called Clara Creek. Clara Creek used to be on the stock route between Morven and Augathella; about 500 miles west of Brisbane. I say 'used to be' because I'm not too sure if it's there any more. Like, even back then, there was just a pub and not much else.

Anyhow, like I said, I was only seventeen and by Queensland law you weren't allowed to drink alcohol till you were twenty-one. But, see, I thought I was a pretty big feller, as you do when you're a teenager, doing the work of men. And that's what I was doing: doing the work of men. Anyhow, I was in Clara Creek this time and I thought I'd go into the pub and have a drink. Now, it's a big occasion for a bloke the first time you go into a pub. Something you remember for a lifetime. But before I did, I took a quick look around, just to make sure that no one who knew me was about. The coast was clear so I hitched up me strides, puffed the chest out and I strode into the pub, trying to look like I'm years older than what I was. Trying to walk ten feet tall and all the while wishing I had stubble on my chin instead of bum-fluff.

A few fellers were in the pub. None I knew. None that knew me. So I fronts up to the bar. The barman comes over, looks me up and down. I go as red as a beetroot. He says, 'G'day. What can I do yer for?'

'I'll have a beer thanks, mate,' I says, in my deepest voice.

Just then, the horsetailer, who was droving with us, he come into the pub and, when he saw me ordering this beer, he calls out, 'Hey, what're yer doin' lad?' Gee, I hated being called 'lad'. Just thinking about it, even now, still riles me.

Of course, with that, the bar goes all quiet. Everyone turns around and they start staring at me and what they see causes smiles to spread over their dials. Meanwhile, I'm wishing the earth would open up and swallow me. But I was still determined to prove myself a man so I said to the horsetailer, 'I'm gonna have a drink.'

'Bullshit, yer are,' the horsetailer calls out. 'Yer under twenty-one, lad.'

So that was that. I was asked to leave the pub. Well, in actual fact, my ego was so bruised by then that I turned tail and virtually ran out of the place. And, when I got outside I could hear everyone in the bar laughing. So there I was, feeling weak as water, as weak as I'd ever felt in me whole life, and I got real steamed up about it.

Anyhow, we had a four-in-hand wagonette in our plant. You know, four horses dragging the wagonette. That's there. So I jumped on this bloody wagonette and I was out of there. And, boy, didn't I hunt the horses along. 'Hey-up!' and I cracked the whip. Oh, I was real steamed up because, see, I thought I was a big feller—a real man—and so, what right did the horsetailer have to come in and put me down like that in front of everyone? I'd been made a real fool of and now everyone was laughing at me. So, yeah, I was chewed up about it and it didn't matter where I was going, just as long as it was out of bloody Clara Creek. I just wanted to get out of there. Get away. Never see anyone anymore. Never come back.

So I was hunting these horses along in the wagonette. 'Hey-up!' and a crack of the whip, 'Hey-up!', when all of a sudden this bloody huge goanna shoots out of nowhere and it scares the living hell out of the horses. And, well, the horses went in one direction, the wagonette went in another direction and I nearly went up a bloody tree.

And I still get flashbacks about that. Because, there I was, thinking I was all grown up and I not only get kicked out of the pub for being underage and be a laughing stock but now I'd have to go back, tail between my legs, and tell everyone that I'd just gone and smashed up the bloody wagonette and lost the bloody horses. Then they'd laugh even louder.

So yeah, that was at Clara Creek. A little place out in the middle of nowhere, on the track between Yo Yo Park and Etona. I'm not even sure if it's there these days, and I wish it wasn't back then, neither.

Coen—Qld

Well, Coen is sort of halfway between Cairns and the tip of Cape York. We were told that a Dutch explorer had named the local river as the Coen, after some Governor of the Dutch East Indies. That was way back in the mid-1670s. But I don't know who the explorer was. Then, a couple of hundred years after that, gold was discovered there and that was really the beginning of Coen. Even some Chinese came in. Then, later on, about ten years after the Adelaide to Darwin telegraph line had been finished, the Overland Telegraph got there. But it was basically a mining place till the cattle station people moved in, which, mind you, upset a lot of the local indigenous people. Quite rightly too, as far as I'm concerned, because you hear some terrible stories about the treatment of the Aborigines, don't you? So there's a mix of people, with about an 80 per cent indigenous population, I'd say. Oh, and also a base of the Australian Inland Mission was set up there; the AIM being the precursor to the Royal Flying Doctor Service and the RFDS still do weekly visits, the last I heard.

Anyhow, we were at Coen to do a gig. This would've been back in about the mid-1990s, thereabouts. It was only a small place. The pub, basically, had a hessian bag and oil drum feel about it. Like, there was the pub and there was a verandah and, because it's tropical, people got served through a window and everyone just sat outside, on old stumps, with empty upturned 44-gallon drums as tables. The beer was kept cold with a generator, from what I can remember. But we only went there a couple of times because everyone smoked, and there was a real odd tree that smelt of cat's piss. A gunya tree, maybe. Anyhow, I just called it the 'cat's piss tree'.

But, oh, it's a beautiful spot. It's really lovely. Cicadas start up at sunset, and over the river there's birds everywhere. And we stayed at the guest house and, oh God, it was the most beautiful place. It had this bougainvillea tree at the side, which was the biggest bougainvillea I've ever seen in my entire life. They even had, like, a magnet with a picture of it. It was enormous. And the lady who owned the guest house, her name was Irene. Irene was an old lady, like, in her late eighties, I reckon, and just prior to us arriving they'd built a new bridge in town and they'd named it after her. I remember that because she said to me, 'You know, Kalyna, the last thing I expected was to have a bridge named after me.' And so she'd been there since the year dot, with her hubby. He'd passed on, but she was telling me about when they first lived in Coen, how they'd drive down to Cairns. Cairns is about 400 k's south and, anyhow, on their trips down to Cairns, the roads were so crap that while her hubby was driving along in the car, she'd be out the front with the machete, slashing through the jungle, clearing the track. True. There were even photos of her as a young lass doing it. Like, things just grow that quick. So if she was in her eighties and this happened back when she was in,

Coen Guesthouse—Coen website

say, her twenties and we were up there in the mid-1990s—what would that make it?—that would've been back in about the 1920s or something.

So she ran this beautiful old guest house. Like, you had the main lounge-dining room, where everyone sat at a big table to have their meals. When we were there, there was about a dozen men who were working on the roads. Anyhow, off that big room were the little rooms where you slept and out the back was the kitchen. And, like, I'm a vegetarian and every night Irene came up with the most amazing, gourmet vegetarian meals. And she'd say, 'Oh, it's not a hassle to cook vegetarian.' And I've always said that. It's easy, you know. You go to some of these outback places and they slap down a bit of crappy lettuce and a pile of greasy chips and think it's a vegetarian meal. But Irene didn't have a problem with it at all, so I loved her to death.

Anyway, she knew we were putting on this show. So that's what we did, though in the end, we didn't do the gig in the river like we usually do, because someone saw a crocodile. So we moved the performance up onto the land, just in case, and that was a great success. And also that week I borrowed a slide projector and we had heaps of slides with us and so, one night, I did this special slide show for Irene to show her all the stuff we'd done in Pakistan and that, and all the other things we'd done around Australia. And she absolutely loved it. She loved it. And all the other people who were staying in the guest house, they saw it too and, oh, I could go on and on about it, but one of the men who was there, I started talking to him and he told me that he was totally illiterate. Like, he could not read or write. I just couldn't believe it because he was in his twenties, like me, and I thought, How could someone in this day and age be totally illiterate. But he was. And when we got back to Cairns, I was talking to a feller about it and he said, 'Well I was illiterate till I was fifteen and I only learned to read and write because this one teacher really persevered with me.' He said, 'I'll never forget her name—Julie Temple.' And we just about fell over because Julie Temple was, like, our really best friend from Adelaide.

But, anyway, getting back to Coen. So we had this great experience there and we'd put on this really great show and we'd put on this slide show and, when we went to leave, we went to pay for our meals and accommodation and Irene wouldn't take any money. None at all. Isn't that brilliant? And we ate like kings. She said, 'No, you just keep your money because you brought so much joy to this community.'

Cook—SA

The most isolated town I've ever been to is Cook, in South Australia. It's away out in the middle of the Nullarbor, a bit over 1000 kilometres from Adelaide and around 1500 k's from Perth. There's no proper roads out that way, nothing but desert for miles around. So to get there you have to travel on the Indian Pacific, out along the Trans Australian Railway Line. To give you some idea, the Trans-line's one of the longest train lines in the world. It's about 4500 k's, maybe a bit less; that's from Sydney to Perth.

So Cook was a railway town, with fettlers and all that living there, plus it was a changeover point for the train drivers and the crew. In its heyday, they say, there could be anything up to 500 people there. Since then, of course, the railways have gone through big changes. So, unfortunately, the town's basically died. I hear that there's only about four people there these days and that most of the houses are abandoned, as is the old hospital and the school. Though, because the Indian Pacific still stops there a couple of times a week, they've kept the small souvenir shop going and there's a place for the train drivers to rest up and get fed, when they change over. But that's about it.

We were out there in the early 1980s, working in schools. We'd spent a few days at Tarcoola then, late one night, we caught the train out to Cook. I'm not real sure but I guess that leg of the trip'd be a bit over 300 kilometres. We didn't have a sleeper or anything. We just sat up in the train all night. So we were pretty stuffed by the time we arrived. Anyhow, we hit the ground running and spent that day with the kids and the next day as well.

But Cook was fascinating. It's so flat that you can actually see the curvature of the earth. And the night skies were stunning. And, even back then, it was still a pretty thriving place with, perhaps, a population of around 100 or 150. And, as most small isolated towns do, people made the best of their lot. Of course, the kids were pleased to see us. The teachers were as well, and everywhere you went you'd get a friendly 'G'day'. The hospital was still open, as was the store and post office. They had a swimming pool and I think there was even a golf course, carved out of the desert, somewhere.

Anyhow, during the day, we worked with the kids in a small Community Centre, and that was also where everyone got together at night. You could get a drink and a feed. And it was a pretty busy place at night too, I can tell you. I reckon, per head of population, it would've held its own as far as drinking goes. So they did a pretty good trade. Oh, and that's right, I remember: something that really confused me was that Cook sort of ran on two separate time zones. Like, because it was a changeover point for train drivers, the Sandgropers stuck to Western Standard Time and the Crow Eaters were on Central Standard Time.

So then, on the night we were returning to Tarcoola, I was mixed up about the actual time of the train's arrival. I mean, with the Indian Pacific only coming by a couple of times a week, I didn't want to miss it. And I remember we were in the Community Centre having a few farewell drinks and nobody seemed to be able to give an exact time as to when the train was supposed to arrive. So I was getting a bit anxious and then I looked out the window and there through the darkness I saw the headlight of the train in the distance. At first it was just a pinprick but, in such clean air, it shone bright.

'Geez,' I said, 'what time do yer reckon the train'll arrive?'

And I sort of expected the feller I was drinking with to take a look at his watch and say something like, 'Oh, at about eight-thirty Central Standard Time.' Or even, 'Oh, in about three-quarters of an hour or so.' But he didn't. Instead he stared out at the light for a while, then he said, 'Oh, mate,' he said, 'you've got plenty of time. The train's still a good six stubbies away.'

So I guess you could say that Cook actually ran on three different time zones. One being Western Standard Time, two

being Central Standard Time and three was local time, where
minutes and hours were measured by how long it took to drink a
stubby of beer. I mean, how much more Australian can you get
than that? What's more, he was spot-on too; right down to the
last drop.

Curtin Springs—NT

Met an old Aboriginal chap once, out at Curtin Springs. Curtin Springs being a small place out on the Lasseter Highway, between Alice Springs and Ayers Rock. It's only about eighty kilometres from the Rock. Actually, Curtin Springs was, and still is, mainly a working cattle station and something I found out about it was that one of the earlier lease holders wanted to name the place Stalin Springs, after Joseph Stalin the Russian Communist leader. But, anyhow, his less-radical kids soon put a stop to that idea and it ended up being called Curtin Springs, after Prime Minister John Curtin. So that's just a bit of trivia, for you.

Then later on in the mid-1950s the new owners, the Severin family, decided to branch out a little and also make it into a stop-over for tourists, who were passing by on their way out to Ayers Rock. To that end they opened up their homestead and they put in petrol pumps and a small store and they called it the Wayside Inn. Like, you could get grog and food and all that there. And even though it might've been a bit of a struggle in the early days, these days it's much different.

Anyhow, I used to travel through there quite a lot so I got to know everyone pretty well and in about '65 I was there and around the roadhouse there were some Aborigines. Now, one old Aboriginal fella in particular got me quite fascinated. As black as the ace of spades he was and he'd always be dressed in basically the traditional Aboriginal garb. Not much more than rags, really. In fact, he looked a pretty pitiful sight.

Now, do you know what a wurley is? It's what the Aborigines lived in. It's like their home. It's a shell-shaped sort of shelter—a bower shelter—made basically from branches and it just sits in the dirt. Then they might have a bit of a fire going out the front so that when they huddled inside the wurley the smoke kept the mozzies at bay and they got a breath of warmth. Anyhow, when the tourist buses arrived, I noticed how this old Aboriginal fella, he'd show them this wurley in the dirt, and he'd have some Aboriginal artefacts laying around and there'd be a few snotty-nosed kids running around the place and, well, these tourists would take one look at him and they'd take a look at the wurley and you could just about see them cringe with the shame and the pity of it all. You know, 'How, in this day and age, could we allow people to live in such wretched conditions?' So to ease their guilt they'd buy, say, a boomerang or two.

'Tank-you, boss,' he'd say, in his thick Aboriginal-English. 'Tank-you, missus.' And he had a beautiful big smile, and so they'd buy something else, perhaps another boomerang or whatever for some long lost uncle they'd forgotten to send a Christmas card to a couple of years ago. Then the old fella, he had a couple of camels and he'd say, 'Want'a ride on camel, missus? I got me kids ter look after.' Then they'd look at these snotty-nosed kids who were hanging around and they'd just

'Now one Aboriginal fella in particular got me quite fascinated'
—Getty Images

about fall over each other to line up and be taken on a short camel ride.

So that's what he used to do and then, after the tourist bus had driven off, he'd disappear till the next bus arrived and he'd be back at it again. 'Wanta see me wurley. Wanta buy some fair-dinkum Aboriginal? Make 'em all meself. Yer gotta buy somethin', missus, ter help me look after all me kids.'

Anyhow, as I said, the old fella sort of fascinated me and so we'd have a bit of a chat every time I went past. Then one day I said, 'Gee, you do a hell of a good trade here, mate.'

'Yeah, boss,' he said. 'Not bad.'

I said, 'Surely you 'n' all your family don't live in the wurley.'

'No, bugga that. I live 'round d' back.'

'Oh, do yer?' I said.

'Yeah, wanta see?'

'Okay then,' I said, and I followed him around the back of the Wayside Inn and there was all his relatives busy knocking out these Aboriginal artefacts—boomerangs by the dozen. Spears by the dozen. And the artefacts they weren't making, he'd had imported and so they were busy scraping off the 'Made in Japan'—or wherever it was—stickers. Oh, it was real mass production.

'I live up there,' he said, and I looked up the way a bit and there's this bloody huge, flash new caravan and alongside it was a flash new car. Without a word of a lie, they would've cost a small fortune.

'God almighty,' I said.

'Yeah,' he said, 'I don't stick 'round 'ere when it gets hot, ay. Went down Adelaide, last holidays. Next time Sydney. Go all over. Big place Australia. But, oh, I tell yer what, boss, I make 'em a killin' outa all them tourist fellers. I make 'em a real big killin'.'

Daly Waters—NT

Daly Waters is a bit over 600 kilometres south of Darwin, just off the Stuart Highway. There's only a few houses and a pub and that's about it really. So I'd say, at a guess, there'd only be about twenty or so people living there and a good few less during the off-season. I know for certain that the bloke across the road from the pub—the one who sells heaps of those wood-burnt signs and all sorts of figurines—well, he disappears after the tourist season and just leaves his handiwork hanging on the verandah so that anyone who happens to pass by can still buy his stuff on an honesty system.

The pub stays open all year round, of course. Actually, the pub's said to be one of the oldest buildings in the Northern Territory. It was built way back in the late 1890s and it's held a continuous liquor licence since 1938. Now, I'm of the opinion that the same feller who built the William Creek pub, in South Australia, most probably built the Daly Waters pub, if not the same architect. It's the same old iron and wooden structure, with the low slung roof, and like the William Creek pub, the Daly Waters Hotel also has all sorts of apparel and memorabilia hanging off the roof and around the bar area. Tons of it. What's more, I'd venture to say that the Daly Waters pub would also be one of the most popular pubs in the NT; especially now, with all the grey nomads. During the tourist season, if you get there any time after four of an afternoon, you may as well forget about staying there. They just pack the place out.

Daly Waters got its name back in the 1860s when John McDouall Stuart and his expedition were getting low on water and they came across a creek and a series of waterholes. That's where the 'waters' bit comes from and 'Daly' was the Governor of South Australia, and as you turn off the highway and go into

'The Daly Waters Hotel also has all sorts of apparel and memorabilia hanging off the roof and around the bar area'—The Hansford Collection

town there's what's called the 'Stuart Tree'. It's a dead looking thing and, apparently, if you look hard enough—or perhaps I hadn't drunk enough at that stage—you can just make out a vague 'S' that Stuart was supposed to have gouged into it. So there's that. Then there's the aviation museum. See, Daly Waters has played a big part in our aviation history. In its time the airstrip at Daly Waters was supposed to have been the largest in the Territory. It was also a landing point during the mid-1920s London to Sydney air race. It became a refuelling stop for the first Qantas international flights. Then during World War II it was used as an air force base.

And I'd also better mention the annual Daly Waters Rodeo. That's a huge event. In fact, one particular time I arrived there on the rodeo weekend and I can assure you, the town wasn't only chock-a-block full of people but just about everyone was chock-a-block drunk. Now, believe me, it's no fun at all walking into a pub when everybody's pissed. You just can't understand what anyone's saying and so then it takes a while to drink yourself to their level.

So that's what I was doing, just sitting amongst this rodeo rabble, downing a few and, with no one I could make any sense of, I started to read the food menu. And here's the interesting thing: on the back of the menu there's a little local history, which is where I got most of this information from. But, apparently, the reason why the pub was built in the first place was not only as a stopover for travellers but also for the many drovers who were taking cattle across from the Kimberley region, in Western Australia, over into Queensland. And I remember reading a quote that gave me an insight into some of the wild times the pub's experienced in its past. It went along the lines of: *'In the early days, the Daly Waters Pub was a drover's rest ... a wild night out for the boys before they tackled the arduous Murranji leg of the trip.'*

So there I was, what, over a hundred years later, in this pub, with this drunken crowd around me, and the thought struck me, Isn't it amazing how little things have changed over the years?

Dampier—WA

Well I went over to Dampier when I was about twenty-one. Dampier's in the north-west of Western Australia, about 1500 kilometres north of Perth. That was in about 1972, when Hamersley Iron was really starting to open up out there in the Pilbara. But after having lived all my life in a small bush town in New South Wales, leaving home and going west was the biggest thing I'd ever done. I can still see Mum standing at the gate, bawling her eyes out, waving me goodbye. I think she thought I was gone for good. But as it turned out it was the best thing I ever did. Like, I love the bush as much as the next man and it's a great place to grow up and all that but, if you stay there, you never know anything else. You get used of the one thing. The blinkers stay on. See, you need to broaden your horizons. Get a bit of life experience.

Mind you, there's a lot of city people who need to broaden their horizons too. Some of them just wouldn't have a clue. Like, I went to the supermarket the other day and I was at the meat department. I'd just bought this nice leg of lamb—I love me lamb—and there was these two women, about my age, and one said to the other one, she said, 'Mary, look at the price of the meat. It's shocking. Those farmers must think we're millionaires.'

And I looked at her. I had me leg of lamb with me. I said, 'Well, one thing's for sure,' I said, 'the cocky's not getting paid that bloody price for it.'

She said, 'Well, who gets it?'

I said, 'You're kiddin'? Who gets it? These bastards get it. That's who. The bloody supermarkets. The big fellers. It's not the farmers. If you think the poor old cocky gets it then yer dreamin'.'

I mean, there's city kids, these days, who don't even know that milk comes out of a cow. True. They think it comes out of a

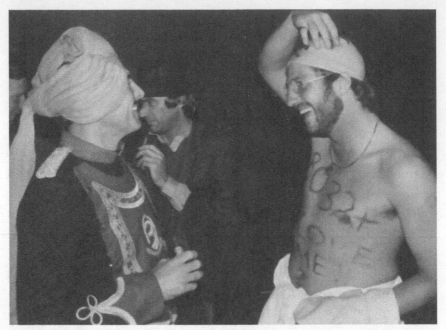

'Let's play a joke on old Vick'—The Hansford Collection

carton or a bottle. So I don't know where the country's going to. To the dogs, that's where. Like, just the other day, on the radio they had this competition where you had to ring in and tell them what the next word in a song was. So they played 'Waltzing Matilda' and they stopped it on the line, 'Up come the squatter mounted on his ... ?' and it took about five bloody calls before someone gave them the right answer. And this was adults. 'Oh, sorry, I don't know,' they're saying, and I'm in the car, in the middle of all this traffic and I'm shouting, 'Thoroughbred! It's a bloody thoroughbred, you idiots!' And I'm sure that everyone sitting in their cars around me thought I was mad. And I was too; mad at the lack of knowledge that a lot of these so-called Australians have about what's supposed to be their own country. So there you go. It works both ways I guess but, for me, getting away from a little bush town and experiencing something different in life was the best thing I ever done.

So, yeah, I ended up in Dampier. Really, Dampier wasn't that big, back then either, but then Dampier's not your usual town. It was built as a port, by Hamersley Iron, to ship out iron ore and stuff from places like Tom Price and Paraburdoo. Dampier only started up in the late 60s, early 70s, and I'm led to believe that, now, it's one of the biggest shipping ports in Australia.

But how they'd set the place up was that I was in the single-men's quarters. Then there was a wet mess, which is like a pub, and you had a dry mess, like the dining area, where you got all your meals and that. The dry mess was part of your board and whatever you got from the wet mess you paid for yourself. Quite a few of us didn't go into the wet mess because there always seemed to be some sort of strife going on—you know, fights and that—so we went down the street to the Mermaid Hotel. The Mermaid was a big pub for a country town. Nice and friendly. There's pool tables, a big bar and a lounge bar. Oh, they had everything.

And, I tell you, back then, money was nothing to some of these fellers that worked out on the mines. I was in the Mermaid one time and two blokes walk up to the bar and one said to the other, 'Toss yer fer a hundred.' 'Heads or tails?' and a hundred dollars changed hands. True. Just like that. And a hundred quid was big money back in them days. Another night I was at a card game and a bloke said, 'I'm skint,' and so they worked out the value of his car—a Volkswagen it was—and he put his car on the card table. Fair dinkum. That was in '72 or '73.

Then the unions; don't get me going about the bloody unions. You won't believe this but one time the men wanted to go out on strike because they reckoned the food in the dry mess wasn't up to scratch. I said, 'Youse blokes don't know what it's like.' You know, I wasn't brought up a fussy eater. Never have been. Never will be. In my day you ate whatever was put in front of you, otherwise you went without. Anyhow, they wanted to go on strike because they reckoned the food in the dry mess wasn't up to scratch.

'Yer bloody mad,' I said.

'No,' they said, 'we're goin' on strike. The food's no good.'

So we went on strike. And do you know what we did? While we were on strike, every morning we'd get up and we'd go to the dry mess for breakfast. After breakfast, we'd go down to the Mermaid. Come back to the dry mess for lunch. After lunch, we'd go back down to the pub, then we'd come back to the dry mess for tea. So we still ate three meals a day at the very same dry mess that we'd gone on strike about because they reckoned the food was crook.

I said, 'You blokes are fuckin' jokin'.'

So it was all a part of learning in life, and we did have some fun. One time I was working in the store and we had this boss, a leading hand. He would've been in his sixties. Pommy, he was. A spritely feller with white hair and a pencil-thin white moustache just like David Niven, the actor, used to have. I forget his name just now. For the sake of the story let's call him Vick Smith. Old Vick'd been a Sergeant Major in the English Army over in India and he still lived the part. Like, he'd strut about barking orders, 'Do this.' 'Do that 'n' be quick about it.' Drove us bloody mad it did. He just never let up. But the thing was, old Vick hated Indians. I don't know what it was all about but it must've come from his army days in India because he was always going on about how much he hated Indians. He just hated the Indians.

Anyhow, this crate had come up from Perth and it was just laying there empty. Size wise, you could squeeze a man inside of it, just. Then we had a bloke there by the name of Pratt. Pratty was a Kiwi, in his twenties. A real funny bugger he was. Do anything for a laugh. Anyway, Pratty said, 'Let's play a joke on old Vick. Let's get one back on the old bastard.'

'Okay,' we said and so we dirtied up Pratty's face a bit and we wrapped a tea towel around his head, like it was a turban. On the outside of the crate we wrote 'Attn: Vick Smith. Urgent Delivery from India'. Then we squashed Pratty inside the crate, nailed the top down and we got the forklift and we took the crate to the main store, to where Vick worked. Hot as buggery it was too. It's always hot in Dampier.

'Vick,' we said, 'there's a crate here, addressed to you. Urgent delivery from India.'

At the mention of India, that got him going. 'Bloody Indians' this and that. He went right off his tree.

'Vick,' we said, 'yer'd better come 'n' open up this crate.'

'Yeah, okay, I'll get to it in a minute,' and he went about his business.

Anyhow, old Vick didn't seem to be in too much of a hurry to open up this crate and so now we're getting worried about Pratty because, as I said, it gets stinking hot up in the north-west of Western Australia and it would've been a hell of a lot hotter if you're stuffed into a bloody crate, with the top nailed down. So we're following Vick around. 'Vick,' we're saying, 'you'd better open the crate.'

'Yeah, all bloody right.'

So he grabs his jemmy, struts over to the crate. Knocks the top off—'Bang'. Up pops Pratty, dark face and turban. He's not looking too good. Pratty looks at old Vick. Old Vick looks at Pratty. And, oh, my God, you should've seen old Vick. Fair dinkum, he just about shit himself.

Denicull Creek—Vic

I'm seventy-seven these days and while I've still got my marbles
I'd hate some of these stories to be lost. See, my dad was a
shearing contractor and I travelled with him to many distant
parts of the Riverina and western New South Wales, and so I met
some real characters along the way. One in particular was a very
well-educated chap called Francis William Carroll. To most he
was simply known as Paddy; Paddy Carroll. Unfortunately, he
lost his parents when he was a little kid and so he was brought
up by his uncle and aunt. Then, in his late teens, he ran away
and he came to work for Dad, first as a roustabout, then as a
shearer. A good shearer, too. A very clean shearer. You know, like
he'd bring them up pink.

Now, other than being a good shearer, Paddy was also a pretty
good storyteller. For example, one of the stories he told me was
about the first time he ever went to Melbourne. He'd never been
to the big smoke before and, for some reason or other, he had to
go there to catch a train up north. Mind you, he'd never been on
a train before either, so he didn't even know how to go about
getting a ticket. So, anyhow, someone from up bush gave Paddy
a ride down to Melbourne and they dropped him off at Spencer
Street Railway Station. Of course, the place was pretty crowded,
which was something else that Paddy wasn't used of, either. The
fewer the people the better was his line of thinking. Anyway, he's
looking around, wondering what to do, when he sees a sign
saying 'Ticket Office'. That's the place, thinks Paddy, and so he
goes over and he joins in the line-up, along with everyone else
wanting to buy tickets.

And, well, I guess you know that there's an outer suburb of
Melbourne called Lilydale. Lilydale? No, you didn't, well neither
did Paddy. So there's Paddy and he's standing in line wondering

Paddy's pushbike
—The Hansford Collection

how you go about buying a ticket. Anyhow, there's this lady in front of him who looks like she knows what she's doing so Paddy thinks, Well I'll just do what she does and I can't go too far wrong. So, when it comes to the woman's turn to buy her ticket, Paddy listens very, very carefully to what she says. First the feller behind the little window of the ticket office says, 'Yes, madam?'

Then the lady replies, 'Lilydale, single, thanks,' and she puts a pound note down on the counter and the feller gives her a ticket.

Good. So now it's Paddy's turn. 'Yes, mate,' says the feller behind the ticket office window.

Paddy puts down a pound and he says to the feller, 'Paddy Carroll, married with four kids, thanks.'

So that's just one of Paddy's stories and, by the way he told it, I never quite knew if it was fair dinkum or not. Like, he'd never smile or grin or anything to give himself away. So he had a pretty laconic sort of manner about him.

Then another story he told me happened at a little place called Denicull Creek. See, back in the old gold-mining days in Victoria, they put a road—a track really—through from Port Fairy, where a lot of the sailing boats used to arrive, right up to Ararat, where a lot of the mining was taking place. That'd be back in the 1850s I'd say. And along this track, each eight to ten mile, there'd always be a pub; you know, a place where a weary traveller could get something to drink, something to eat and have a place to stay, after a long day's walk or ride or whatever. So along this particular road, about five mile south of Ararat, was the small town of Denicull Creek.

To give you some idea, as you come over the Dividing Range from Ararat, heading south, there's a fairly steep gravel road going down the hill into Denicull Creek. Of course, this story happened long after the goldmining days. By now the area was used more for sheep grazing. But, anyhow, at the bottom of the hill there was this huge bend that swept past the Denicull Creek Hotel and by a huge stand of pine trees.

Anyhow, Paddy was riding his pushbike back from a weekend at Ararat and when he got to the top of the hill he decided to take his feet off the pedals and freewheel for a bit, just to make up some time. But before he realised it, he'd built up such a speed that he couldn't get his feet back on the pedals to slow himself down. And seeing how they didn't have brakes on the handlebars, back in them days, all Paddy could do was to hang on for dear life. So, down this hill he freewheeled, gathering speed at the rate of knots. And by the time he got to the bottom, and started into this sweeping bend, he was going so fast that he already had the bike lying down on its side. So, to save himself from a complete disaster, he decided he'd have to take the bend a little wider. Which he did by riding the bicycle off the road and up along the verandah of the pub, between the pub wall and the verandah posts. But then, at the end of the verandah, there was a little bit of a ramp where they offloaded the beer kegs, then there was this huge stand of pine trees and Paddy said, 'I remember getting to the end of the verandah, to where the ramp was, but that's the last of it because everything went black.'

Anyhow, he finally regained consciousness on his way to Ararat Hospital, then he stayed there for three days, recovering.

Following that, he spent two days recuperating in an after-care home. And when he went back to collect his bike, he said, 'You wouldn't believe it, there it was, stuck up in the fork of a pine tree, with its wheels still spinning.'

So, old Paddy would've had to have been travelling at a fair clip, ay?

Elliston—SA

I'd say it would've been around the end of June 1972 that a mate and I went over to the west coast of South Australia to do a spot of fishing. Anyhow, we ended up at a beautiful little place on the Eyre Peninsula, called Elliston. From memory, I think the pub we stayed in was called the Elliston Hotel.

Now, I've found out a couple of quite interesting things about Elliston, the first being that Elliston's one of the very few places in Australia that's been named after a writer. Her name was Ellen Liston. She was a governess over there during the 1850s and she had a few books published. So in gratitude to her it was originally known as Ellie's Town and that later got changed to Elliston. Then something else I discovered was that, back before it was named Ellie's Town, it was known as Waterloo Bay, and that name came about after a mob of Aborigines were herded up to the top of a cliff by some white settlers and given the choice, 'Either jump or be shot.' Then, from that incident, one of the white fellers concluded how the Aborigines had met their Waterloo. Hence the name Waterloo Bay, and the bay's still known as that.

Anyhow, all that aside, I've got a story about our stay at Elliston. See, when we went to the bar, my mate kindly offered to buy me a glass of Grandfather Port. Now, up until that stage, I'd never had a taste of that particular port before and, mind you, I've never had a taste of it since. So we had this glass of Grandfather Port then, as what happens, we had a few more and at some stage of the evening we got talking to the publican.

'So yer like yer Grandfather Port, ay?' he said.

My mate said, 'Yes I do, very much. It's a bit expensive but it's a nice drop.'

Anyway, the publican says, 'Well, you and yer liking for

Grandfather Port reminds me of an old story I was told, from many years ago.'

'Yeah,' we said.

And he told us a story that went something like this: see, pre-myxomatosis there was an old rabbiter who'd set up camp somewhere out of Elliston and he scraped out a meagre living by selling skins to the local dealer plus the occasional carcasses to the butcher and to some of the locals. Then, like so many did back in those days, this feller kept a shotgun close at hand, just in case he came upon a snake or got attacked by a dingo. Actually, rumour had it that, around Elliston at the time this story took place, there was a particularly vicious rogue dingo who'd been known to have, and I quote, 'ripped a few people to shreds' as the publican described it.

Anyhow, one day the old rabbiter had come into town to sell his skins and carcasses. Now, something I forgot was that the only transport this feller had was an old pushbike. That's all, an old pushbike. So he'd strung the carcasses across the handlebars and down along the pipe thing that goes between the steering column and the seat, and he'd stacked the rabbit skins in a wheat bag and tied it down, tight, on the carry-frame at the back of his bike. Then he slung his shotgun over his shoulder and off into Elliston he pedalled. It was a couple of hours ride or something. This was in the middle of summer and so he was pretty parched by the time he arrived in town and he was even more parched by the time he'd gone around and sold all his skins and his few carcasses. But by now he's got some money in his pocket and so he ends up in the pub.

'What'll yer have?' says the bloke behind the bar.

The old rabbiter says, 'Oh, I'm pretty flush so I might have a glass'a that Grandfather Port, over there.'

So the barman poured the old rabbiter a glass of Grandfather Port, which he downed. Then he downed another one. Then another. And by midnight this old rabbiter's blown all his hard-earned money on Grandfather Port, so he slurs, 'See yer,' to the barman and he staggers outside, slings his shotgun over his

The Rabbit Trap—The Hansford Collection

shoulder, gets on his pushbike and he heads out of town the long way. By 'the long way' I mean that the bike was zigzagging so badly from one side of the road to the other that, by the time he would've gotten back to his camp he would've almost covered twice the distance.

So there he was, snaking his way down this old dirt track. It's a nice moonlit night, but it's all getting the better of him. He's not seeing too well. In fact, you could liken him to being as blind as a bat, plus he's starting to feeling as crook as a dog. So he decides to lay down beside the dirt track to sleep it off. And it was while he was snoring away he thought he heard a dingo growl and, when he sprung awake, there, just a few feet from his face, were these two bright shining eyes. It's the rogue dingo! he thinks, so he grabs his shotgun and he gives it both barrels, straight between the eyes. 'Boom … Boom.' There's this hell of a racket, then all's quiet.

'Gotcha,' he said, then he went back to sleep.

It wasn't until mid-morning, with the sun pelting down, that the old rabbiter woke, with a hell of a hangover. The worst he's ever had in his entire life. 'I'll never touch another bloody drop of that bloody Grandfather Port again,' he swears. Then he recalls shooting the rogue dingo. He has a look around. But, no, not a sign. No dead dingo. No blood. Not even a paw print.

'Well, bugger me.' Then it was only when he went to get on his pushbike that he saw that the handlebars had been shot, clean off. So he must've woken up in the night and seen the moonlight reflecting off the handlebars and, in his drunken state, thinking they were the eyes of the rogue dingo, he'd inadvertently blown his own handlebars off.

So that's the story. Now, whether that's true or not, I don't know, but the publican was dead right about one thing: a night on the Grandfather Port gives you one hell of a hangover and so, like the old rabbiter, I swore that I'd never touch a drop of the stuff again.

Ferewana—NT

All Ferewana was, was a little bloody roadhouse cum pub about halfway between Camooweal and the Three Ways turn-off, just north of Tennant Creek. If I remember rightly, the Barkly Highway around Ferewana went as straight as a die for something like thirty-seven mile. The Barkly was all bitumen. The Americans done that during the war. They also bituminised from Alice Springs, right up to Darwin. Then all the bores that were put through that way were done by old George Gory. But, anyway, to give you some idea, there was nothing else out along this 600-kilometre or so stretch of bitumen, apart from Ferewana. That was the only place.

The actual roadhouse was a bit off the highway, about a hundred metres, and the bloke that owned it was a character called Ferewana Bill. I can't think of his surname because we only used to call him Bill or, if anyone was talking about him, they'd call him Ferewana Bill. A short stocky sort of bloke he was. Even back in the 1960s he was only probably in his late thirties, early forties. Not an elderly man by any means.

But there was no town there at Ferewana, just Bill and he looked after the roadhouse side of things as well as the pub. It was all in the one. To give you some sort of picture, out the front there were some apple-pine trees. They used to grow all out around that area. Then there was a bowser, maybe two. The roadhouse itself was nothing flash. Just a low on-the-ground place. Fibrolite and tin. You'd walk through the front and Ferewana Bill had a little bar on the side, to the right, where you could get a beer or whatever. Then you went to the left to pay for your fuel. Out the back was a toilet. Bill also used to live out the back somewhere. From memory, he was there, mostly, on his own. I don't even think he had a woman with him those days but there were always a few dogs around. Then, of course, the black fellas used to wander in and camp around the place too because, not that far down the road, there's the turn-off that shoots up to Borroloola, up in the Gulf.

So that was Ferewana. But this Ferewana Bill, what he used to do, the bugger, he had a generator that ran all his power, see. So between, say, 11 o'clock and 2 o'clock—around lunch time—he'd run the generator to get the fridges a bit cold. Then he'd turn the thing off and he wouldn't start it up again till five through to seven of an evening. Like, he'd get the beer a bit cold and then he'd turn the generator off, which also meant you couldn't get fuel between those hours. No power, no fuel. So if you lobbed into Ferewana at two-thirty of an afternoon and said, 'Oh, Bill can I get some fuel?' he'd say, 'Sorry, I can't give yer fuel yet, not till I start me generator up at five.'

And if you asked him why he couldn't start the generator up there and then he'd go into this big spiel about how it'd cost a fortune to start up the generator just to fill up one vehicle with fuel. So you'd say, 'Oh, okay,' and then, of course, there'd be nothing for you to do till 5 o'clock other than have a beer or two or three. So you'd get on the grog with him and so he'd make some extra money out of you that way. Then, by the time 5 o'clock rolled around, you'd be nice and relaxed and you'd say, 'Oh, well, I'm on the grog now so I may as well stay 'n' have a few more beers.' And before you knew it you'd be feeling hungry and you'd say, 'Oh well, I may as well have a feed.' So he'd make even more money out of you with the feed.

Then after you'd had a feed, you'd have a few more beers and before you know it, you'd be there all bloody night, drinking and going on. Then the next morning you'd get up and Ferewana Bill, he'd start up the generator, fill you up, and away you'd go. And that's what Ferewana Bill used to do so that he'd make a few extra dollars. Still, I guess he had to make a living too, the poor bugger.

But I remember one time, back in 1965, I got stuck there with a good mate of mine, Kenny McEwen, and we had another bloke with us called Ray Somebody-or-other. I can't think of his surname just now but this Ray feller, God he was a funny bloke. Now I was never a gambler but Ray used to bet a fair bit because he'd come to me and say, 'Graham, I've done me dough on the nags. Can yer lend us a few bucks' and I'd give him a few bucks and the next payday he'd give me back the twenty quid or whatever it was. Ray come from Victoria, from a place called Curyo. It's up near Swan Hill somewhere and Ray was a great impersonator. Like, out of the blue he'd say, 'And the time at 3 CO Curyo will be three o'clock on the third beep. Beep. Beep. Beep,' and you'd swear that it was coming out of a wireless. Oh, he was as good as gold. But, anyhow, not only could Ray mimic the time signal but he could also take off racing commentators. Like, he'd make up some horses' names and then he'd call a race straight off the top of his head. He'd say, 'They're neck 'n' neck half-way down the straight. With twenty yards ter go it's still anyone's race. They hit the post. It's so-and-so by the nose.' Oh, he used to do it well.

Anyhow, so it's 1965, we're stuck in the bar at Ferewana, Kenny, me and this Ray plus a few other blokes as well. We're all waiting for Ferewana Bill to turn the generator on and by this stage we'd had a few and this Ray feller pipes up, 'And the time at 3 CO Curyo will be three o'clock on the third beep. Beep. Beep. Beep. And now to the third at Randwick.' So then he starts giving this racing commentary and he did it so well that, after he'd called two or three more races, all these other blokes were placing bets on the horses that Ray was calling. Like, he'd tell everyone what horses were running in the next race and they'd place their bets and he'd call the race as if it was for real. I mean, true, we were all pretty pissed but, gee, he done a perfect job of it.

So then we all ended up staying overnight at Ferewana. We had a little old bloody caravan thing or we might've just camped on the floor of the bar. I can't remember. But that's the way it was back then. Everyone made their own entertainment. And we were in no rush. We used to work underground at the Mount Isa mines so we were pocketed up so if it was today or tomorrow it didn't

*The Barkley Highway. A
six-hundred kilometre or so
stretch of bitumen*
—The Hansford Collection

worry us, you know. Time didn't seem to mean as much, those days, as it does now. In those days none of us were in a hurry. And anyhow, at Ferewana, even if you were in a hurry you'd still have to wait. You had no choice. Ferewana Bill saw to that.

Yeah, so that's Ferewana; population nil, these days. It's gone now and so has Ferewana Bill. When they built another big, new, flash roadhouse up the road a bit he just closed up and went. I heard somewhere that he went back down to Alice Springs, working for the Department of Works. But I'd just love to know where the man is these days because, gee, they were good times. Like I said, no one seemed to be in a hurry.

Fitzgerald—Tas

I can remember being told a story. I guess it would've been in the 1940s. Anyway, there was a railway's depot at the end of the Derwent Valley line called Fitzgerald. Fitzgerald's a little scattered town out in the middle of the woop-woop. The main road was only a bush track up on the hill, a couple of miles above the railway station. It's in rainforest country so it's mainly timber industry. But, oh, it was a wild and woolly place.

Now most of the railway chaps were single men and they lived there in a barracks, which was stuck in the middle of a 'Y'. A 'Y' in Tasmania is the track where you turn engines. It's called a 'triangle' in other states of Australia. Oh, there's lots of funny things in Tasmania that I can tell you about, like someone calling someone a 'rumun'. That's short for rum one. It's a Tasmanianism you won't hear anywhere else in Australia and it means you're an 'odd bod'.

Anyway, this barracks at Fitzgerald was very small. They only had enough room for four or five single men's bedrooms with a combined kitchen-dining area which had a fuel stove. And of course, being single, all these fellows drank lots and lots and lots of beer, to such an extent that supplies would run out on a frighteningly regular basis. Now you've got to remember that roads around that neck of the woods were virtually non-existent so there were very few cars around. But the nearest pub was at National Park, which is the famous Mount Field National Park, where trains ran on a regular basis.

So on a Sunday the crews would have one of the locos steaming away in the engine shed, all banked up, ready to run. Then, when they run out of grog, they'd all hop aboard and away they'd go. Oh, there'd be about eight or nine of them all squeezed in the cabin. So there'd be quite a crowd. Anyhow, they'd tear off down the track, hoping that nothing else was on the line and they'd head for National Park.

Now, just past National Park, away from the road, there was a cutting and that's where they'd hide the engine. They'd just bank it up, put the handbrake on and off to the pub they'd go. Then, before they headed back to their barracks, just in case of an emergency, they'd buy a barrel of beer, roll it down the track, load it onto the engine, then they'd go at breakneck speed back to Fitzgerald which, as you might imagine, would've been a hairy-scary trip.

But near where they used to park the loco, there was a house and, I don't remember the lady's name, but she'd see all these goings-on and she'd inform the railway office in Hobart about how these fellows were up to no good. But of course, in those days, the grapevine was extremely efficient so each time some official or other came sneaking around, these fellows would be acting like angels. But, anyhow, because they knew this lady was dobbing them in, whenever they saw her standing on the platform, waiting to catch the train, they'd just give her a wave and shoot straight past.

Then there was another train driver called Doc. Doc lived in a camp down behind the barracks that we'd named 'Skid Row'. So you can just imagine what it was like. Anyway, Doc kept a cow near the barracks so that whenever the crews wanted milk they'd just go out and milk this cow. Now Doc looked after this old cow like it was a pet, you know, so it was always hanging around the barracks. Then, of course, they had a vegetable garden there, which was another one of Doc's pet projects. Now having a vegetable garden was very common with railway blokes. They had gardens all over the place. It's known Australia-wide that railway men were good gardeners. Anyway, these blokes were on the booze one night, as per usual, and, at one stage, one of the train drivers, old Rastus, he staggered back into the common room and yelled, 'Somethin's out there's eatin' the friggin' lettuces.'

And old Doc, who was in his usual drunken state, replied, 'Don't worry, Rastus, I'll sort it out.'

'Doc kept a cow near the barracks'
—The Hansford Collection

So Doc grabs his shotgun and stumbled outside. Next thing they hear is this almighty 'BOOM!' And you can just imagine it; Doc, coming back into the barracks and standing at the door, with his big hat stuck right back on his head, the barrel of his shotgun still smoking. Then he looked around the room for a bit, wide-mouthed, with a bewildered look in his eye.

'What's up, Doc?' the fellers asked.

'I'll be stuffed,' Doc slurred. 'I think I just shot me own bloody cow.'

Fitzroy Crossing—WA

My name's Phil O'Brien and I've written a few books about my many experiences. One's called *101 Adventures that got Me Absolutely Nowhere* and another one's called *The Minor Successes of a Bloke that Never had a Real Lot of Luck*. So do you want to hear one of my stories? Okay, so this one came about in a roundabout sort of way really. It happened at Fitzroy Crossing, a nice little place in the north of Western Australia, about 250 k's east of Derby. Now, I'm not really sure how the town started but I think it was used as a stock crossing across the Fitzroy River, for drovers and that, during the dry season. It's got a mostly all-Aboriginal population and I was told that from right back in the late 1800s, when the first whites arrived, there'd been a lot of trouble, especially around the Geikie Gorge area. Like a lot of Aborigines were rounded up and killed and that.

But anyhow, see, one day I decided to do this big trek from Darwin across to Broome in my little old Datsun. This was in the early 1980s. There was no great reason behind it other than it being an adventure. But being young and naïve, I set off in the wet season, which was my first big mistake 'cause I was forever getting bogged. Then another time I ran out of fuel and got towed by a road-train. That was pretty hairy. If you can imagine; there's these three massive trailers, packed full of cattle, then tailing on behind that was about six foot of rope and me being dragged along in the little Datsun. It was terrifying.

So it took me a couple of weeks longer to get to Broome than I thought and then, when I got there, the cops went and defected the Datsun and they ran it straight off the road. So I didn't have any transport. But I met up with some people who'd come up from Perth and we became friends. They were on the bones of their arses as well and so we made a bit of a camp in the bush, halfway between town and Cable Beach. It was all bush back then. Four miles of it. Now it's all houses and resorts. And so we were living out there and we'd walk into town, to the Continental Hotel, just to be in the pub atmosphere. It was a good pub but, seeing we couldn't afford beer, we just drank ice water. Then, when things got real bad, we pinched a twenty kilo sack of spuds out of the kitchen of the pub and we lived on them for a couple of weeks; you know, cooked on the campfire.

So the future wasn't looking real good. Then, when I was in the Continental one time, I heard about some work going with this oil exploration mob, out in the Kimberleys, so I went down to the Commonwealth Employment mob and I got the job. About five of us got employed; me and some Aboriginal fellers. They weren't the blokes from Perth I was camping with. The Perth blokes stayed in Broome. When I left they were throwing rocks at coconuts, trying to knock them out of the trees, to get a feed.

Anyway, me and these Aborigines, we went out with this oil exploration mob, somewhere around Christmas Creek Station. I can't remember exactly where and neither can I exactly remember what the actual blue was all about. But there was this almighty blue, and me and the Aborigines told the oil exploration boss where he could stick his job and so we walked off and we hitched a ride into Fitzroy Crossing, with some station people. Then the Aboriginal blokes hitched back to Broome.

Fitzroy Crossing was just a little place back then. Pretty wild. But, see, I didn't want to go back to Broome and end up living out bush again, eating spuds and coconuts. I wanted to get back to Darwin so I went up to the pub. I think it was called The Crossing Inn or something. It was an old pub, anyway, up on a bit of a hill. It might've even been one of the first buildings in Fitzroy Crossing. But all around the pub, like, going for hundreds of metres in every direction, there was just this sea of empty beer cans. Cans everywhere. So I went into the pub. It was all Aboriginal. I was the only white bloke. There was no problem with that. They welcomed me in. You know, the Aboriginal people are very friendly, honest people, and I remember, blaring out of the juke box was Shakin' Stevens singing his hit song 'This Old House' and, like, the whole night, all there was, was Shakin' Stevens singing 'This Old House'.

I only had what I was wearing: a pair of thongs, a pair of shorts and a good King Gee work shirt. Then I also had a towel and a radio-cassette player. I had no money so I sold the radio-cassette player for sixty bucks, which wasn't bad in those days, and I started drinking into that. But, see, 'cause I now had money, everyone was trying to hit me up for a beer. And they all had their own style. Like, one bloke said he was a kadaitcha man—a powerful medicine man—and he reckoned that, in the olden days, whenever he wanted to get rid of someone, he used to point the bone at them and they'd die a slow death. But now, since he'd been to Vietnam, he said, 'Now I just shoot 'em. Bang! 'n' they're dead. Saves time.' And so he hit me up for a beer for telling me that story. Then another bloke come up and he told me that if I bought him a beer he'd watch my back. Like, he'd protect me and make sure no one robbed me or nothing. He reckoned he used to be a real good boxer and, to prove it, he sparred around a bit, shadow boxing. So I bought him a beer, too.

Anyhow, I just charged on there and, oh, it was great. But before long all me money was gone. Then near the end of the night a young bloke and his girlfriend turned up in an old HT Holden station wagon. I can't remember where they came from or where they were going but I got talking to them and they said, 'Well, look, if yer've got nowhere else to sleep you may as well crash in the front seat of our Holden.'

So that's what I did. I choked out in the front seat of their Holden and they bunked down in the back and when I woke up in the morning all I had on was me shorts and thongs. Some bugger had reached in the car and stole the King Gee work shirt, clean off me back. Like, nicked it. It was a good shirt too. I was pretty much stuffed then. The future wasn't looking real good and all I wanted to do was to get back to Darwin. So I really had to pull something out of the bag and that's when I got the idea of talking the young bloke with the girlfriend into going for my old job, out with the oil exploration mob. At first he wasn't that keen so then I bullshitted it up to make it sound like it was a really great job, with great money, great blokes, great conditions and, in the end, he fell for it. So we drove out to where the exploration camp was and the boss took him straight on. Like, with me and the Aborigines having had the big blue with him and walking off, he was stuck for workers.

So the young bloke got the job and then I took off with his girlfriend. I talked her into going to Darwin. And didn't we have a great time, ay. I tell you, she was a real hot potato, she was.

Ganmain—NSW

My name's John Bartlett. I was born in 1923 and I grew up in a little place, out near Wagga Wagga, called Ganmain. Back then it would've only had a population of about 100–120 people, tops, and, as kids, we were number one at playing football. We used to travel all over the place and we'd beat the lot of them. But I'd like to tell you about my dad, John 'Ted' Bartlett. See, before coming to Ganmain, he worked on the Berembed Weir, which is where the Murrumbidgee Irrigation Area (MIA) water comes out of the Murrumbidgee River, near Narrandera. Dad had a horse and a plough and a scoop and he was helping make the weir and the system of channels that supplied water to all the farms. And because it was a government project you had to belong to a union so, later on, when he died, he left me all his union tickets and those are now in the Mitchell Library, along with the overall story of the MIA from 1913, when it was first laid out.

So when Dad finished up there, he came to Ganmain. Actually, Ganmain was first called Boggy Creek because it was a watering hole between Coolamon and Matong. Then in the early 1890s, when a town started to grow around the new railway station and water tank, it was renamed 'Ganmain' after a huge sheep station in the district called the Ganmain Run. Now, something quite unique to Australia would be that the actual creek—Boggy Creek—went right up the main street of Ganmain. So it's just lucky that it only run when there was a tremendous rain, and that was pretty rare because, as a kid, I can only remember it flooding just the once.

Anyhow, when they found out that the area was suited to wheat and oats, Mellor & Murphy came along and they set up the biggest chaff mill in the Riverina, at Ganmain. So Dad was contracted by Mellor & Murphy as a hay carter and he did one load per day. Now, of course, back then they didn't have any of the fancy machinery they have today so what they did was, when the crop was ready for harvest, it was cut off down near the soil, with a reaper and binder and bound up into sheaves. Then the sheaves were stacked up in little stooks out in the paddock for about a fortnight, till they dried out. There were eight sheaves in a stook.

Then, after they'd dried, hay carters like Dad would come along and have workmen with pitchforks throw these dried sheaves up onto a large frame that was built onto a massive horse-drawn wagon. Dad's wagon had four six-foot-high wheels and there was a massive overhang so you could stack as much hay as possible on them. Really, it was like building a huge hay stack on top of the wagon. And the biggest load that Dad ever took to the mill was fourteen ton, which is a hell of a load.

Of course, this was getting into the Depression times so labour was never short and I remember the hobos coming through and asking Dad for a job. Now, what Dad had done was that he'd stuck a pole out the side of a tree, about fifty foot up in the air and so, if he needed a workman, instead of an interview he'd say to the feller, 'Here's a pitchfork. There's a sheaf of wheat. If you can throw it over that pole, up there, in the tree, you've got the job.' A sheaf of wheat would've weighed about twenty pound. And, naturally, if they couldn't throw it up and up over the pole in the tree, they wouldn't have had a ghost of a chance of being able to pitchfork the sheaves as they got stacked taller and taller on top of the wagon.

Anyhow, after Dad'd loaded his wagon, he'd take the hay into the chaff mill where they'd put it through a thrasher to take the heads of wheat off, and that'd go into bags, to be railed off and be made into flour. The rest would end up as chaff, which was fed to horses and other stock. See, nothing was wasted because, back in the 1930s, just about everyone in the district had a pony and trap. So really, Ganmain started out as pretty much just a railway siding for the transportation of grain and hay. In its time it was said to be one of the biggest wheat growing areas in

Welcome to Ganmain—The Bartlett Collection

Australia, which is why it got known as the 'Sheaf Hay Centre on the plains'. These days, there's even a big mock-up of a hay stack in the main street.

But it was a pretty hard life because Dad'd head out at about 2 o'clock of a morning to yoke up his twenty draughthorses. He had three wagons like I described; one wagon would be in his horse yard, one'd be being unloaded in at the chaff mill, while the third one was being loaded out in the cocky's paddock. And he'd rotate his three wagons with the same team of twenty horses. And he knew every horse. Every horse had its name. When he'd go down to yoke them up he'd say, 'Righto, Dolly, you're next' and Dolly'd walk over and he'd put the traps on. Then, when they were all done, away he'd go with his twenty draught-horses, set up in pairs. And Dad never had reins or nothing to control his team of horses. No whip. No stick. He'd just talk to them, and each horse knew exactly what to do when it was called to 'come over' or 'move up' or 'slow down' or whatever.

Then after he'd finished his day's work he'd bring the horses back to the horse yard. He'd see to them first, then on the way home he'd stop off at the Ganmain Hotel for a drink. So it'd be a long day, from about 2 o'clock of a morning and he'd end up getting home at about 8 o'clock at night then every Saturday he'd go down to the horse yard and make his own horse shoes and shoe the horses. He'd only have the Sunday off. He wasn't religious or nothing; just a hard-working old bushie. Though, now I'm thinking about it, with having fathered seven kids—five girls and two boys—the occasional Sunday might've been pretty busy as well, ay?

Anyhow, so Dad hauled hay right up till 1934 which was when the 4-ton Chevy trucks came in. His team became irrelevant then, and so they went into the history books. Then seeing he'd worked building channels and that for the MIA he got a job at Deniliquin, working on the channels down there.

But see, I was always on about Dad and the old days out at Ganmain and so about three months ago I took the family down to show them where we come from. There was three carloads of us. But the old railway station had gone. There's just a dirt mound where the platform and the big old waiting room used to be. Also, the big old square metal water tank that they needed for the steam trains, that's no longer there, and a lot of the track's gone. But the school's still there, and I remembered that one main street used to have two pubs; the Royal and the Ganmain, which was where Dad used to drink. Actually, the Ganmain had a bit of a history. It was first built in the late 1880s and in 1908 it was destroyed by fire and rebuilt again. Then it was destroyed by fire again in 1930 and rebuilt. The Royal's now shut down but I think it was also destroyed by fire and rebuilt at some stage. So there seems to be some sort of a pattern here. Anyway, the Ganmain Hotel's still going so we stopped in there for a drink in Dad's honour.

But, of his three wagons, I remembered that two were sold at his equipment sale, back in the Easter of 1934, and when I took the family down to where he had his old horse yard, there was the third one, still sitting there, abandoned, by the side of Matong Road. And though it was in a pretty sad state of disrepair the family were absolutely amazed by it, being city kids or almost. So we got pieces of wood off it and a couple of the bolts out of it and we brought them home. But, no, they weren't disappointed. They thought it was a great day, a really great day. And so did I, because all those things are important to all of us.

Gascoyne Junction—WA

These days I'm retired, but I've done a little bit of country teaching in my time; about thirty years to be exact. Yeah, so it's just a bit more than a little bit, I guess. But I remember when we went to Gascoyne Junction. Gascoyne Junction's about two-and-a-half hours drive east of Carnarvon, which is up on the central coast of Western Australia.

I sort of applied for the position. Though, in saying that, you could describe it more as an 'appointment by choice' really. See, in those days, being in a one-teacher school was a step along the promotion line. And that's the way the wife and I saw it. Looking to the future. So I applied, in order of priority, for about twenty-seven placements, with Gascoyne being the twenty-seventh on the list. And I got it. But you didn't argue with the system. You just took it.

At the time my wife was pregnant with our third child and, that first day, she cried all the way, from the time we left Carnarvon and we hit the gravel road, out to Gascoyne Junction. Oh, it was a hot, dusty, dry journey, with an overloaded vehicle. Absolutely terrible. And when we finally arrived, the house was like an oven. I mean, the house had been designed specifically for those areas. It had the cyclone shutters and the windows where you could open the bottom and let the breeze blow through. But we'd been told it had air conditioning and, yes, it had an air conditioner alright; the only trouble was, the bloody thing didn't work. Then the house relied on the town's power supply which turned out to be a generator that was housed in a big shed about two blocks down from where we lived. Then, that used to crash. So much so that the pub had its own subsidiary power as well, just in case, which was a wise move.

So we'd arrived at the Shire of Gascoyne Junction and, while I was there, the school only averaged about six pupils. There weren't that many people living in the town itself; just the shire clerk, the police sergeant, the shire foreman, a couple of shire workers and the publican, plus their families, of course. But you made the most of it, and it was a strong, active community. For example, people came from near and far for the yearly Gascoyne races. A dirt track, of course. As for the horses, some were brumbies and some were well-bred, country-class horses. The main event was the Gascoyne Cup. But the occasion was made more unique in terms of the social events afterwards. The ball was the main attraction and we had midnight motorbike scrambles, sing-a-longs around campfires, we'd listen to the old fellers from off the various stations telling stories and before you knew it you'd be barbecuing some snags at three o'clock in the morning, with a beer in your hand. Those sorts of things. So it was a pretty lively sort of place.

It was all sheep country, at that stage. With Gascoyne being one of the better pastoral areas there was some very high class Merino wool around, especially at Bidgemia and Jimba Jimba stations. Bidgemia was run by the McTaggarts and Jimba Jimba used to be run by the Vivashes. Anyhow, I used to go out to Jimba Jimba and help with the mustering. You know, get on the bike and things of a weekend. I didn't make any money out of it. The mustering I did was just out of pure enjoyment.

Then, because I'd worked in shearing pens before I went into teaching, when Sandy McTaggart was at Bidgemia he used to fly me out to some of his outlying stations and we'd press out the straggler wool at whatever shed they were shearing at. The McTaggarts paid me. At that stage it was a dollar-fifty a bale, which wasn't going to make me a fortune. Still, it was about forty cents more than what I'd got in the shearing pens. But, you know, they flew me out. I stayed there. I pressed the wool. They flew me back. I'd head off on the Friday and be back on the Sunday. So it was all in my own time.

So all those sorts of things kept you busy and actively in with the local community. Then we also used to run the Saturday night pictures. We'd order the movies up from Perth and they'd arrive in these big cans, on these big spools, and we'd hitch the spools onto the projector and away they'd go. That was at the school. Outside, usually. We didn't get much rain. We just provided the projector and the screen and everyone brought their own chairs and that along. It got a bit chilly at times but, on the warm nights, there'd be no better place to just sit and watch a movie.

It's all about community, really. Getting involved. Of course, the pub also provided a bit of night life. Some very interesting times were had at the Gascoyne Hotel, I can assure you. The pub itself was a sort of a corrugated iron construction and when the Gascoyne River flooded, the pub got flooded as well. Really, any time it rained, the roads were pretty well impassable. No bitumen; all gravel and clay so then, when it rained and they had to close the road, the tourist buses would be stranded too. Oh, they'd be heading from Carnarvon through to Meekatharra or out to some of the station country; maybe Mount Augustus or down to the Landore Station Races, depending on what time of year it was.

But one incident that comes to mind was when one of the tourist buses got stuck at Gascoyne Junction. I'd say there would've been about fourteen to twenty people. I can't really remember. But it'd rained and they'd closed the road and I'd been down the pub having a few sherbets, chatting away, and so, to entertain these stranded tourists, I drove back home in my HK Holden station wagon, grabbed the projector and the screen, and came back and set a movie going inside the main bar. Anyhow, while the film was running, I got a little bit pie-eyed and fell asleep, sitting on the floor. I can't recall the movie—obviously— but they'd just wake me up when it was time to change the spools. But, oh, if I reckoned that the drive home and then back to the pub, with the film gear, was a slippery enough affair, you should've seen me in the morning. Because it'd rained all night, the road had become so muddy that it took me about three hours to drive home. And I only lived 300 metres from the pub.

Georgetown—Qld

To give you a location, Georgetown is exactly a hundred mile south-east of Croydon. Croydon being up in the Gulf country of Queensland. Then the next town, heading east, would be Mount Surprise. That'd be about eighty mile. This is in miles. I don't understand that other language. But away back in the early days, Georgetown had a big gold rush. Then a copper rush happened not long after. So that's what got Georgetown going; gold and copper. Then after the copper had run out, the area went over to beef cattle. There's some quite large stations around the area. It's not bad country either, except the Milky Creeper has crept into it, these days.

Now I don't know how big the place was, or how many pubs there were in those early days, but there was only one pub in my time. It was one of them beautiful old-fashioned two-storey places, with the wrought iron around the verandah and the bat-wing doors, like they had in the American cowboy films. All western Queensland had them back then. Then there were stables down the back of the pub where people could put their horses and that. I went through there many times back in my droving days.

Okay then, so this was during the 50s. I was going through Georgetown and I saw this sign outside town advertising a drinking donkey at the pub. From memory, the sign itself was a crude sort of painting of a donkey, with someone holding a beer, and it said 'The Famous Drinking Donkey—at the Georgetown Pub' or words to that effect. Apparently a lady had found it wandering out along the Croydon–Georgetown road. He'd been gelded. He was pretty young, but he was in a very dire situation. Very distressed and very poorly. So that's what happened and, in the end, he took a liking to beer and so he became a local identity

'The Famous Drinking Donkey'—The Hansford Collection

up at the pub. People knew of him even down around Cairns and all them places. You know, they'd say, 'If you ever go ter Georgetown yer must go 'n' have a beer with the donkey.'

The publican's name was George Dickson. George was a very good friend of mine. Every time I'd go through Georgetown, I'd call into the bar and it was, 'Oh, g'day, Goldie. Good to see yer,' and he'd introduce me to everyone and sort me out with a drink straight away. We were great mates.

Anyhow, so I goes into the bar and there's the donkey having a beer with a tourist. See, the way they done it was, they'd hold up the stubby and the donkey would just guzzle it down, like there was no tomorrow. Of course, all this did wonders for George's beer sales. And, not only that, George also had a stack of film stored behind the bar and, for a price, the tourists could have their photos taken drinking with the donkey; you know, with their arm around his neck and, if I remember correctly, George had also put a couple of holes through the top of an old cowboy hat for the donkey's ears to go through. So, yeah, he was a real novelty. What's more, George was making a real killing on it. Oh, and that's right, as it turned out, this donkey wasn't only an alcoholic but he was also addicted to nicotine and after he'd had a few beers he'd go around the place looking for cigarette bumpers to eat off the floor. You know, lick them up off the floor. So this donkey not only provided George with a massive boost in beer sales and from the supply of film, it also saved a lot on George's cleaning bill.

Anyway, it was about ten o'clock in the morning when I arrived and so I said to George, 'How many's he had today?'

George says, 'Oh, about twelve or fifteen.'

I mean, twelve or fifteen stubbies by ten o'clock in the morning is a fair bit of grog because, if I remember correctly, the stubbies back then were a fair bit bigger than what they are these days. So I said, 'Boy, I couldn't drink that many in two days.'

But, that's how it went. The donkey would drink all day and night with whoever wanted to buy him a beer. Then, after closing time, George would let him out the back door and he'd stagger down to his stable to sleep it off. And then, of a morning, he'd be there at the back door, bright eyed and bushy tailed, waiting for the bar to open so he could go through the whole thing again.

Anyway, after I'd spent some time with George, I moved on. But I was later told that one day while the donkey was up at the bar, drinking with the tourists, the council came along and they dug a big trench right across the backyard, between the back door of the pub and the stables, where the donkey lived. So then, after closing time that night, when the donkey wobbled off in the direction of his stable, down he went into this trench.

Now the trench itself was about three feet wide and about nine or ten feet deep. So it was pretty deep, and it was pretty narrow. And unfortunately, when the donkey fell down the trench, it somehow fell backwards, so he ended up stuck there all night, on his back, with his legs sticking up in the air. Then, when the council fellers arrived the next day, they came across this upside-down donkey, stuck in their trench.

'Well, I'll be blowed,' they said, and they went back to the council depot to organise a crane.

Anyhow, after a lot of to-ing and fro-ing and a lot of mucking about, they eventually hoisted the donkey out of the trench. And do you know what? That donkey would never, ever drink alcohol again. True. They tried dragging him up to the bar and forcing him to drink and everything. But, no, he wouldn't touch the stuff. He'd given up the grog, totally, and so George had to go and pull the sign down.

Great Ocean Road—Vic

My father-in-law, Colin Cooper, was one of those real gems. Col was born in Colac, spent his childhood in Lavers Hill and Beech Forest. Now, I know it's not what you'd describe as the 'outback', but he lived and worked in many small towns throughout Victoria and one of those places was out along the Great Ocean Road which, these days, is a much visited part of Victoria even though the Twelve Apostles are now only eleven. But, of course, back in Col's time, the Great Ocean Road drive wasn't as popular as it is today.

Now, I've actually forgotten the name of the town he was living in at the time but it was just a small place, just off the highway, somewhere around Lorne. And the way Col told the story was that, one day, he was working at the local garage in this tiny place. Anyhow, the garage only had the one petrol bowser, which was usually enough because customers were so few and far between. So Col was sitting in his little office sort of thing, reading the newspaper, catching up on all the horrible things that were going on in the world, when a bloke drove in. Col reckoned that the chap looked the dead-spitting image of one of the gangster types he'd seen a picture of in the newspaper; you know, European, with the black suit and dark sunglasses.

'Hey, you, fill it up'a,' this bloke called out, in a none too friendly tone.

'Okay,' says Col and he walked out of his office sort of thing and he started filling the car up with petrol.

Now, this was a long time ago so I'm not sure what the biggest and latest cars were back then but, anyway, it was something like, let's say, a Fairlane. You know, the types that either gangsters or lost rich tourists drive.

'Nice car yer got,' said Col, in an attempt to be friendly.

'Yeah, maybe,' replied the owner, obviously none too interested in anything someone like Col might have to say.

Anyhow, as Col continued filling the car, this shifty sort of bloke happened to notice that attached to the garage was an old corrugated shed which was where Col did a bit of car servicing and where he kept whatever mechanical bits and pieces he'd come across over the years. 'You never know when a piece of junk might come in handy, do you?'—that was Col's philosophy. So when the bloke saw the shed he said, 'You wouldn't happen to have'a spare hubcap for'a car like'a mine, would you? I've'a lost d' one on d' front'a driver's side.'

Of course, being one of the latest model Fairlanes, there was no way that Col would've had one but, anyhow, Col said, 'Maybe. I'll have a bit of a poke around after I've finished filling up your car.'

'Yeah, okay,' said the bloke. Then he said, 'Well, look'a, while you're doing all that I might'a go 'n' have'a bit of' a look 'round this'a dump.'

Well, to call the town a dump sort of hurt Col a bit. I mean, he wasn't what you'd call one of those real sensitive types but this was the place where he and his wife had lived for yonks. They'd raised kids and everything there. It was a good, friendly community. No crime. Great lifestyle. I mean, what more could you ask for? But before Col could think of anything to say in reply, the bloke had locked his car in the middle of the service way and off he'd wandered.

Anyhow, Col finished filling up the car. He knew he didn't have any hub caps to suit the latest model Fairlane so he went back to his little office and continued reading the newspaper. Half an hour later, the bloke hadn't returned. An hour later, still no sign. Now, where this little town was, the petrol bowser might only get used once, maybe twice a day, and that's only when things got busy. 'But you never know, do you?'—which was another of Col's philosophies. And with having the one and only petrol bowser being taken up by this flash car, Col could see that if there was a sudden rush on petrol he'd be in strife. 'It's bad for business,' as he'd say.

But what could he do about it? Nothing, so he kept on reading the paper. The only trouble was that, the more he read of the newspaper, the more horrific the news became. And the more Col read those sorts of stories, the more peeved he got about the world in general and, in particular, the more he got peeved that some shifty-looking bastard, from God knows where, could come along in his flash car and take up the one and only petrol bowser at his precious petrol station.

Anyhow, half an hour later and Col had had enough, so he went out to the Fairlane and he took the hub cap off the back passenger side of the vehicle and he stuck it on the front driver's side, to make it look like he'd found a new one. No sooner had he done that than Col noticed the bloke coming back down the street. From the unsteady way he was walking it was obvious he'd been down the pub for the last couple of hours. Anyhow, Col held his temperament and, when the bloke arrived, he pointed to the replaced front driver's side hub cap and he said, 'There yer go. All done.'

The Fairlane—The Hansford Collection

The bloke gave a nod of recognition. 'How much'a is that?' he grunted.

'Oh, just pay for the petrol 'n' we'll call the hub-cap an act of customer relations.'

Without another word, the bloke paid for the petrol then he jumped into his Fairlane and he took off back out and onto the Great Ocean Road, leaving Col to wander back into his office and continue reading his newspaper. Yet, somehow, the world seemed like a much brighter place.

Anyhow, life drifted on in its usual manner until a couple of weeks later. It was a weekend and Col was in his little office at the garage, newspaper spread out, reading about all the terrible things that were going on in the world, when in pulls this flash new Fairlane. Out steps the same bloke—European, black suit, sunglasses—and he's not looking too happy at all.

Blimey, here's trouble, Col thinks to himself.

Anyway, the bloke has a quick shifty sort of look around the place before he comes striding over to Col who's now trying to make himself invisible behind the newspaper.

'Hey'a, mate,' the bloke called out, 'you wouldn't have another one'a them hub caps'a, would you. I gone 'n' lost the one off'a d' back passenger's side now.'

Halls Creek—WA

This might sound like a little bit of an odd one, mate, but I'm hoping you might be able to help me out. Now, if you don't mind, I'd prefer it if you didn't mention the name of the actual town where this happened. It's just that, if me mates found out, it'd upset them. I mean, the chances are pretty slim anyway, I guess, because, if the truth be known, I don't think they've ever read a book in their lives. Same here. You know, by the time you've finished work you're usually pretty knackered and so there's only enough time for a few beers and a bit of a yarn with your mates, then go home for a bite to eat before you hit the sack. No time for reading books. Still, I guess, it'd be okay to say that the town's in the Kimberley area of Western Australia. God's own country, I tell you.

Now, I don't know much about the history of the place because me and me mates, we're just workers, out on the roads, but I think they found gold here once upon a time and also drovers used to come through this way because it's at the top of the Canning Stock Route, which has probably given the town's name away. But who gives a bugger. It just shows how desperate I am. But that's all I'm saying.

Okay, now, this all happened about a year or so ago, right. It was a Friday night and we'd knocked off from work and we were in the front bar. There was Bluey, Tail-lights, Tugga and me. The nickname of Bluey is pretty obvious, because he's got red hair. Then Tail-lights because, if there's any trouble, that's all you'll ever see of him, is his tail-lights, and Tugga, well, you can work that one out for yourself. But that's all beside the point because on this particular night there was a bloke sitting over in the corner, drinking by himself. We'd never seen him before but, to give you some sort of idea, I'd say he would've been about fifty—

around our age. It was pretty obvious he wasn't a bush sort of feller. He was more city. You know, like he could've come from Darwin or somewhere, where they dress up a bit more, and he had a briefcase, so he was some sort of a business feller or other.

Anyhow, we never like to see a man drinking alone so we took him over a beer and said, 'G'day'. 'Thanks,' he said and then we got talking about this, that and the other and, somewhere along the line, I saw that he had a book there with him. So I asked him about it and it turned out to be one of yours. I forget what it was called but it was a Great something-or-other. I haven't read any of them, myself, personally, but this feller seemed to be quite a fan of yours, so that's how I remembered your name: Swampy Marsh.

Now I forget the bloke's name but the thing was that, after we got talking to him, somehow it got around to his personal life and he started telling us how he'd only recently been through a rough patch with his missus. Same old thing; she was unhappy, he was unhappy, and, you know, how, after thirty years of being married he'd started to lose the urge, so to speak. Of course, we could all relate to that. I mean, Blue had been married for about thirty years. Same with Tail-lights. I'd been married just on twenty-two years, as the wife continually reminds me. Tugga, of course, is still single. Anyhow, it seemed like the feller really wanted to talk about it, so Bluey asked if they'd split up.

'Oh, God no,' he said, 'we sorted it out 'n' now we're closer than ever.'

'How's that?' we asked.

He said, 'Well, this feller sold me a special ointment.'

'Is that right?' we said.

'Yep, heaps better than Viagra,' he said, and he sort of gave us that type of look that made it clear as to exactly what he was on about. Then he added, 'So good, in fact, that me 'n' the wife ended up buying the company that made the stuff.'

'Gee, have yer got any with yer?' asked Tail-lights.

'As a matter of fact,' he said, 'I've got a little bit left here in a sample jar,' and he pulled this small red jar out of his coat pocket. I mean, it didn't look too fancy. There was a printed label glued on it that read 'Johnson's Pawpaw Magic'. Then below that it was wrote how it was good for just about everything—including you know what—and then right at the bottom there was a telephone number.

'Open it up,' he said. 'Take a look.'

So we unscrewed the lid. Just a tiny little jar it was. The ointment was slightly greasy—a bit thicker than Vaseline—but it had a slight tingle to it. And it had a flowery sort of smell that you'd reckon a woman might be attracted to. The bloke said how it was made up from 95 per cent concentrated pawpaw and the other 5 per cent was some sort of a secret magic ingredient that— how can I say—well, if you rubbed just a little bit it on yourself, it got things up and going, if you catch my drift.

'No kiddin',' we said.

'As true as I stand here,' says the bloke.

So, naturally, we were pretty keen on getting ourselves a jar.

'Gee, you'll be lucky,' the bloke said. 'I sold out in Broome, in only two days, 'n' I'm just on my way back to Darwin to pick up another batch.'

But, anyhow, he dug around in his briefcase and, as luck would have it, he found four sample jars. That's all he had left; just the four sample jars.

'So how much is it?' asked Blue.

'Oh,' he said, 'a sample jar like this retails for around a hundred dollars.'

'A hundred fuckin' dollars,' says Tugga. 'Christ, yer could buy a hell-of-a-lot'a beer fer a hundred dollars.'

Then the feller said that, because he appreciated how we'd gone out of our way to make him welcome, he'd give us a 'mates-rates discount' which, when he calculated it out, worked out to be fifty dollars a jar. So we borrowed some money off Ted, the publican, and we bought ourselves a jar each. Just a sample jar. Even Tugga.

'You'll never regret it,' the feller said and he told us that, when we run out of that lot, we could get in touch with him via the telephone number on the bottom of the label and he'd organise a shipment over for us right away at the same mates-rates discount.

So, to cut a long story short, we forked out a pretty hefty sum of money for these four tiny sample jars of this Johnson's Pawpaw Magic then we downed our beers and said 'Cheerio' to the bloke and we left the pub a fair bit earlier than usual.

Anyhow, next morning I gets this phone call from Blue. 'We've been diddled,' he said. 'The bloody stuff doesn't work. I've rung the other fellers. The same thing. We've been taken for a ride.'

'Oh yeah,' I said. 'Even Tugga?'

'Yeah,' said Blue, 'so we're goin' round to the pub to sort this feller out 'n' get our money back.'

'Oh, yeah,' I said.

'Are yer comin'?'

Now, here's the tricky bit. See, while it mightn't have worked for the other fellers, in my particular case, it did work. In fact, it was the best night that me and the wife had had for yonks. But what could I do, ay? I just couldn't tell me best mates that it'd worked fantastic for me. That'd only make them feel like they was duds, wouldn't it? Anyhow, best mates always stick together so I said to Blue, 'Yeah, the stuff was bloody crap. I'll be ready in ten. Pick me up on yer way through.'

But, as it turned out, when we arrived at the pub, the feller wasn't there. Ted told us that he'd left town earlier that morning on some sort of urgent business. So that was that. This bloke had got away with a couple of hundred quid and the ointment didn't work ... well, not on me mates, it didn't.

So that's basically the story and that happened about a year ago now and I've been trying to get in touch with the bloke, for him to send me over some more of the ointment. The only trouble is the telephone number that was wrote on the jar doesn't seem to work and I can't find hide nor hair of Johnson's Pawpaw Magic in the telephone directory. So things've been pretty desperate on the homefront and that's why I've rung you; you know, just on the off chance that, if he reads this story in a book, he'll get in touch with you and you can put him on to me. Thanks.

Harrismith—WA

Definitely one of the highlights of my career was my time teaching in small towns in Western Australia. Many just one-teacher schools. Actually, at one place, there wasn't really a town at all, just a school building stuck out in a wheat paddock. But as Head—and only—Teacher, teachers like us were responsible for the education of those attending the seven primary grades plus you may also have to keep an eye on a couple of high school correspondence students as well. Not only were we responsible for teaching the three R's, you can add sewing teacher, art and craft teacher, music teacher, physical education teacher, manual teacher. You name it. Plus there were the duties of gardener, cleaner, nurse, registrar, office lady, free milk dispenser, librarian and, on occasions, bus driver. Oh, and in one particular school I was even responsible for mothercraft. And being just nineteen myself at the time, you might imagine my surprise when a young girl asked me, 'Sir, what's the best milk for babies?' No, it wasn't sunshine milk or cow's milk.

Taking all that into account, those teachers—and it was really only men back then—they really provided a first-class education and, what's more, that education might well have been achieved in schools with no electricity and very little funding. As a result, students were not only given a sound grounding in the three R's and other subjects but, because it was impossible for the teacher to constantly attend each grade, the students had to learn to work on their own. So they became very independent, which is very important. And it was that amazing sense of 'community' that became very apparent to me. If anyone was in trouble, everyone rallied around to help, and that kindness and thoughtfulness was transferred to the children.

And if the town wasn't large enough to have its own hall, all the community gatherings were held at the school. Though, usually, there was some sort of community hall. Even today, scattered throughout the country, you'll notice that, though many of the towns have gone, the local hall still remains. And, mind you, these halls weren't usually aided by government grants or shire help. Most were built from the efforts of the local residents. So, of course, on the weekends there'd be a dance at the local hall or at a hall nearby.

The township of Harrismith, in the south-east of WA, was a case in point. It was a single-teacher school—me. We didn't have piped water so there was no garden. There would've been about twenty-six children in the school, ranging from Grade 1 through to Grade 7. With only four families living in the town, the balance of students came from the outlying area. But still Harrismith managed to have a fully functioning and active town hall. It even had a pub. And as there were no other pubs within fifty miles, it was aptly named the Oasis. The Oasis looked like a very old large house with a shop front. Actually, it's still a going concern— modernised, of course—and, interestingly enough, it's owned and run by one of my ex-students. These days it serves a nice ice-cold beer, top counter meals and has rooms at a reasonable price. Other than the modernisation of the pub, the only other big change is that the old generator, which supplied all the electricity back in my day, has been replaced by Western Power. Otherwise the town's still pretty much the same.

So the pub's still there and the old town hall's still there. And it may seem strange to us now but, back in those days, the usual procedure was for the women to remain in the hall all night while, between dance brackets, the men went outside where they'd stand around in groups and have a cigarette and a chat and they'd knock the top off a King Brown—as a 26-fluid-ounce bottle of beer was called—then they'd take a swig and pass it on to the next bloke. This 'male only' ritual generally allowed enough time for at least two cigarettes each and four bottles of beer to be drunk by each group before they wandered back inside to partake in the next dance bracket. It was all bottled beer back then, bought at the local pub, taken over to the hall, and kept cold thanks to the efforts of the same generator that was keeping not only the hall lights but the rest of the town going as well.

Mind you, not all always went to plan. I remember after one particular dance night my wife and I were woken by the news that the hall was on fire. With only four families in the town we soon joined the rest of the onlookers, inhaling exploding asbestos dust and what-have-you, and discussing how the fire could've started. Then the following day we all mucked in to clean the mess away. Of course, back then, we didn't have a clue that asbestos was such a danger.

And it was that wonderful community of Harrismith that, when I suggested I'd like to take a group of present and ex-students to far-off Canberra, they were right behind me. It was to be a 2000-mile round trip. The neighbouring town of Tincurrin was also invited and the two communities joined together to raise funds for the trip. One of the top money earners was a 'bottle drive'. See, these King Browns were worth tuppence each upon return. And seeing how they'd never been collected before, over the years, everyone, including the pub, had simply stacked their empties away. So there were literally thousands of bottles and we ended

One of the top earners was a 'bottle drive'—The Hansford Collection

up sending two enclosed railway carriages away to Perth. Yes, two enclosed railway carriages.

Twenty-nine children between the ages of ten and seventeen were chosen to go. It was during the August/September holidays of 1967. My wife was the chaperone and I was the teacher. The cost for each student was seventy-five pounds and for a group of farm kids who were preparing to travel all the way across the Nullarbor there was all sorts of excitement and expectations. One that really stands out: Vicki's mum saw her packing an empty jar into her case. 'Why the jar?' asked the mum, to which ten-year-old Vicki replied, 'I'm going to bring you back some snow, Mum.'

On departure day the children were transported by car the 200 miles or so to the Perth railway station. Then it was Perth to Kalgoorlie, change trains, Kalgoorlie to Port Pirie Junction, change trains, Port Pirie to Adelaide, change trains, Adelaide to Melbourne. From Melbourne we travelled by bus to Canberra. In all it had taken a total of four days. Then we spent a week sightseeing. And the kids were rapt, the real highlight being the snowfields. I don't think any of them had seen snow before. So it was an experience. An educational one at that. One they'd never forget. And, of course, something like that was only made possible due to the spirit of co-operation and togetherness that's alive and well in small country towns everywhere ... aided, of course, to some degree, by the men's enjoyment of the contents of the ubiquitous King Brown.

Humula—NSW

I live in a small place between Wagga and Tumbarumba, called Humula. I guess you could describe it as being on the south-western slopes of New South Wales. Twenty k's and you're up in the mountains. Basically, Humula's a small timber town, with surrounding farms, and by the time this happened—crikey, it'd probably be around the early to mid-80s—the town only consisted of the timber mill, a club, a shop and that's about all.

The Humula Citizens' Club's just a little sports club, really. And like the town itself, the club was going through a bit of a tough time and we needed new members badly. I'd been a long-time member and then, further down the track, I wanted to help out a bit so I got myself voted onto the Board of Directors. Then, being on the Board, I started doing a couple of nights' voluntary work, behind the bar and that, to try and help give the club a kick-along. But it sort of turned into a bit of a trap. You know, you'd go up there and have a few beers and the next thing you'd know, you'd had a few too many and it'd be one or two in the morning.

So this was one of those sorts of nights. A few of us were still at the club, chatting and drinking and it's getting pretty bloody late. There was me and a couple of other Board members, Peter and Smithy. Then there was another bloke there with us, Bill Millard. Bill was a cocky from up the road. He'd done a bit of droving. The Millard family had been in the area for years. See, everyone knows everyone in a small community. Anyhow, so Bill Millard was there with us this night and his dog, Fred, kept coming in the back door. And no sooner would we throw the bloody thing out than it'd find its way back inside again. We just couldn't stop it. Anyhow, it got to the bloody stage where we said 'Enough's enough' and so when we threw it out again we locked the back door. Now, perhaps we were too far gone to have locked the back door properly. I don't know, but the dog somehow got back inside. So I said to Bill, 'Bill, yer know very well that yer have to be a bloody member if yer come into the club, so if that bloody dog comes in again, we'll have to nominate him.'

So we threw the dog back outside again. This time I double checked that I'd locked the door. We got back down to business and, blow me down, next thing, the dog's found its way back inside again. It might've even come through a window. I'm not sure. We'd had a few. I said, 'Bugger this, it's obvious the dog wants to be part of the show. We'll have to nominate him.'

So we dug out a nomination form. 'What'll we call him?' So, seeing how the dog's name was Fred and Bill Millard was the bloke who owned him we decided that the dog's name should be 'Frederick Aloysius Millard'. Then we had to give him an occupation so we wrote down 'drover', which was pretty true because he'd done some droving with Bill at one time or other. I nominated him—'proposed by Arthur Webb' and Smithy seconded the proposal. Then we stuck the nomination form up on the noticeboard. See, the procedure was that you've got to have the nomination on notice for something like twenty-eight days. That's just in case any of the members have some sort of objection before it comes up before the Board. If no one objects then, the way it goes is that, if you're considered a good, strong, honest, upright citizen of the community, you became a member. So this Frederick Aloysius Millard, he's now up on the noticeboard—occupation, drover—and we all agreed not to tell anyone that it was a dog.

Anyway, the notice of proposal had been up there for about twenty days and Peter, one of the director fellers who'd been there on the night, said, 'Arthur, what are yer gonna do about this dog?'

I said, 'Buggered if I know.' And so it just stayed up there.

So it's nearing the date of the bloody Board meeting and it still remained a well-held secret, which is pretty rare for a small bush town. Now the President, Sylvester Sykes, was a very pedantic sort of bloke. Everything was run in a very efficient manner, to the strict letter of the law. And the woman who was the Treasurer, an old girl called Patsy, she was even more so that way. Probably, at that stage, she would've been about fifty-five or sixty. She'd never married and she was as straight-laced as you could get. Our families had been friends since we'd been in the district, which was about forty years or something. Actually, Patsy's brother and my father had been the founders of the club, back just after the war.

Anyway, Peter says again, 'Arthur, what are yer gonna do about it?'

'I don't know,' I said.

Anyhow, time's up and we go along to the bloody meeting of the Board of Directors. I was there, of course, so was Peter and Smithy. And I just couldn't look at anyone or I would've burst out laughing. So Sylvester Sykes, the pedantic President, opened the meeting. Then came the Treasurer's report, expertly prepared and presented by old Patsy. Next the correspondence and, when we finally got to the general business, someone went out and got the bloody nomination forms off the board. Of course, I'm looking down at me boots, trying not to laugh, and, like, just for the lack of not doing anything, not making a decision, here I am jammed into this bloody corner. So I'm thinking, What the bloody hell am I gonna say?

Of course, Sylvester Sykes doesn't have a clue that we've nominated a dog. So he received the proposals, then he got up and we went through them, one by one, in alphabetical order. Like, Sylvester would say, 'Joe Anderson', then he'd asked around to see if anybody had anything good, bad or indifferent to say about Joe Anderson. If it was good then it'd be a show of hands. 'Yeah, alright', and Joe'd become a member and he'd start paying his fees which, as I said, were much needed around the place.

Right, so we go through a couple of nominations. They were okayed. Then Sylvester reads out, 'Frederick ... Aloysius ... Millard.' He looks around, waiting for comment. Dead silence. Oh

'Frederick Aloysius Millard'—The Hansford Collection

shit, I'm in trouble now. I'm trying not to laugh. But it's starting to get the better of me. So I'm looking down at the floor and I'm twisting buggery out of the skin on me knee, hoping that the pain might stop me from cracking up.

'Arthur,' says Sylvester Sykes, 'you nominated this Frederick Aloysius Millard so can you shed some light on the feller?'

But before I can say anything, old Patsy, she jumps up and says, 'I know this Frederick Millard. I think Bill Millard's father, old Doug Millard, introduced me to him about twenty years ago.' Then she said, with an odd sort of Mona Lisa smile, as if she knew something about this Frederick Millard that none of the rest of us knew, 'and I remember him as being a little bit strange.'

Oh dear, poor old Patsy. She'd mistaken this Frederick Aloysius Millard for one of old Doug's brothers who was, how would you say, a very eccentric character, indeed. And I'm thinking, Too right he's a little bit strange. For starters the bastard's got four legs and he barks. But, no, I didn't say anything. I couldn't speak. But seeing the Millard family were well known around the area there was a show of hands and this Frederick Aloysius Millard became a member of the Humula Citizens' Club.

Anyhow, I got out of there as quick as I could. Then, about two nights later, I get this phone call. It's from Sylvester Sykes, and he's sounding none too pleased. 'Arthur,' he says, 'I've been informed that you nominated a dog.' He said, 'Don't you realise that we're going to be the laughing stock of the whole country? Not only that but we're going to have to cancel his membership forthwith or else we could lose our licence.'

'Sorry, Sylvester,' I said.

'Arthur,' he said, 'I'll never forgive you till the day I die.' Then he hung up.

Oh, bloody hell. Then, of course, when the news got out, poor old Patsy, she suffered badly, too; you know, with thinking that Bill's father, Doug, had introduced her to this Frederick Aloysius Millard years before. So I wasn't in the good books for a while, especially where those two were concerned. Anyway, that's the story and, to the best of my knowledge, Frederick Aloysius Millard is the only dog to have become a member of any Citizens' Club in Australia.

Hungerford—Qld

Well, my name's Ian McKechnie but everyone just calls me Mac. At the moment I'm eighty-one. Actually, just before I came down to the pub, they were talking on the wireless about how the average age for dying, from all over Australia, was eighty-one. So now I'm a bit worried about not making it to eighty-two. But we'll see. I live just over in Hanson Street. A neighbour calls it Handsome Street. He's looking for a wife so he reckons if he calls the street Handsome instead of Hanson he might have a better chance of getting a woman to come out here to Hungerford to live with him. But I reckon he'd have to be very lucky, ay?

I've lived around the area since 1951. Don't mind if I drink, do yer? Came out working for a pastoral company and when the property was cut up in about '56 I went and worked for a couple of blokes for a bit then I went earth moving, all around this area. Within a hundred mile or so. But when I first come to live in town, the telephone was all manual. You know, you'd have to ring up the telephone exchange and they'd put you through to whoever. Back then, the exchange opened at 9 o'clock and it closed at 6 o'clock, and on the Saturday it opened at six and closed at midday, then it never opened again till the Monday. Well, you could ring up on a Sunday but it wasn't compulsory for them to be there and, if they did, you were supposed to pay some sort of an opening fee. But most times nobody rang of a Sunday, unless it was an emergency.

But there's not too much here apart from a few houses, the pub, a small police station and the Dog Fence. Only about seven people live here, then a couple come up each winter because they don't like the cold down south. So that's nine. There's never been many more than that, really. Oh, one time, there used to be a chap working here on the Dog Fence, a boundary rider. People by the name of Bevis and he had eleven kids. That really jumped the population up. Their kids did School of the Air. Actually, the Dog Fence's supposed to be the longest man-made thing in the world. Longer than the Great Wall of China, even. It was first done to keep the rabbits in check but these days it's more to keep the dingoes away from the stock. So, she's a pretty long fence to keep an eye on. But the feller Bevis and other boundary riders, they only look after a couple of hundred mile of fence, either way.

But being right on the Queensland–New South Wales border, Hungerford first came about because of all the drovers and shearers and all that coming through. The old Cobb & Co. had a depot here and even Henry Lawson; the poet feller walked the 150 mile, all the way up from Bourke, just to prove himself as the poet of the outback. That was back in January 1893. But he didn't like the place. He reckoned it was even a pity Burke and Wills found Hungerford in the first place. He thought it was the arse-end of the earth. They say he didn't even like the beer, and he was an alcoholic and there were two pubs to choose from back then. But, I mean, he must've been bloody mad to come up here in the middle of summer, ay?

There's only the Royal Mail Hotel here now. It's just a normal old-fashioned sort of pub; thick walls, low ceilings, corrugated iron, and out the back is where the stables were. Of course, there was no power in them early days so they had a compressor-engine driving an old brine, tank-operated, cold room. And, over the years, there's been quite a few publicans come and go. Some good, some not so good. I remember when people named Barclay owned the pub. Old Roy Barclay. Anyhow, old Roy's eldest son was Terry Barclay. Terry's passed away now but he would've been the same age as me if he was still alive. So he didn't even make it to eighty-one. But, old Roy Barclay—the father—he was a very excitable sort of bloke and, of course, seeing there wasn't electricity, there was no lights around the pub and one night someone come haring into the bar. 'Hey, Roy,' they said, 'there's some shearin' fellers beltin' the livin' daylights outa young Terry, down the back'a the pub.'

So old Roy's out the door like a shot. 'I'm comin', son.' He races down the back. It's all in the dark and he sees these fellers fighting. So 'bang'. He king-hits the first one he comes across. Down the bloke goes and the other fellers, they take off. Then old Roy, he hears the feller he's just flattened start groaning. And you know who it was? It was young Terry. His son. Old Roy'd flattened his own son in the dark.

So yeah, we've had a lot of publicans over the years. But it's tough. The current feller's taken on the mail run to try and make ends meet. That takes, near on, two full days and two half-days of the week so his missus runs the pub while he's away. See, first he has to go up to Cunnamulla to get the mail. That's about a 600 kilometres round trip, and there's all the mucking around in-between. Then, when he finally gets back, he spends a couple of half days delivering the mail within a hundred mile radius of Hungerford.

But the pub's the hub of our social life. It's a family sort of place; very quiet during the summer then in the winter we get a hell of a lot of tourists through. But, see, with the drought and one thing and another, station properties can't employ anyone. There's a property out here that's a bit under 400,000 acres and they used to employ at least fifteen men. Like, there'd be the boundary riders, there'd be the ringers, the cooks and that. Now just two or three blokes run the whole show. And it's running the same number of stock. I reckon a lot of it's to do with motorbikes. The days of the horse are gone. I remember, at one time, they tried to give the place a bit of a lift by bringing the sports-gymkhana days into Hungerford. That was round the late '60s and they had about 160 horses here. Oh, at times there'd be twenty to thirty horses in a straight race. Then they'd have bullock riding, flag bending and that. Gee, it was a great day. Then after the gymkhana they'd auction some of the horses off for the Flying Doctor Service, you know, as a fundraiser. But then the motorbikes started to come in and now there's just a few kids' ponies. Last time we had a Hungerford Cup, a drover feller from Cunnamulla, Les Cable—he's retired nowadays—he brought

The Dog Fence at Hungerford—The Marsh Collection

three horses down and got first, second and third in the Cup. Yeah, so it's fizzled.

Still, it's all to do with change, ay. Some's good, some's not so good. I mean, when we got electric power, that was good. That was about thirty year ago and most people went out and bought a television set and a video player. Like, even though we couldn't watch live TV, we could still watch videos. So that's what we done. Then, I can tell you exactly when we first got live TV. It was just before Haley's Comet came over, back in the mid-1980s, because Aussat came out and they set up a satellite dish over behind the hall. Oh, then everyone was watching anything that was on the TV, even *Play School*; grown-ups, the lot. It was such a big thing for us. But the thing was, the live TV was coming down to us from outer space, via this satellite. Anyhow, so there we were, all excited by finally getting live television and I remember quite plain, one night, some feller coming over and saying how they'd just knocked the satellite out of the sky. So we all went outside and, lo and behold, there it was, with a big fireball trailing it. Gee, we were disappointed. Then the publican came out and he was laughing. 'What the bloody hell's up with you?' we said.

He said, 'The feller gotcha. It's April Fools' Day. They haven't knocked the satellite out of the sky at all. That's Haley's Comet going over.'

So that's when we first got live TV.

Kalgoorlie and Kambalda—WA

My name's Bill 'Bones' Hanson. How the 'Bones' came about was that, see, when you work on the mines, you lose a lot of weight. So back in the earlier days, when I was pretty skinny, one of the barmen at the Federal Hotel in Kalgoorlie nicknamed me as 'Bones', and it stuck.

Actually, I was born in South Australia, up in the Riverland, then my old man come over to Kalgoorlie when the Depression was on. I was only a kid then. I went to a school on the wrong side of the tracks—East Kalgoorlie—and I was the biggest dunce in the class so I left as soon as I turned fifteen. Then I had a few jobs before I went underground. The first job was pumping petrol. That was during the war. In them days you had to hand pump the petrol up into a glass bowl at the top of the bowsers to measure it, then it'd drain out from there, into your car. After that I went on a dairy farm down the south-west of Western Australia, at Busselton. I was there for about eighteen months, on seven and six a week, then I thought, No, I'll go back to Kalgoorlie.

I was seventeen by then and I went underground and that's where I stayed all me life, more or less. First, I was just cleaning up around the place. Then I went bogger driving. I was pretty good at it too, I might add. Then I went on as a machine miner. That's drilling holes with a sort of jackhammer-like thing. I also used to be a development miner. He's the feller who digs out the mullock before the stoke miner comes in and takes the ore out. See, mullock generally doesn't have any ore in it, so you've got to go through that to get to the ore.

Kalgoorlie's all gold. Then another place I worked at was Kambalda. That was nickel. Kambalda's a smaller place about 60 k's out of Kalgoorlie. I was an air-rig miner out there. I bore rock-drills for the form work, to hold the ground up. I went out there in about 1970, when I was in me late thirties, early forties. Kambalda had only been going for about three years. But we didn't live out there. I mean, there was a town and that there with a bit of a shopping centre and a pub. But, see, a lot of the Kalgoorlie people were happy enough in their own little dunghill so they didn't want to go out there to live. So we'd take it in turns, using our cars, and we'd travel out and back with about five blokes in each car. You'd be up early and pick up the fellers and you'd get out there at about half past seven, to start at eight. Knock off was at half past three. A seven-and-a-half hour shift.

Like it was hard work but a lot of things had humour in them. One time we had a Pommy union rep who had the exact same model Holden as me. Same green colour and everything. And I was coming home one afternoon, from Kambalda, with a car load of fellers. I was driving my car so I was pushing it a bit; you know, going well over the speed limit. Anyhow, I come over a rise and there's this traffic cop booking some poor bloke on the side of the

Underground mining—The Hansford Collection

road. Next thing, I flash past, and the mob in my car said, 'Hey, Bones,' they said, 'aren't yer gonna slow down?'

'Not likely,' I said. 'I'm gonna go faster so he won't bloody catch me.'

So I planted the foot. Then a bit further along we came across the union rep. He was heading back to Kalgoorlie too, but he's plodding along, well under the speed limit. Like I said, his car was the exact same model Holden and everything, as mine. So I shot past him. Then I found out later that, after the copper had booked the first bloke, he'd took off after me and when he'd seen the union rep's car, he pulled him over for speeding. The union rep said, 'Mate, yer bookin' the wrong bloke,' because, see, it was me he should've been booking, not the union rep. But he didn't dob me in or nothing so I guess he was a pretty good sort of bloke for a Pommy union rep.

Then another thing: see, the crib is the place where you go to have your dinner, underground. Anyhow, one of the miners—an Italian feller he was—he really enjoyed his coffee with his dinner. So, one time, while the Italian feller wasn't looking, one of me mates grabbed his thermos and poured the coffee out, into another thermos, then he went and filled it up with hot water. And so, when the Italian feller went to drink his coffee, he said, 'That'a silly bloody'a woman'a mine, she's'a fergot ter put'a d' coffee into 'd' thermos.'

Oh, he went real crook over it. He was going to give his wife a good going over about it. Then, just as he was going to throw the hot water out, my mate said, 'Don't throw it out. Take it home 'n' show yer missus how she'd only put hot water into yer thermos. Like evidence.'

'Yeah, good'a idea. Like'a evidence.' So he put his thermos back in his crib bag and, when he went back to work, me mate emptied the hot water out of the Italian's thermos and he poured the coffee back in. So you can imagine what happened when he got home and he went crook on his wife for not putting the coffee into his hot water, ay? Especially when he showed her the evidence. She would've thought he'd gone off his rocker.

Yeah, so they were good days. But then, when they went to the open cut mining, they tramped a lot of us underground fellers. I was fifty-nine by then so the chances of getting a job was pretty slim. But a mate of mine, Boris, he got me a job driving a bus and I done that for two-and-a-half years. But then I needed a change of life so I ended up being a trades assistant, doing nothing much. I'm seventy-seven now. I'm out of it all. But I get the shakes now and then because I've got a bit of Parkinson's disease. But we all stick together. Did back then. Still do today. See, the mining community always look out for each other. Like, there was this publican in Kalgoorlie and this mining bloke had broke his leg. So his leg was in plaster and he was on crutches and he come into the pub. It was just before Christmas and the publican said, 'God almighty, man, whatever happened ter you?'

The feller said, 'I've broke me leg.'

'Are yer on compo?'

'No, I'm not.'

So the publican, he goes to a cabinet and he pulls out a turkey and he says, 'Well, mate, it looks like yer battlin', so yer can have this turkey.'

And the bloke with the broken leg said to the publican, 'Listen, I don't take charity from nobody.'

'Mate, this isn't a charity,' says the publican. 'Yer've won it fair 'n' square in the raffle.'

'But, I haven't got a ticket in the raffle,' says the bloke with the broken leg.

'Well, that's okay,' says the publican, 'it's not bein' drawn till tomorra'.'

Katherine—NT

Yeah, Katherine's in the Top End of the Territory. It's about 300 k south of Darwin. I'm led to believe it was named after the daughter of one of the supporters of John McDouall Stuart's expeditions and there was some sort of mix-up because the daughter's name was Catherine with a 'C' and not Katherine with a 'K'. But anyway, it was first settled around Knott's Crossing. There was the overland telegraph and the workers' quarters, a small post office and a tiny one-room police station, all across from the Sportsman's Arms Hotel. Then, back in the mid-1920s, they put through the railway bridge more to the south-eastern side of the river, where they thought it'd be less likely to flood. So Katherine sort of gravitated towards there. But there's been some rippers since: '57 was a huge flood and you might've heard about the one in '74. That was on the telly and all that, with a big relief operation.

But I drifted over to Katherine in the mid-90s. Kirby's Back Bar was the nerve centre of town. It's where all the workers used to meet. If you wanted a job you just went to Kirby's and you'd get the word about what's going on around the place. That's where I heard about the job of taking tourists out on the Katherine River, on an evening–night crocodile trip.

'Do you know anything about crocs?' they said.

'A bit,' I said, and so they gave me the job as the tour captain of an old boat.

It was a pretty serious little show. The boat could take about forty people and I had an Irish deckhand, Big Al. Big Al was a backpacker. He was only a little bloke but he had a real deep voice. I don't think he had any qualifications or anything. All I know is that he knew absolutely nothing about crocs and he knew absolutely nothing about boats. I think he got the job because he was also hanging around Kirby's Back Bar. See, that's how it sometimes happens in the Territory; if you're in the right spot at the right time, you get the job. It doesn't matter if you're qualified or not; everyone usually gives you a go and you can either handle it or you can't. Like, I didn't even have much experience on a river, with boats. I'd done a bit of fishing, but that's all.

So I was the captain and Big Al was the deckie and the tour went for about three hours. We'd pick up the tourists, late-arvo, and head off down the Katherine River looking at all the different stuff, like the birds and the sunset and you might see a few freshwater crocs—Freshies. So I'd talk a bit about that. Then, when we got to this really nice sandy beach, we'd get everyone off the boat and we'd light a fire and we'd have a stew in a pot that we'd cooked earlier that day. We'd whack that on the fire and, while it was warming up, we'd open a couple of big casks of red and white wine.

Then, when everyone was nice and relaxed, we'd have a few little pilchard type of things in a bucket and we'd go to the water's edge and tap on the bucket and, like, there's about three or four good sized crocs that used to live there, right, and they'd walk out of the water and come up to where the fire was and they'd lay near the fire and we'd feed them some of these pilchards. Freshies are a little bit more social than Salties; not so aggressive. But we never told the tourists that. Still, you never know, do you? And so we'd feed them and everyone'd drink some more plonk and get stuck into the stew and, you know, the crocs'd still be laying there and everyone'd just forget about them and party on and walk around them and fall over them, then we'd head back later that night.

No one ever got bitten or nothing but, me and Big Al, we still managed to have a few accidents. Like, the boat was really old and so the motors would smoke up and everyone'd be coughing and going on. And the lights weren't much chop neither so, coming back in the dark, Al used to have a spotlight and, like, he's meant to light up the river so I could see where we're going.

Beware of crocodiles—The Marsh Collection

But he didn't have much concentration. He'd always get distracted and he'd be shining the spotlight around in all directions, just looking about, and so I couldn't see much. One night there was a big paperbark tree overhanging the river and Big Al's meant to be, like, illuminating it for me, but he wasn't, so I hit the side of the tree and a big branch snapped off and it fell on four German tourists. I mean, if it'd hit them on the head it would've killed them but, luckily, it just took all the bark off their shoulders and their backs and that, so we only had to take them to hospital.

Then another time I was coming back in the boat. For some reason Big Al wasn't with me that night so I had this pretty fat sort of bird holding the spotlight and I was pushing it a bit so we were going along at a fair rate of knots. Next thing, Bang! I rammed straight into a log and the boat come to a dead stop and this lady got catapulted clean out the front of the boat and she did about three somersaults before she levelled out and piked into the river. And when we fished her out, she still had hold of the spotlight. You wouldn't believe it, ay? She just took to wing. So she had to spend ten days or something in hospital, which she wasn't too happy about.

So that's what I done when I was in Katherine. But it's a great place and it was a really good tour, even if I do say so myself. You know, it was just out in the wild a little bit and so all the tourists loved it ... well most did, anyway.

Kempsey—NSW

We really need to be sitting around and having a few beers for me to tell stories. But, anyway, here goes. First of all you might ask just why a place like Kempsey should be part of a book about outback towns and pubs. Well, I'll tell you later. But first I'll give you a brief rundown about the place. Kempsey's on the north coast of New South Wales, between Port Macquarie and Nambucca Heads, just inland, on the Macleay River. The Dunghutti people were the first to live in the area and they're still very much a part of Kempsey. Actually, one of Australia's best Aboriginal artists, the late Robert Campbell Junior, was from Kempsey, and his artworks hang in many of the better known national and international art galleries.

The first white settler was a fellow named Rudder. Around the mid-1850s he named the place Kempsey, because the countryside reminded him of the town Kempsey, back in Worcestershire. The first white settlers were attracted to the area because of its high quality cedar and rosewood. Then, as time went by, came the grazing. Dairying started up in the early 1900s. Crops like maize have always been a staple. Beef is a major product and Kempsey's considered to be the 'home' of the Akubra hat. Also, many locals are well known: people like the author Thomas Kenneally and Tommy Woodcock, Phar Lap's devoted strapper. And, here's the point of the whole story: Slim Dusty, Australia's greatest country music performer, was born and bred around the area. And, of course, if anyone or anything other than the Akubra hat symbolises the outback of Australia it's the late and great Slim Dusty, and that's why I think Kempsey should be mentioned.

As a matter of fact I went to the RSL Club just last Sunday night and a few past and present local performers held a concert,

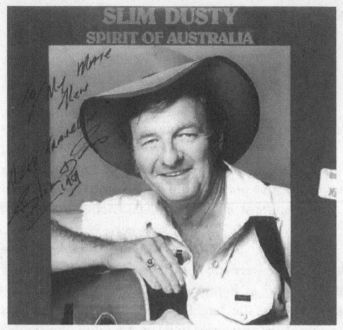

'The late and great Slim Dusty'—The Hansford Collection

which was pretty much attributed to Slim Dusty. And the auditorium was chock-a-block. And I tell you, it was probably one of the best music nights you're ever likely to see. Just brilliant. The fellow who compered the show, and got it together, he'd won a golden guitar at the Tamworth Country Music Festival, as an instrumentalist. Another fellow, Amos Morris, he'd also just won a golden guitar at Tamworth, for best bush ballad. Then, have you seen the TV show *Australia's Got Talent*? Well, another young local feller, who's only gone sixteen, well, he's in the Grand Final. And he's the best guitar player I've ever heard. So there was a fair bit of class amongst them and, actually, the violinist on the night had been the fiddle player in the Slim Dusty band. So, as I said, even though Slim Dusty may have gone, his influence is still alive and well in Kempsey, as it is throughout the outback areas of Australia, where his songs will continue to be played in clubs, pubs and around campfires for many, many years to come.

Actually, I'm a bit of a musician myself. Of course, nowhere near as talented as the people who played in the concert at the RSL. I started in 1959 and played drums in a dance band for twenty-five years. Mostly it was old time stuff; dances like the Canadian Three Steps, Gypsy Taps, Barn Dances. That sort of thing. There were five of us in the band; drums, piano, guitar, trumpet and saxophone. And for quite a while we played at the Kempsey Bowling Club and every Wednesday night they'd come down and broadcast a live session over the local radio station.

But, gee, we used to have some fun. I remember in the mid-to-late '60s we had a fellow named Mike. Mike was with the Tick Board and he'd come down from Kyogle because there was an outbreak of cattle tick in the area, so we snared him to play trumpet in our band. So we were at the Kempsey Bowling Club this particular night and we decided to play a bit of a prank on the audience. We had a spare trumpet lying around the place so, while Mike hid down behind the piano and played his trumpet, one of his mates stood up on stage and pretended to play the spare one. You know, he just mimed playing the trumpet, while Mike was down behind the piano actually playing one. I mean, the bloke couldn't play for nuts but, he'd had a few drinks so he put on this big miming act of playing the trumpet and, oh, didn't he make an impression. In actual fact, when he'd finished, I went down to the bar to get a round of drinks and about four people came up to me and said, 'Geez, Tony, yer ought'a sign that new feller up. He's a hell of a lot better bloody trumpeter than what Mike is.'

Yes, so they were all convinced that Mike's mate was a far better trumpeter than what Mike was. But no, as I said, this feller couldn't play for nuts. Mike was doing it all from behind the piano. But, gee, those were the days.

Kingoonya—SA

Well Kingoonya, in South Australia, was always just a rail maintenance town and that's all. It came into being during the construction of the Trans-Australian Railway Line, across the Nullarbor. And something that's quite unique about it is that the pub—and I've only ever known it as the Kingoonya Hotel—was owned by the same family, the Brett family, right from the day it was built, in 1914, right through till it shut down, which was in about the late 1980s, I'd say. But, in my time, in about 1982–83, other than the hotel, Kingoonya only had a bakery and a little shop and, to the best of my knowledge, the population never got above fifty.

But then, see, when the concrete sleepers were inserted into the Trans-line and the rails were 'continuously welded', the track required much less maintenance and so the Railways closed down a lot of those small places across the Nullarbor, like Tarcoola and Rawlinna and the rest of them. But, even then, the township of Kingoonya somehow managed to struggle on for a bit till it eventually withered away, like a slow death, and they finally had to close the pub. Though, the good news is that, with the better roads and better transport these days, a lot of the buses go out to Kingoonya before they turn off and go south, down to the west coast of South Australia. And they tell me that the little pub, she's up and running once more, though I don't think the Brett family are involved in it.

Anyway, my story is back when I was working through the area, a good friend of mine was working at Kingoonya, a bloke called Terry Sharpe. Terry was the Road Foreman, in charge of a group of about sixty men, inserting something like 1500 of these cement sleepers per kilometre of the rail line. Anyhow, I was the Superintendent-in-Charge of the continuous-welded-rail across the Trans-line and, Terry and me, we had our camps adjacent to one another. Now, Terry was a former policeman and military man, and I don't know whether you know any military people or not but, usually, you can tell them a mile off because that's all they talk about—the military. Still, he was a bloody hell of a good bloke and a real bloody wag.

So, this day, I was in the camp and the next minute a bloke comes running across to me and he's pretty anxious and he said, 'Yer'd better go 'n' see Sharpie, he's been shot.'

'Oh, Jesus no.' Anyway, I went and saw Terry and here he was, in his room, laying on the bed. So I said to him, 'What the hell happened to you?'

He said, 'I've just been shot.'

'Oh yeah, how?'

'Well,' he said, 'I was over at the pub and there was some sorta argument with a bloke about a bloody dog 'n' the bloke walked away 'n' he came back with a .22 calibre rifle. So I thought I'd better take it off him. You know, disarm him. So that's what I was attempting to do when he shot me.'

A railway camp—The Norris Collection

'Jesus,' I said, 'where did yer get shot?'

At that, Terry looked a bit embarrassed, then he mumbled, 'In the backside.'

Now, like I said, because Terry's ex-military, he's forever talking about his service days and what he did do and what he didn't do and what he should've done and what he would've done and whatever. Very proud of his time in the military. I said to him, 'Well, thank Christ there's not a war on.'

He said, 'Why's that?'

I said, 'Because you'd be labelled a bloody coward.'

Now, being ex-military and being a coward is about as low as you can get. So now he's pretty agitated. He says, 'And what the bloody hell do yer mean about me being labelled a coward?'

I said, 'Well, if yer got shot in the arse then, obviously, yer must'a been runnin' away.'

Anyway, he wasn't too pleased about that. But, the long and the short of it was that, being ex-military, his pride was bruised and so he refused to go and see anyone about it.

So he's still got this bullet in his bum and he's staggering around the place, like a bear with a sore head, and so his blokes are coming to me and they're saying, 'Look, Ted, you'd better go 'n' talk to Terry, he's getting crankier by the minute.'

So in the end I went and seen him and I said, 'Fer Christ's sake, Terry,' I said, 'come on, I'll take you into Woomera.' Woomera being the nearest hospital. I said, 'We'd better get this bullet taken out 'n' get you fixed up.'

But, no, he still wasn't too keen on it. Perhaps my remark about being called a coward had got to him and he was out to prove some point or other. I don't know. He said, 'I tell yer, Ted, there's no way I'm gonna go all the way ter Woomera just ter have some inexperienced nurse dig a piddly little bullet outa me bum.'

So I said, 'Terry, you know what's gonna happen, don't you?'

'No. What?'

'Well, if we don't get that bullet taken out, mate, your epitaph's gonna read something like you see in the American old west, up on Boot Hill somewhere.'

'What do yer mean by that?' he said.

'Well,' I said, 'your headstone's gonna read "Died of friggin' lead poisoning after being shot in the bum". Now, mate,' I said, 'is that the image yer want'a leave about your life?'

Anyway, that convinced him. 'Yeah, okay,' he says and so I took him into the hospital at Woomera and they cut this bullet out of him. So that was it. He survived and now lives in Launceston, in Tasmania, and if you ever get in touch with him and ask him about his days in Kingoonya, I reckon he'll say something along the lines of it being 'a pain in the friggin' arse'.

Kojonup—WA

Okay, well my dad would be able to tell this story far better than me but, anyway, it goes something like this. See, after the Second World War there was a large migration from Europe to Australia and a lot of those migrants came to Western Australia, seeking a better life. Many of them went to country towns where they helped out on farms or worked in shops. They did all sorts of things. Mostly it was the men who came first and, once they were established and had made a little money, they'd bring out their families or the women they were betrothed to. This particular story is about such a gentleman, an Italian, who'd recently arrived in Western Australia. He couldn't speak English, but he'd heard that there was work down in the south-east of the state, near a small town called Kojonup. Kojonup's about 250 kilometres from Perth, sort of, on the way to Albany. The nearest major regional centre, Katanning, is about thirty or forty k's away.

The actual name of Kojonup comes from the Aboriginal word 'Koja', which means something like 'stone axe'. It was originally settled away back in the late 1830s because of its potential to become a prosperous sheep farming area, in as much as it had natural springs and the local stone was suitable for building. And it has been quite prosperous over time, though possibly less so these days, as with all farming.

Be that as it may, when this Italian gentleman heard that there was work around the area, he left Perth and he walked and he walked and, late one evening, he arrived in Kojonup. He was extremely tired, he had no money and he didn't have anywhere to stay so, when he saw a vacant building, he decided to sleep there the night, then set about looking for work the next day. All he had with him was a small suitcase, packed with just the basic necessities. That was all he had. For the sake of the story you could say that, in his suitcase, he also had a photograph of the woman he was betrothed to over in Italy. His sweetheart. He was a long way from home, lonely, and alone in this strange country. Anyhow, he bedded down in this old building, kissed the photo of his sweetheart goodnight, then drifted off to sleep. She'd soon be with him and they'd make a good life together, with many children.

It was sometime later in the night that the people of Kojonup were woken by a blood-curdling scream. Not just the once, but it continued, piercing the night air like a dagger through the heart. Terrible it was. It'd raise the hairs on the back of your neck. And so it wasn't long before people came rushing out of their houses to see what was happening and they found this man, this Italian gentleman, cowering outside the vacant building. He had no suitcase. Nothing. He was shaking and crying but he didn't seem injured or anything, so the locals asked, 'What's wrong? What happened?'

But the Italian couldn't understand what they were saying. He spoke no English. They spoke no Italian.

Someone said, 'Perhaps he's been on the grog 'n' he's got the DTs.'

But, no; there was no smell of alcohol. Garlic, maybe, alcohol, no.

'Looks frightened to me,' said someone else. 'Perhaps there's something in the building? Could be scared of mice?' And so, through a series of mime actions they tried to get this Italian gentleman to go inside and show them what the problem was. But, try as they may, there was no way he was going to enter the vacant building. He remained, huddled on the ground, white with fear.

And that's where he stayed until they managed to round up someone who understood a little Italian. So this fellow, the one who could interpret Italian, he arrived and he asked the gentleman what was wrong. And the Italian told him how he'd arrived in town. He didn't have anywhere to stay. Then, when he saw the vacant building, he decided to bed down in there for the night. So that's what he did and he'd been asleep—sound asleep—until he'd heard a noise and when he opened his eyes, there, looking down at him, was the ghostly figure of a nun, holding a lamp.

'That's incredible,' said the locals.

And when the fellow who was doing the interpreting asked the locals 'Why?' they said that the building had once been used by the church, as a hospital, and there'd been nuns caring for the sick.

And it was incredible too because there was no way the Italian gentleman could've known any of that. Like I said, he'd only recently arrived in Australia so he wouldn't have known anything about the history of Kojonup. And, here it was, he'd been woken by this vision of a nun holding a lamp and it'd scared him so much that he refused, and still refused, to go back inside the building, not even to get his photograph.

'After the Second World War there was a large migration from Europe to Australia'—The Hansford Collection

Kulgera—NT

About twenty k's over the South Australian border, into the Northern Territory, there's this really little place called Kulgera. It's the exact central point of Australia—or that's what they told me at the pub. But, anyway, this happened back sometime in the late '70s. It's all cattle country out there and I was working out on a place for this elderly couple. Real old staunch station people, they were. Strict to the letter. At that stage I was only young, about nineteen, and I'd been working hard for about three months straight, in quite primitive conditions, without seeing a girl or having a beer or anything.

Then come the time for the Kulgera Easter Race Meeting. Now, the Kulgera Easter Race Meeting's the biggest thing that happens in that part of the country and so all the people from off the cattle stations and that, they come in for this big weekend and they stay down at the campground. It's like a big get-together. And the tradition was that when the younger station workers, like me, came into town, we had to hang out with our bosses; you know, set up camp for them, get the fire going, get some water. See, in those days, the boss and his wife were like royalty. With total respect, that's how you were meant to treat them. These days it's a bit more relaxed but, back then, you were expected to be a good ambassador for the station. You know, not play up or nothing.

Anyway, when we got into Kulgera, lots of other station bosses and their families were there and, like, they're all fairly well-to-do and so they're all dressed up and that. So they're all at the campground. Then just up from the campground, by the racetrack area, there was a little hall. That's where all these prim and proper station people were going to have this big function that night. Then just up from the hall was the pub, right. That's where the jackaroos and the jillaroos and the other station workers hung out.

Now, like I said, I'd been three months, living out in pretty rough, isolated conditions so the last thing I wanted to do was to be sitting around with the station bosses and their families, eating sandwiches and talking bullshit. You know, I wanted to get up to the pub and have some fun. So I made up an excuse about how I had to go and make some phone calls.

'Don't be long, young feller,' said the boss, 'you've still got duties to attend to here.' Oh, something I forgot; my boss always had a cigarette hanging out of his mouth—always.

Anyway, I said, 'Okay,' and so I left the campground and I walked past the little hall, then up to the pub. And the place was just rocking and so I started drinking and, well, time just vanished. Next minute, like, it's midnight. I'd been there for hours, you know, just getting on the grog and talking to people more my own age and that. It was just great. Then, about midnight I looked around and there was just the one unattached girl left in the pub. She had a bloke with her but he'd passed out. So she's at a loose end. I'm at a loose end.

Now, I don't know how we hooked up, but we did, right. She might've been, you know, who knows, but her bloke's choked out so she knew she wasn't going to have any fun with him. But we somehow hooked up and I talked her into coming down to the campground for a bit of romance. My swag was back down there. She said, 'Okay,' and so we headed off, past the hall where the posh function was being held. Then, halfway between the hall and the campground, it just got too much. You know, it'd been months and months, and it's a starry night. Very quiet. Dark. I've got a girl who's keen. The crickets are singing in the background. It was just so romantic and so, right on the side of the road, we started to consummate our relationship. If you can imagine, it was like a scene out of *Gone With the Wind* and *Debbie Does Dallas*, all rolled into one.

Anyhow, so that's what we were doing and, without realising it, the function at the hall had just finished. But I'm so lost in the moment that I didn't even notice all the station people—the old aristocracy—had got into their cars and had started to head back down to the campground. The first I knew about it was when I heard a car horn beeping and I looked up and I saw a woman go by with her hands covering her little kid's eyes. Then, when the next car rolled by, there's my boss, in the passenger's seat, with his eyes popping out of his head and his cigarette falling out of his gob. And just from the look on his face I had a pretty good idea that I'd done me dash. But then, like I said, it'd been quite a while so, after all the cars had gone by, you know, me and this girl, we still had a little bit of lead in our pencils, sort of thing, and we headed down to where my swag was, in the campground. Being dark, no one could see what we were up to and so now it's like Act II of *Gone with the Wind* and *Debbie Does Dallas*.

Then, somewhere along the line, I fell asleep and the girl must've got up and took off because, when I woke up, like, it's broad daylight and I'm just laying there on top of me swag—stark naked—and there's the boss and all his station people, pointing at me and going on. Well, that was it then. I knew I'd get the sack for sure. So I just got up and I got dressed and I rolled me swag and I got out of there and hitched to Alice Springs. Like, you could say, I more or less ran away, really. And that was it for Kulgera.

Kynuna—Qld

Do you want to hear about when me dog got stolen twice in the one night? This was back in about '61, when I was out at a place called Kynuna. Kynuna's sort of in the north-west of Queensland, out along the Winton to Cloncurry road. Actually, it's near Dagworth Station where Banjo Paterson heard about the suicide of that feller beside Combo Waterhole and that all ended up as the 'Waltzing Matilda' song. Well, Combo Waterhole's just south of Kynuna. So it's all in that area; big sheep country, or it was when I was there shearing, about seven mile out of town, at a place called Mimong Station. That was with a feller called Bill Fisk. I was only young back then. Just learning to shear. Actually, I might've even got me first pen there.

Kynuna was only a real small little place, then; just a pub, a store next to that and about three houses. The pub was called the Kynuna Hotel. It's called the Blue Heeler Hotel these days. It's a big-time trucking stop now. Huge. You wouldn't know the place. I mean, these days, the pub's about four or five times bigger than what it used to be. Back then, if you got ten people in it, it'd be crowded; you know what I mean.

But, see, I had this dog called Blue. He was only about three or four. A half-coolie he was, or so I'd been led to believe. He looked pretty good, actually. He was the colour of a blue and white cattle dog. But the thing was, he'd only work for me. He wouldn't work for anyone else. Not a soul. Absolutely hopeless. I was the only one he'd work for and so he was handy to have around the shed and the paddocks and that. And, anyhow, it got to the weekend and a few of us had organised to go into the Kynuna pub. Then, before we went, Fisky said, 'Garry,' he said, 'put the dog around ter get a killer fer Sunday.' A killer's a sheep that you kill for your own tucker. So I done that. 'Come on, Blue,'

Where's me dog?—The Carter Collection

I said, and I chose a killer out of them—a wether—then I showered up to go into Kynuna.

We didn't have cars back in them days so the publican from the Kynuna pub said he'd drive out and pick us up; like, he offered to take us in. Mind you, he didn't say anything about bringing us back; only that he'd take us in. It was a business thing. He made a lot of money out of us. Then just before the publican was due to arrive, I called the dog so I could tie him up. Nothing. So I called some more, 'Blue ... Blue,' but he wasn't about. So, seeing how I didn't want to hold up the other blokes, in the end, I thought, Oh, well, he won't go far. He'll just hang around here. He'll be okay.

So the publican come and we go into Kynuna and, when we pull into the pub, blow me down, sitting in the back of a ute is me dog, Blue. Me dog's there, see, and he's got this guilty look on his dial. He sort of looked at me and I sort of looked at him and he started wagging his tail. I said to the fellers, 'Shit, look, someone's stole me dog.' So I went into the pub and I found out who owned the ute and I said, 'Hey, that's me dog yer've got out there, in the back of yer ute.'

'Oh, is it?' they said. 'We just saw him on our way inta town 'n' he seemed like he'd be a pretty keen worker so we picked him up.' See, out at Mimong, the shearing quarters was only a couple of hundred yards off the road and as it turned out, these two young blokes were driving along and they spotted Blue wandering about, and they were looking for a good working dog so they nicked him.

'Sorry about that, mate,' they said.

So I went and grabbed him out of the back of the ute and I took him around to the back of the pub. There was a little sort of beer garden type of thing there at the back. I tied him up. 'Blue,' I said, 'stay.'

Anyway, we started drinking, then by about two in the morning we're well on the way, if you catch my drift. But, like I said, we didn't have a lift back to Mimong. Now, somehow, there was a semi-driver. I forget how it happened but he must've pulled in for a beer and we must've got talking to him because he said he'd run us back out to Mimong.

'Thanks,' we said.

Then, just before we're about to leave, I went out the back to get me dog. He's gone. The bugger's gone again. I called and I called, 'Blue ... Blue.' But, nothing. Shit. So then I'm ranting and raving about what a thieving mob of bastards everyone around the place is. Anyhow, there was nothing I could do about it just there and then or I'd miss the ride back to Mimong. So I said, 'Bugger it', and I went back around to get this lift back out to the shed. My shearing mates had already gotten onto the back of the semi so I just climbed in the front, into the cab part, and, blow me down, there's me dog sitting in the cab, as large as life, looking pleased to see me.

I said to the truckie, 'Yer've nicked me bloody dog, yer thieving bastard.'

He said, 'Oh, well, he was just wandering about, you know, 'n' he looked like he'd be a pretty good dog.'

'Christ,' I said, 'that's a bit low; nickin' a bloke's dog.'

But I didn't go on about it because if I'd upset him, he might've changed his mind about taking me back out to Mimong and I didn't feel like walking, not with the state I was in. Anyhow, he was real nice about it. Like it was, 'Sorry, mate. I didn't know it was your dog' and all that sort of stuff. Real apologetic he was. You know, 'Oh, yer can have him back' and all that.

'Too right I'll have him back,' I said.

Anyway, he dropped us off back at Mimong; me and Blue and me shearing mates. But the crux of the story is that, this dog'd only work for me, see, and, here it was, he'd been nicked twice in the one night and he would've been absolutely hopeless to the thieving bastards, anyway. They were trying to steal a dud dog, really.

Lake Cargelligo—NSW

Shit, sure as eggs are eggs I'll tell you something about Lake Cargelligo that's wrong and you'll put it in print and I'll get heaps. Now, there was a local history called *The Dusts of Time* but I just can't find it so I'll just have to try my best without it. So, here goes: Lake Cargelligo is a natural lake on the Lachlan River, about a hundred kilometres south of Condobolin. For many, many generations, the Aborigines would've used the lake as a food and water source. It was first discovered by whites—by John Oxley, in fact—in 1817, though it wasn't settled until the mid-1800s. Gold was found in 1873 but the high water table restricted exploration. See, they didn't have the technology back then. Around town, legend has it that there's still plenty of gold down there. Mind you, I haven't seen any sign of it and I don't think anyone else has either. But, you never know.

When the lake's full it covers about 1500 hectares and is about three metres deep. So it's pretty big. In the early 1900s the State Water Board cut channels from the river into the lake to try and ensure permanent water for the township. Previous to that it'd existed on a cycle of drought and flood. Unfortunately, the community's also had the same sort of swings and roundabouts; you know, thriving when wheat, wool and cattle are going through good times, suffering when they aren't. And over the years there's been a lot of suffering. So I hope that's sufficient information, though now that there's sealed roads leading out here, our hopes are on the rise that the beauty of the lake might attract the tourists.

Anyhow, I was born here and we had the farm here and all that sort of stuff and, well, this happened, back in a winter about twenty years ago, when it was okay for just about anyone to go out and shoot kangaroos for dog meat. It's a true story. If you like, I can give you the names and addresses of the people involved. Actually, I had a drink with one of them tonight. But, anyhow, about twenty years ago these young bucks had gone out and they'd shot a couple of 'roos and they'd brought them back into town, in the back of their ute. Then before they went home they decided to drop into the Australia Hotel. Now, I won't mention any names but, when these young bucks arrived at the pub, there, slumped over the bar, working hard on drowning a monumental hangover, was a local identity who we'll just call 'Jack', for the sake of the story.

Of course, as in all small towns, gossip travels quickly, so these young bucks knew that Jack's wife had left him a while back. One rumour had it that his excessive drinking may've had something to do with it. Another was that some of his personal habits had gotten out of hand. Either which-way Jack remained oblivious to just about everything beyond the bottom of a schooner glass. So, knowing of Jack's post-marital predicament, these young bucks decided to play a bit of a joke on him.

Now, just off the main bar was a smaller bar, with an open fire. It was known as the Ladies Lounge because that's where the women used to go and have a shandy while they waited for their husbands to finish off whatever they were doing in the main public bar. Very patient women in Lake Cargelligo, I can tell you. All gems. Salt of the earth. They'd have to be. Then, between the Ladies Lounge and the main bar, other than a doorway, was a small servery-window, where the ladies could order drinks from the barman.

This particular night the Ladies Lounge was empty. So these young bucks went back outside and they got this dead 'roo out of the back of the ute and dragged it into the Ladies Lounge. The publican's wife, a very attractive woman, was in on all this so she went upstairs and she got an old dress and hat. She tied the dress around the 'roo, then she put the hat on its head, tucked its ears up underneath, then tied a bow underneath the chin. When all was done they propped the 'roo up against the wall, over near the fireplace. They placed a shandy on the table next to it then they turned off the lights. The room was now only dimly lit from the open fire. Then, after a couple of minor adjustments, one of the young bucks stuck his head into the main bar and he called out, 'Hey, Jack, there's a sheila out here in the Ladies Lounge who reckons she know yer.'

At hearing this, old Jack's head lifts off the bar and he comes to life, a bit.

'Fair dinkum?' he slurs.

'Yeah,' says the young buck, 'she's in here waitin' ter see yer.'

Well, all of a sudden, Jack thinks his luck's changed. A bit of a twinkle comes to his eye. A couple of months of trying to drown your sorrows can be pretty tough, especially with all the sorrows Jack had. So Jack grabs his beer, eases himself off his bar stool and he staggers around to the Ladies Lounge as fast as his legs could carry him, which wasn't fast. But he's eager, very eager. When he arrives he sees this apparition—this sheila—over in the corner, romantically lit by the flickering flames of the open fire. His heart skips a beat because what he sees, he likes the look of; the type that might just be a bit of a goer if she was chatted up right, you know, by a real gentleman like himself. To make a top impression, Jack licks his fingers and tries to flatten down his balding hair. Straightens himself up a bit. Tucks his stained pullover in a bit. Attempts to rub the toes of his thongs on the back of his pants, to shine them up a bit. Then he wobbles towards the fireplace.

When he gets there, he has to lean up against the mantelpiece that goes over the top of the fireplace. One hand's gripping onto the mantelpiece, the other's gripping on to his beer and there, just past the other end of the fireplace, is the sheila that's been waiting for him. In an attempt not to sound overly eager, Jack decides to start up a friendly dialogue. 'G'day,' he slurs, 'nice night but a bit on the chilly side, ay?'

No answer, so he decides a different tack to see if she's a city type or more the rural type. He'd been to the city once. Perhaps he'd met her there. He says, 'Do yer reckon it'll rain?'

Still no reply.

'Well, yer certainly the quiet type, ain't yer, girlie' he says, as he shuffles a little nearer. He struggles to adjust his focus. He scratches at his chin, trying to sort it all out. Then finally he gives up and he says, 'Look, pardon me, love, yer face looks familiar but, fer the life'a me, I just can't place yer.'

Launceston—Tas

Now this story isn't about a little outback town or nothing but it's a little ripper about a pub in Launceston, Tasmania. The Apple Isle. Nice place, Launceston, lots of gardens and stuff. Pretty old. Don't know its history. Wouldn't have a clue. It's in the Tamar Valley, that's all I know, and I even stand corrected on that. I'm no historian. I'm a worker. An ex-shearer.

So it's the Commercial Hotel, Launceston. Early 60s. And this story's as true as I stand here, holding up the bar. See, the Commercial was one of the most popular pubs in Tassie because it was totally a union pub. Totally. If you were in the AWU, you were in. Not a worry. Even if you hadn't booked a room, it didn't matter. They got you in somehow. Then in the morning, if you could manage it, you fronted up to this huge kitchen-hall for breakfast and, boy, didn't you get a real good feed: bacon, eggs, sausages, chops, the lot. Whatever you wanted. But what the pub was really known for was their beautiful Sunday lunch. Just about everyone who had a union ticket would turn up for this feed, this Sunday lunch. Oh, they'd come for miles.

Okay, so we go into Launceston, a few workmates and me, and we go down to the Commercial. It's a huge, big, rambling hotel. Typically old style. Two-storey. We gets there on the dot of ten o'clock and the place's already packed. Absolutely packed. Lunch's about one. But, it doesn't matter, we show our ticket and we're in. Any rate, we have a few beers then we get stuck into this lunch. Absolutely beautiful. Everything you'd ever want and more. Then after lunch a mate and me decide to go for a bit of a poke around. Me mate's name's Ted. So we wander up to one of the rooms and, lo and behold, there's about twenty blokes playing poker, which, mind you, was a highly illegal activity. Any rate, I'm a bit buggered, right. A bit wobbly on the perch. So I just finds myself a spare bed and hits the sack. When I wake up I need some fresh air. 'I'm goin' fer a walk,' I say.

'I'll come with yer,' says Ted.

So that's what we do and somehow we end up down near Victoria Bridge. I don't know how we got there but we did. We hung around there for a while then we start thinking that we'd better go back to the Commercial and see what our workmates are up to. Now, by the letter of the law, pubs had to close up pretty early in Tassie, especially on a Sunday. So, by the time we get back, everything's sort of dead. The blinds are drawn and the place looks like it's closed down.

'Shit, what are we gonna do?'

Then we hears this racket coming from inside the pub.

'There's somethin' goin' on in there,' Ted says. 'Let's have a look.'

'Okay.' So we find the fire escape and we're up that. At the top of the fire escape there's this open window. In we go, straight into someone's room. 'Sorry, mate,' we say to the feller who's trying to get some kip. Through his room we go and down the old winding staircase, into the bar. And that's where everyone is. They're still drinking and carrying on.

So we settle back into the swing of things. After a while we see that the barman's falling off his perch. The barman's the owner. He's the publican. We give him a bit of a shake. 'How's about another beer?'

'Go fer it,' he says. 'I've had it.' Then he locked the till up, stuck the takings in the safe, and called out, 'Go fer yer lives, fellers. It's now an honour system.' Then off to bed he staggered.

Any rate, someone took over the bar and everybody just put their money down and that was that, we kicked on. Now, buggered if I know what time it was but, see, there's this bloke there with a big, red, woollen, fluffy sort of jumper on and he was starting to make a bit of a stir of things. A big, loud sort of feller he was. A real performer.

'Who's that?' I said to someone.

'Oh,' the feller said, 'he's the Birdman.'

And by geez he was a strange character. No exaggeration, this feller, the Birdman, he was at least twenty-four stone. Fair dinkum. Any rate, I just thought they called him the Birdman because of his fluffy jumper. But no, the feller next to me reckoned they called him the Birdman because, when he got good and pissed, he somehow got it into his head that he could fly.

'Pull the other one,' I said.

'Just you wait,' the feller said.

Any rate, just inside the entrance of the Commercial, there was this big, ornate staircase that winded up two tiers, to the residential part of the pub. So, Ted and me mate, we order a couple of jugs and we go and sit over with the rest of our mob. I'd say there would've been about a dozen of us at this wooden table. And it just happened that this table was right near the entrance, which also just happened to be under the landing of this staircase. So we're at this table and suddenly the Birdman calls out for everyone to shut up. Then, when all's quiet, he announces, 'I'm goin' fer a fly.'

Everyone gives him a bit of a cheer. 'Go fer it Birdman!' they started shouting. Apparently he was well known in Tassie and so they start a slow hand-clap to egg him on. So the Birdman got off his bar stool and he wobbled over to the staircase and proceeded to stagger up the two flights of stairs, right up to the top. Then, when the Birdman attempted to climb up on to the balustrade, high up, right up above our table, our boss grabs the remaining couple of jugs of beer from off our table and he calls out, 'Stand back, fellers!' Which we did, and pretty quick, too. So there's the Birdman, away up on this balustrade, two floors up. Everyone's slow-clapping him.

'I'm gonna fly,' he calls out. The clapping stops. There's dead silence. Everyone's eyes are on him. The Birdman balances himself on the balustrade. He fluffs up his big red jumper, gives a bit of a squawk, then he dives out into the air, arms spread wide like they're supposed to be wings. He manages a flap or two but it doesn't work. Down he comes, belly first, right smack-bang through the centre of our table. Splintered it.

Christ almighty, he didn't move a muscle. 'He's dead,' someone called out.

Then comes a ruffle of his woollen jumper. A shake of his head. He staggers to his feet. He's got this funny sort of grin on his dial. He looks straight at our boss, who's standing there, still hanging onto the two jugs of beer.

'What do yer reckon about that, then?' the Birdman slurred.

'Well, mate,' our boss replied, 'I must say that I was very impressed with the take-off but I reckon yer'd better brush up a bit on yer landings.'

Louth—NSW

A few years ago, a long-time mate of mine, Andrew Hull, and myself, Tonchi McIntosh, decided to pool our musical, writing and research abilities and go on a trip along the Darling River. Our aim was to stop off at towns, properties and pubs along the way to collect stories that we could later work into poems and songs.

Our first stop was Louth, which, as it happened, also ended up being the last town we visited on that proposed sojourn. I'd say that the population would've been well under fifty. If you look on the internet you'll see where Louth's advertised itself as being 'a tiny and insignificant little settlement on the banks of the Darling River' where the biggest event that happens is Louth Turf Club's annual race meeting. Though we did note that a certain Robyn White has added that there's more to Louth than what may greet the eye, including: 1) a complete lack of unwanted unit developments; 2) a crime rate next to none; 3) there's no terrorist warnings pending; 4) everyone in town is friendly; 5) the beer at the pub—Shindy's Inn—costs at least as much as it does in a ritzy pub in Sydney and, to top it off; 6) Shindy's also sells the best chips for at least a hundred kilometres.

Now, considering that the nearest place downstream, Tilpa, is just on a hundred kilometres away and the nearest place upstream, Bourke, is also about a hundred kilometres away, Andrew and I arrived in Louth with no expectations other than to follow up on a lead that a nearby sheep station was the first place in the world to use mechanical shears. But then we came across an amazing story. A story that, in itself, provided us with enough material to more than fill a CD that we've since called *Firestone*.

So, to the story: it all began in County Louth, Ireland, back in the 19th century, with a man named Thomas Andrew Mathews. Thomas was a wheelwright and shipwright by trade. His wife's name was Mary and they had five children. But then news started coming through about the big gold strike in Australia. So, lured by the hope of striking it rich, Thomas left Mary and the kids in Ireland and he headed for the Australian goldfields. As happened to so many, he had no luck in the goldfields and so his trade drew him to the Darling River, where he soon realised the potential of the place.

See, around the mid-1850s, the area around Cobar and Bourke and all those places was opening up. The wool industry was kicking in and the paddle steamers were doing a roaring trade up and down the Darling. So there was steady work for the gum-cutters who supplied the wood for the paddle steamers. Like, they'd chop the wood and they'd leave it in a pile by the riverbank. Along with the wood they'd leave their details in a pouch, such as who they were and, of course, the cost of the wood. Then, when the steamer captains collected the wood, they'd leave an IOU in the pouch for the gum-cutters to cash in, which they usually did at the nearest pub. Anyhow, Mathews thought, 'Here's a go' and so, in 1859, he bought forty acres of land between Bourke and Wilcannia where he built a pub to cater for the passing river- and land-based trade, which included a stopover point on the Cobb & Co run. Things went extremely well and so, five years after arriving in Australia, Thomas sent for Mary and the children.

Now here's an important part of the story that will later unravel: when Mary and the children travelled to Australia they did so in the company of a Peter Hoey Finn. Finn was a monument builder and he was later to play an integral role in the story.

Anyhow, by the time Mary and the kids arrived, a bit of a town had sprung up around where Thomas lived. Mary soon warmed to her new home and named it Louth, after their county in Ireland. But such was Thomas' influence on the place that he became known, far and wide, as the King of Louth. Now, apparently, he wasn't noted for being a very kind or caring man. In fact I gather from his family—some of them still live in the arca—that he was quite a hard man who had long absences from home. So Mary reared the family and she ran their pub—The Daniel O'Connell—and, well, basically, she virtually ran the town while her husband wasn't there. But then, at the age of forty-two she became ill with pneumonia and, with no medical care within cooee, she died in Louth.

So now, here's the interesting bit. As I said, Thomas Mathews wasn't noted for being a kind or caring man. In fact, he could be a tyrant. But what he did, after his wife's death, seems to have been an eternal gesture of burning love. See, he had built a very special monument to his wife in the Louth cemetery. From what we could gather it was most probably in collaboration with Peter Hoey Finn, the monument builder who'd travelled to Australia in the company of Mary and the children. This assumption is on the basis that Finn's eldest daughter later married one of Thomas and Mary's sons. So there was a close connection there.

To give you some idea of the monument, it's a pillar, standing, say, eight metres high, which is surmounted by a huge Celtic cross, made of Victorian granite from Philip Island. From all accounts, the stone very nearly didn't make it to Louth cemetery because the steamer carrying it, the *Jane Eliza*, got stranded by falling water levels in the Darling River and remained stuck there for three years. So the granite finished its journey by bullock dray.

The granite itself has a gold fleck. When it's polished you can almost see your face in it. So, when the sun's just above the horizon, the light reflects off the cross and it's just like a spotlight. Oh, it really makes the hair rise on the back of your neck. But because the reflected blaze can only be seen from certain places at different times of the day and the year, the cross was forgotten until the 1950s when two kids, who were out gathering firewood for drovers, saw what they thought was the light of a bushfire. So they ran back into town, screaming about a fire in the cemetery. But, of course, by the time the townspeople got there, the light had faded, the reflected blaze had disappeared and the kids were in strife for raising a false alarm.

But the really fascinating thing about the monument is that it's been designed and positioned to such an amazing degree of accuracy that, every year, on the anniversary of Mary's death, the reflected light falls in a path that leads straight to the door of the Mathews' old house. What a story, ay?

Lyndhurst—SA

Lyndhurst. Yes, well, Lyndhurst's about 600 kilometres north of Adelaide. It's at the end of the black top—the tarred road—that runs up from Port Augusta, Quorn, Hawker, Beltana to Leigh Creek, where the coalfields are, then Lyndhurst's about thirty kilometres north of that. From Lyndhurst you can either head on north, through the ghost town of Farina, up to Marree, where you can hook into the Birdsville Track. Or, if you turn right at Lyndhurst, you're on the Strezelecki Track, and that goes up through Innamincka, up into western Queensland.

Actually, they reckon the infamous cattle duffer, Harry Readford, sort of 'pioneered' the Strezelecki Track when he duffed something like 400 head of cattle from a property in western Queensland and he brought them down that way, into South Australia. And seeing he did that in the early 1870s, it was a pretty huge feat because, only ten years or so beforehand, Burke and Wills had died out in that area. Anyhow, from that particular adventure, people realised they could bring cattle down the Cooper Creek, then down the Strezelecki Track, to the railhead at Lyndhurst.

So, back in the old days, Lyndhurst was a railway town on the old Ghan line. These days the old Ghan's gone so there's not much left in the town. But, for me, I've got some wonderful memories of the place and in particular a big fundraising event we ran. Prior to that I'd been involved in smaller events, you know, making a bit of money here and there. But it was to be the first of many major fundraising ventures from which I've won a 'Northern South Australia Outstanding Contribution Award'. And I'm very proud of that because all the stuff I get involved in brings money into the area and that's vitally important for so many of these smaller outback places.

Anyhow, a best mate of mine, Alan Dunn, used to own the Lyndhurst Hotel. Dunnie was one of the most famous publicans in Australia. Huge he was; twenty-eight-and-a-half stone. He always reckoned it'd be easier to walk over him than around him. He was a big, big boy. A real outback identity. Known by everyone. But the fact of the matter was that Lyndhurst's only source of water came from the north coalfield at Leigh Creek, through to a tank on Myrtle Springs Station, via a little one-inch pipe.

Now, the tank on Myrtle Springs was set up in such a way that the outlet to Lyndhurst was above the outlet to the sheep trough and, when it was hot and the sheep got thirsty, the water level soon dropped below the Lyndhurst outlet. So we were constantly running out of water. I mean, it used to recover a bit in the night when the sheep weren't drinking, but during a particularly hot spell it'd take days for the water level to get back above the Lyndhurst outlet.

So that was the problem and Dunnie and I decided to raise some money to build a new pipeline to Lyndhurst. That's when we came up with the idea of the Strezelecki Stomp. Actually, I remember we had a band come up from Adelaide, called Misty Mountain. They were a fantastic group and two nights later, after they'd returned home, all their gear got burnt down in a shed and they never played again. But, anyhow, we blocked off the street for the dance and we had roasting spits, with sheep and pigs. Plenty to drink. Lots of fun. Terrific atmosphere. And you won't believe it but, along with the help of a development grant, we raised enough money to buy the entire length of pipe to do the job, which was about twenty kilometres. Then six of us volunteers went out with some volunteered equipment and we laid the two-and-a-quarter inch polly pipe from the north coal field, up to the tank on Myrtle Springs Station, then on to Lyndhurst. And so many people were, and still are, thankful for that because Lyndhurst's never run out of water to this day.

So yes, that was fantastic though, unfortunately, Dunne's no longer with us. He died as the result of a car accident with a road train. But then that got me going on a thing called the Alan Dunn Memorial Fund. Heaps and heaps of functions later and we'd raised enough money, again with a development grant, to build a brand new hall in Lyndhurst. So, when you drive through Lyndhurst these days, there's this beautiful hall sitting on the corner of the Strezelecki Track. You can't miss it. But, gee, he was a great bloke. A top bloke, and it's a great little outback town, too.

Marble Bar—WA

My name is Hans. I am from Germany. A paediatrician—a doctor for children. I love Australia, particularly the outback. I try to come here twice, three times a year and I remember this tour of Western Australia. I start from Darwin, to Katherine, to Kununurra. I've seen the Bungle Bungles. Drive over the Gibb River Road to Derby, then to Broome, then to Port Hedland. While I am visiting the RFDS Base in Port Hedland I receive an invitation for a consultation flight to Marble Bar. I remember Marble Bar. Oh, yes, it was one of my favourite places, I think. It is located 1500 kilometres north of Perth, 200 kilometres south-east of Port Hedland.

It was a fantastic flight into the blue morning sky. The landscape is really outback. It fascinates me every single time, even though I have seen it many times before. Down there was the desert. I could see dried-out rivers and few vegetation. Red soil. Interesting brown mountains. That is what I love about the Australian outback. It's not like Germany. You look to the horizon and you see, just like you'd say, 'nothing'. But to me it is 'everything'.

I have read very much about Marble Bar. It is an old gold-mining town from the late 1800s. I am told it once had a population of over 5000 but today there is less than 400, maybe. The gold rush has gone but there is still a little gold, some tin, silver, lead, zinc, copper and jade. Marble Bar is known as the hottest place in Australia. For over 160 straight days in the summer months of 1923–24 the temperature has never dropped below 100 degrees fahrenheit or 37.8 degrees centigrade. This record still exists, I believe. Also the temperature has never dropped below zero degrees centigrade. But today the sun is shining but it is very, very cold for the hottest place in Australia.

Windy and cold. Not below freezing, but it feels like this. You cannot dress only in a shirt. You must have a coat, maybe from leather. I think it is about fifteen degrees centigrade. Our crew wasn't prepared for the cold either, especially not our pilot, Walter. Walter was only wearing a thin short-sleeved pilot shirt. I am freezing, just looking at him. Therefore I snuggle into my woollen jacket. Walter borrowed a leather jacket.

Walter and I borrowed the nurse's Toyota to have a look at the surroundings. First we go to the natural wonder where the town got its name, to the Marble Bar Rocks and the Marble Bar Pool. The pioneers who discovered this area misinterpreted the rock of this place and thought it is marble. But it is a stone known as jasper. At the western side of the town an exceptionally colourful barrier of jasper is crossing the Coongan River. The glass-clear pools underneath this barrier are a popular place for bathing and look very inviting for a quick dive. But it is so chilly we only enjoy the impressing colour of the rocks.

Marble Bar is a very historic town, with many old buildings. At its centre is the Iron Clad Hotel. It is a traditional Australian pub. I like this pub but I don't have a drink. How Australians can drink cold beer on a cold day, I don't know. Opposite of the hotel you can find the Marble Bar Roadhouse. Oh, it fascinates me because it is everything: it is a gas station, it is a supermarket, it is a post office, it's a visitors' centre. All in one. A cosy institution.

On top of a hill, there is a huge water tank. It is called Water Tank Lookout. From there you have a fantastic view. You can actually climb up this hill as well. I am thinking we should have done that, to get a little warmer. On our way back to the RFDS station we pass the Government Building. It is architecturally, the most impressive building in town. Built with natural stone from this area. Today it is host for the police station and the central management of mines of the rich Pilbara goldfields.

Back at the RFDS we have a little break. Out of my own interest I ask Matt, the doctor, about some of the dangerous animals of Australia. These subjects may sound a bit strange to Australians but it is very unusual and interesting to us Germans.

First I ask, what to do if someone has been bitten by a snake? Usually the species of the snake is not known. As the venom of the snake is using the lymph stream to make its way through the body, first of all, one has to ligature the affected limb to hinder the flow to the body. This must not be done too tightly. If you don't know the snake species you get a screening of the bite in the hospital or of a urine sample to figure out the species. This is a very important step when deciding which antidote must be given. There is an all-purpose antidote but that is not easily tolerated by the body and can cause an anaphylactic shock.

Australian spiders can also be venomous. The redback likes to sit at places you wouldn't expect; underneath the table, in the sandpit, in your garden. The venom is not necessarily dangerous but it hurts a lot after contact.

Crocodiles must also be thought of. The water is the habitat of the crocodile, therefore the croc can move a lot faster in water and can attack the victim more easily. All crocs bite when they are tormented or hungry. Saltwater crocs, or Salties, can get seriously dangerous. When they bite, the jaws snap shut incredibly fast and hook up like a hinge, with a locking device, so the prey won't get lost. The croc then tries to pull the victim into the water. You can't possibly open the jaws of a croc. The freshwater crocodiles, or Freshies, also bite but at least they cannot eat a person.

After lunch we visit the Flying Fox Lookout, a most stunning view over the Coongan River. Due to the dry season, it is hardly running water. There is a long, thick, steel rope tightened across the river. When water is running, a man is let out to the middle of the river, along this rope, to measure the depth of the water. This is meant to be useful for building a dam. But these plans have been dropped for the moment. Downstream of the Coongan River lies the Chinaman's Pool. This waterhole or water pool is so beautifully embedded into the landscape that you could actually stay there for a picnic and a swim. But not today.

When we came back to town, the consultation time was nearly finished. Then we set off. After a warm farewell, the small aeroplane—a Piper—lifts off the gravel road, into the blue sky. On the flight back everyone is quiet as they hang onto their own thoughts. I am remembering Marble Bar. I remember the pub, the Iron Clad Hotel, and a sign outside reading, 'No alcohol to be taken into these premises'. At first I think they have got that the wrong way around but then, no, it is the Australian humour, I am told.

Marree—SA

Well, take Marree for example: a small town, in the desert country, 700 kilometres north of Adelaide, fifty metres above sea level and with an average annual rainfall of just over 150 millimetres—six inches on the old scale. Though, mind you, with the drought, it's been very rare that the average has been reached. And it's got a history, a great history, from right back when the Arabunna Aboriginal people roamed the area. Even today, they've got a community centre in town.

So then, the first explorer to come through was Edward John Eyre. That was in the early 1840s. Then twenty years later John McDouall Stuart passed by and he named the place Herrgott Springs, after an assistant who discovered some springs there. Now, I don't know but, somewhere along the way the spelling got changed to Hergott Springs—minus an 'r'—because, when the Overland Telegraph Line came through, ten or so years later, and set up a maintenance camp, that's how they spelt it.

Hergott Springs then became a busy outpost and, with it being a meeting point of both the Birdsville and Oodnadatta Tracks, the Afghan cameleers began to use it as a staging post to go north with their camel trains. That's how the train got known as the 'Ghan'. So then, by the time the railway reached the camp, in the early 1880s, Hergott Springs was declared an official town. That's the way it stayed until just after World War I when, with all the anti-German sentiment and stuff like that, it was renamed Marree. Marree, in the local Aboriginal language, is supposed to mean 'place of possums' though no one I know can ever remember seeing too many possums around the place.

Anyhow, one of the legends to come out of Marree was Tom Kruse. Tom used to do a mail run from Marree up to Birdsville. You might remember how that was featured in the award-winning 1950s documentary *Back of Beyond*, which showed Tom in his old truck, a Leyland Badger, going through hell, high water, sand dunes and a number of breakdowns along his trek up to Birdsville.

But then, when the railways shut down in the early 80s, it was just about curtains for Marree. These days it's a pretty lonely and isolated sort of place with a few old corrugated iron houses here and there, and wide streets that seem to disappear off into nowhere. Someone even wrote a poem about Marree which, if I remember, goes along the lines of:

'A corrugated-iron town, in the corrugated-iron air, where the shimmering heat waves glare out onto the red-hot iron plain, and the steel mirage beyond.'

So Marree's somewhat fallen into decline, so much so that, these days, Lyell and Shirley Oldfield just about own everything in town, apart from the beautiful old two-storey pub, and Lyell even used to own that. In actual fact I was only talking to him a while back and he said, 'Burgie, do yer remember where yer were on this day back in the early eighties?'

I said, 'No.'

He said, 'It's the anniversary of my wedding.'

'How could I forget, Lyell?' I said, because, see, Lyell had the Marree pub back then and I was living down in Lyndhurst. Anyhow, I'd been invited to the wedding so up I went to Marree and, oh, we had a very big night in the pub, the night before. A raucous night that went into the early hours. And so the next day everyone's pretty hung-over and they're getting ready for this big wedding and Lyell's nowhere to be seen. No one could find him. He'd disappeared. So I went out the back and there's Lyell in his bloody tails—like, in his wedding outfit—fixing this busted bloody polly pipe that fed the water to the pub. It's a mess.

I said, 'Lyell, what's up?'

He said, 'Well, I can't leave the pub with no bloody water.'

'Gee,' I said, 'you can't be late for your own wedding, mate, so how about you piss off 'n' get married 'n' I'll fix the pipe up?'

He said, 'Are yer sure?'

'Just leave it with me, mate. I'll fix the pipe. You go 'n' get married.'

'Gee, I feel bad about that,' Lyell said.

'Well don't,' I said. 'Just piss off. You'd better not keep the bride waiting.'

Anyhow, off he went and by the time I got the pipe fixed, I'm running late. So I go and clean up and get dressed and, when I turn up for the wedding, there's Lyell but there's no Shirley. Shirley's gone missing.

Now, as it turned out, they'd decided to go all out for the big occasion and have Shirley arrive in a horse and sulky. The only trouble was that, when the horse came to the old Ghan railway crossing it thought it was water and so it decided not to cross this water. So Shirley's stranded in the buggy, and not wanting to get her dress and all that dirty, the wedding party and what-have-you, well, they got out to try and get this horse to cross the railway line. But when they pushed the bloody thing, it wouldn't budge. So they pulled it and it still wouldn't budge. So then they tried to drag it over the railway line but still it wouldn't budge. It just wouldn't cross the railway line. No way. Then, all of a sudden, the horse went skittish. It bucked and it kicked and then it shot around and took off in the opposite direction, with Shirley, done up to the nines, hanging on for dear life. So now everyone's screaming and yelling and going on as Shirley disappears off into the distance.

Anyway, to cut a long story short, they finally caught the bloody thing and they calmed it down and they, somehow, coaxed it across the railway line and Shirley turned up at the wedding very late and a bit worse for wear. So, as it turned out, Lyell could've stayed back at the pub and fixed the bloody pipe himself.

I said, 'Yes, Lyell, I remember that day. How could I ever forget it?'

McKinlay—Qld

In the mid-90s we were doing gigs throughout Queensland and we ended up at a small place called McKinlay. McKinlay's about 100 kilometres south-east of Cloncurry, in western Queensland. I didn't know anything about the place; you know, that the McKinlay pub was the one they used in the film *Crocodile Dundee*. Like, I'd never even seen the film so I couldn't work out why all these bus loads of people would turn up and take pictures of the pub and talk about it as being Walkabout Creek or something.

It was a pretty substantial pub. Timber, with the usual big outback verandah. Inside, it was quite beautiful. You know, richly decorated. I've got the colour green in my head. I think it might've had a green paint job or something. Then there was lots of paraphernalia on the walls; interesting stuff, not just the half-naked XXXX girls like you see in most of those outback pubs in Queensland, but, like, lots of flotsam and jetsam of outback stuff and they had these nice tin chairs out on the verandah and I remember they had a goose. Yes, that's right; instead of having, like, a pet dog, they had a pet goose walking around everywhere. I was actually a bit scared of the thing at first but, in time, I got used of it and it was quite friendly.

Then, what else was in McKinlay? That was about it really; just the pub and the community hall and there might've been a store or something. But that's about it. They used to have a school there but it'd been closed down before we got there. And apparently, when the school was closed, nobody informed whatever government department it was that puts in air conditioning and carpet and so, one day, these blokes rolled up and had a look and said, 'Well, it's on the job list.' So they laid down all this brand new carpet and they put in a new air-

Crocodile Dundee—The Hansford Collection

conditioning system into this school that'd been shut down. And, when the guy told me that, I said, 'That's disgusting. What a waste of money, you know. It's stupid how people can't think for themselves,' I said, 'and especially for a building that doesn't get used.'

And the guy said, 'Oh, it gets used alright.'

I said, 'Oh, well, that's okay then.'

'Yeah,' he said, 'we use it as a polling booth every three years or so, when there's an election on.'

Anyhow, we spent a week there, staying in portable dongas out the back of the pub, while we helped put this performance together for everyone in the district. Like, it was a big fire event with lanterns and movement to music and dance and stuff. But the thing was, we hadn't been paid for something like six weeks. There was this big cock-up with the system. And, like, we're artists. We don't have any spare cash lying around. This was before mobile phones and so, most nights, we were in the front bar making phone calls, trying to sort it all out. And the promoters over in Brisbane were saying shit like, 'Well, why don't you use your savings?'

And I'm like, 'What savings?'

'Then, what about a credit card?'

'Don't have one.'

You know, we were getting nowhere. We were really up the creek and in the end I was making all these desperate phone calls to our mates. 'Hey, can you lend us some money?'

Anyway, so there we were, in McKinlay, and the publican guy, he couldn't believe that I'd never seen *Crocodile Dundee*. He just couldn't believe that there was someone still alive in Australia that hadn't seen the film. So, one night, he set the TV up in the lounge and he came and grabbed me and sat me down so I could watch it. Then afterwards I said, 'Now I understand why all these bus loads of people are coming here and taking photos and going on about this Walkabout Creek place.'

So that was it. That's how I got to see *Crocodile Dundee* and stay in the pub where some of the filming went on. But, anyway, none of that helped us get paid and so, like, in the end, we're dead broke. Not a cent. Then, just as we were about to leave town, the publican went over to the till and he grabbed something like a couple of hundred dollars out and he gave it to us.

'Here,' he said, 'pay us back when yer get things sorted out.' And, like, we'd only known the guy for a week. How good's that, ay?

So that was McKinlay. There was hardly anything there, in the town, and I believe that now they've even moved the pub over to the highway so that they can cash in on it being the *Crocodile Dundee* pub at Walkabout Creek. Yes, they physically moved the building because not enough tourists could be bothered driving, the something like 500 metres, down the track to the pub, yeah.

Meekatharra—WA

The region from Meekatharra, down through Cue, Mount Magnet and Yalgoo, is known as the Eastern Goldfields of Western Australia. Now, why on earth it's known as the Eastern Goldfields, I don't know, because it's north and west of Kalgoorlie. But, anyhow, that's what it's known as and there's been mining going on for more than a hundred years and more recently, because of modern technology, they've started to rework the old mines and extract more gold.

Other than that the area's also served the pastoral industry. One time it used to be full of sheep though, these days, whoever's running stock generally runs cattle. It's just too hard to make wool profitable, what with current market prices plus the costs associated with the long distances and so forth. So a lot of the country's now been closed down for restoration and some of it's been taken over by the Aborigines. So, even though both the pastoral industry and the mining industry aren't what they used to be, Meekatharra's sort of still alive.

Back in the early 1950s, I was working out there as the overseer on Belele Station. Belele's a famous station settled by the Lee-Steere family. And, of course, all through that country back then they needed horses for stock work so they were pretty interested in horses. And also, some of the owners of these places were quite well educated, with a bit of 'old' family money behind them, and so they bred thoroughbreds and raced them. So, for most of the pastoralists and graziers, race meetings were the biggest social events of the year. Actually, Sir Ernest Lee-Steere, who owned Belele, bred horses and though they weren't bred out on Belele, he bred one by the name of Eurythmic that won both the Perth and the Caulfield Cups, back in 1919, and he had another one, Maple, that won the Caulfield Cup in 1928. And I

Bush race meetings are popular throughout Australia—The Carter Collection

can remember there were large framed photographs of both those horses in the manager's dining room at Belele.

Anyhow, so they used to have races there at Meekatharra twice a year, as a part of the Eastern Goldfields round. Like, they'd have a meeting at Meekatharra then, a week or two later, they'd hold another one at Cue then a week or two later at Mount Magnet and a couple of weeks after that at Yalgoo, and they'd go on down to Geraldton.

So, anyway, this's just a little pub story that springs to mind. It took place in the Commercial Hotel in Meekatharra. I was Clerk of the Course at the races that year so it would've been about 1954 or '55. It was late in the evening and the Commercial was absolutely packed with all the racing crowd from far and wide. I was drinking in the main bar with a group that included a bloke called Bill Broad. Now Bill was a big feller, about six feet three and very solid. Tall and solid. He came from a station near Yalgoo, 270 miles west of Meekatharra, on the road to Geraldton.

Bill would've been in his late thirties, early forties. Then there was a woman with us, Mavis. I'd say that Mavis would've been in her mid-to-late forties and she was the girlfriend of one of the bookies. Actually, she wasn't a bad looking sheila. A tiny thing, about five feet two in her shoes. A bit on the cheeky side, too. So we're drinking away and Bill says, 'Hey, Mavis, what about sleepin' with me ter'night?'

Anyhow, Mavis stepped right up close to Bill. Of course, Bill's towering over her. Mavis looks him up and down, with a bit of a cheeky grin. Then she tilts her head right back so that she could see up into Bill's face and she said, 'Oh, I dunno, Bill, I'm not sure we'd be able ter see eye-ter-eye on too much.'

Menindee—NSW

I knew a real character once, Ron Healey. An eccentric old bugger. He had this shock of white hair, a big bushy moustache, weather-beaten skin. And he had all this cactus—prickly pear—growing in his front yard. Great big bloody things they were and I remember when someone gave him a pair of bright green Speedos—swimming togs—and he'd stand there, with the hose, watering the cactus, dressed in nothing but his bright green Speedos. Oh, it was a sight to behold. He looked just like Moses, you know, with this shock of white hair, a bushy moustache and dark leathery skin, but just standing there in this pair of bright green Speedos. Hilarious. And something else I used to laugh about was that he had a dog he'd called Arsehole and, when he'd take it for a walk, you could hear him shouting, 'Come on Arsehole! Get a wriggle on, Arsehole!' And I was with him one day and he said, 'Yer know, I've had two Arseholes but I reckon the old Arsehole was much better than this new one.'

Yes, so that was Ron. He's gone now, but he'd been around a lot. And he loved his poetry. Just loved his poetry. On the spur of the moment he'd hop in his ute and go bush, getting inspiration. Loved the bush. He also enjoyed telling a yarn or two and he had a few up his sleeve, too, I might add, and one of them was when he was living alongside the Darling River, at a place called Menindee during the Depression.

Menindee's in the far west of New South Wales, a bit over a hundred kilometres south-east of Broken Hill. In Ron's time, there would've been less than a hundred people living there. It's a pretty arid area. Actually, it's quite an experience to go through country that you'd swear hadn't seen a drop of rain for years, then suddenly come across a series of lakes, fed by the Darling River, that hold up to four 'Syd-harbs' and almost cover ten times its area. You wouldn't credit it, would you? Away out there.

Now, I believe the name Menindee comes from the Barkindji Aboriginal people's place-name of Minandichee and right from when white fellers arrived you could describe its history as being 'ill-fated' to say the least. For instance, back in the 1830s, one of the first explorers through the area, Major Thomas Mitchell, shot a few Aborigines, including a woman and a child, after they tried to nick one of his kettles. Later on, Charles Sturt also had his problems when he travelled up the Darling during his ill-fated attempt to discover a non-existent inland sea. Then there was the terrible killing of a whole tribal group of Aborigines when one station property fed them bread that'd been laced with arsenic.

So things were pretty uncomfortable when a feller named Tom Pain and his family arrived. Tom opened the Menindee Hotel, which later became known as Maiden's Menindee Hotel because it was in the Maiden family for several generations. It's still open, and I believe it's now the second-oldest pub, still in continuous operation, in New South Wales. Also, Maiden's Menindee Hotel was where Burke and Wills stayed on their ill-fated expedition north to the Gulf. In fact, they gouged an arrow shape in a door post that pointed the direction they were going to take and for many years, until that part of the pub burnt down, the room where they stayed was still there.

So that's a bit of background about Menindee and when Ron came to live there it was during the Depression era and people were setting up humpies and lean-to's along the banks of the Darling in an attempt to try and survive. Food was quite plentiful. There was always underground mutton—rabbits—and the river would've been in far better condition than it is now, so you'd have your beautiful cod and perch and freshwater lobster. Quite a little community grew there. In fact, Ron said that one of the most enjoyable Christmases he ever spent was when a group of his fellow down 'n' outs strung an old wireless aerial up into a tree and listened to Christmas carols while they shared a lunch from whatever they could scrape together.

Then, having to be the sorts who'd have a go at anything in an attempt to make a quid, these people did whatever they could. One little enterprise Ron had going was that he'd catch cod and what-have-you and, to keep them fresh, he'd run a wooden peg through their lips, toss them back into the river, then tie a line from the peg to a tree. Then, when the train came through, one of the crew would buy the fish off him and take them into Broken Hill and sell them there. So Ron'd get his couple of pence or a shilling from that and he'd go and buy his flour, tea and other supplies before settling in for a few beers at the Maiden's Hotel.

So they might've been poor but they were survivors. Like, one day, Ron was sitting beside his humpy, dressed in rags, watching the river flow by, wondering where his next feed might come from, when he looked up and away in the distance there's a bloke in this small punt—a small wooden rowboat. He was sort of pushing his way downstream, gondolier-like, with just the one oar. And as this boat drifted nearer it became obvious that the bloke'd stolen it from somewhere because he didn't have a bloody clue what he was doing. What's more, as the feller got closer, Ron could see that he was definitely 'not from around these parts'. He was dressed more like a city-type down 'n' out. You know, an out-of-work salesman or whatever, wandering around, desperate to make a quid.

Anyhow, when this bloke finally paddled nearer, Ron saw a crumpled bag of clothing in the punt; like, as if the feller had tossed whatever he could grab into this old bag and did a runner, out bush, before the police or whoever could nab him.

'And how are you, my fine sir?' is how this bloke announced himself to Ron.

'G'day,' Ron replied. 'What's up?'

'Today, my friend, amid these deeply depressing times, is your lucky day.'

'Why's that?' Ron asked.

Then this bloke rummaged around in his old bag and pulled out a brand-spanking-new silk tie. 'Because, sir, for just today only, I am willing to sell you this authentic silk tie for a mere shilling.'

And Ron was telling me, he said, 'I just couldn't believe it. There I was, in the middle of the Great Depression, without a penny to me name, sitting beside me humpy, out in the middle'a nowhere, dressed in rags, wondering where me next feed's gonna come from 'n' this bloke's done a runner 'n' he knocks off someone's punt 'n' comes floating down the river, flogging, of all bloody things, brand-new silk ties. 'N' yer think I'm mad because I water me cactus in me Speedos 'n' I've got an Arsehole for a dog!'

Mintabie—SA

If any place is to be described as being the true outback, the opal mining town of Mintabie's it. It's situated, gosh, I'd say a bit less than a couple of hundred kilometres south of the Northern Territory border and about 300 kilometres north of Coober Pedy. So the climate's fairly tough. You know, from below zero, up into the high forties. But the jewel in the crown of Mintabie is that it's got a very rare version of black opal. See, it's rare that you get black opal anyway but the Mintabie black opal has a crackling in it which is different to the black opal they get at, say, Coober Pedy.

Then Mintabie's also quite unique in that the opal fields and the township are on freehold Aboriginal land. Actually, it's said that the Aborigines first found opal there, back during the First World War. But, see, it's all limestone country, which makes it very hard to dig, so it wasn't till the mid-70s, when heavy machinery was introduced, that Mintabie really came into its own.

As far as the population goes; when I arrived in 1991 there might've been 100, 150 people, max, plus stacks of dogs in all shapes, sizes, breeds and conditions. Of course, if the welfare mob arrived in town, you know, families disappeared out bush and others vanished down their mines till they'd gone. Other than the Aborigines, who came and went a lot, I'd say it would've been about 90 per cent Croatian, with some Koreans, a few Aussies and one Serb. And because the Croatian–Serbian War was on at that time, the one Serb was considered to be the bravest man in town. Then the ratio of women to men was about 20 per cent female to 80 per cent blokes. So, like the one Serb, the women had to be pretty brave as well. If they were young they'd work in the pub, as bar staff, and if they were not so young

'*Outside the Mintabie pub were half a dozen or so palm trees, I presume from the Afghan days*'—The Marsh Collection

they'd work in the kitchen at the pub, and the rest; well, if you didn't have a baby to look after, or multitudes thereof, you'd work at the school as an office person or a typist or a teacher's aide or whatever.

It was a generator town. All generator. There was no grid power and, with there being such a hotch-potch buildings, a lot of places shared a generator. The planning authority didn't really exist in Mintabie so some of the living conditions were pretty basic. You know, you'd sometimes go out to dinner and it'd be all candles. No power at all. There were a few caravans here and there and what houses there were were mostly put together from just timber uprights, clad with a sheet of corro—corrugated iron. Pretty much like a Coolgardie safe, really. There'd be no lining on the inside walls. Dirt floors covered with, you know, with whatever bits and pieces they could find. Like, there'd be a bit of old furniture, an old iron-framed bed, laminex table, a couple of old chairs and a sink, that was held up with upturned 44-gallon drums. It was all bore water, pretty much, which had that bore-watery sort of smell. Like, you'd have a shower and your hair felt like nails.

There were two stores. One was a down-in-the-dumps, tacky place that was seen as the Aboriginal's store. The other one was a bit more ritzy because it had fluoro tubes in the fridges and they'd stock stuff like soy and other bits and pieces for the Koreans. Then there was a post office, a rip-off merchant who fixed your car, a health clinic and the pub. The health clinic was run by the Uniting Church's Frontier Services, together with the Royal Flying Doctor Service, and they'd move between the other Aboriginal lands and Marla. It was a sort of cluster so the clinic nurse wasn't always there. I know that because, the very first day I arrived, a car'd run over a small dog and its back leg was hanging by a thread and I nursed it for like four hours till the clinic nurse arrived back. She took over then and sort of stitched it up and put a brace on it. Then, basically, it hobbled around like that for the next month or so, and it survived.

But only a month or so prior to me getting there a million dollars worth of opal was pinched off a table in a caravan. The thief just grabbed it and pissed off out of town. Of course, the word got around like lightning so the chase was on. Anyhow, the thief ended up chucking them out the window and kept on driving, so they let him go. Yeah, they got the opals back. So when I got there they were still a bit shaky about newcomers. In fact, it was lucky that I did look after the injured dog because it just happened to belong to one of the wildest kids in town. So I got on famously from then on. I'd saved this kid's dog. I could do no wrong. I started off at hero status from the very first day. Yeah, so thank God for the dog incident. It got me through a tight time.

Then the pub had a Fred Flintstone look about it. It was made from big rock boulders held together by cement and, in an attempt to give the place an exotic feel, out the front were half a dozen or so date palm trees, I presume from the old Afghan days. So it was a unique place, in a unique community and it was just a case of, when the barman was about to shut up for the night, and put down the cage over the front bar, everyone'd buy two or three beers and they'd wander into the lounge. From then on we'd just help ourselves, pretty much. Of course, the generator'd go off well before midnight so then you'd be sitting around, playing cards by candlelight or by lantern till all hours, because someone was determined to win back the money they'd lost. Or some bloke's lonely and he needs someone to talk to so there's a real shaggy-dog tale being told and it just keeps going on and on and on and you can't leave because you just might miss out on a great punchline. Then, and at the end of the session, it was 'the last person to leave, just shut the door, please' and the next morning they'd basically hose the place out and we'd start all over again.

So yes, as I said, I arrived in '91, which was when the Croatian–Serbian War was going on overseas. Oh, it was classic, that was, because the only news they got about the conflict was during the evening news on ABC or Impaja television. So all the Croats'd gather at the pub and they'd get stuck into some sort of homeland brew that had the Croatian chequered flag on the label. Like, it must've been like rocket fuel because it really charged the guys up with patriotic fervour. Oh, they'd even start singing the Croatian national anthem. Well, by then, most of them would only be able to gurgle it out. Then, when the news came on, if it was good news there'd be big cheers and if it was bad news they'd swig down their drink then smash their shot glasses up against the wall. So she was a pretty wild sort of place.

Now I can't remember what the one and only Serb was doing while all this was going on. Hiding somewhere, I presume. But there was a lot of that real deep nationalistic sort of stuff going on. Actually, the son of the publican, a young Croatian feller in his early twenties, he left Mintabie to go back to Croatia and join up with the army and he proved to be a bit of an inspiration because, over the next six months, maybe another dozen young guys left as well. But, really, Mintabie didn't offer too much. You'd hear them say, 'Oh there's nothing going on with the opal 'n' there's no women around the place so I may as well go 'n' do my bit for the homeland.' Very slim pickings; no opal, no women, high testosterone, so off they'd go full of bravado. Mind you, just how many got further than Adelaide, I don't know. I'd imagine a good many of them arriving in Adelaide and taking one look around and saying, 'Bugger the war, there's women here' and they'd decide that Adelaide was a pretty cosy place to live in comparison to Mintabie or Croatia for that matter. So I'd say some of them wouldn't have quite got past the first bordello.

But, really, the prettiest thing about Mintabie, and I'll never forget it, was when I first flew in. It'd rained in that area not long beforehand and, looking at Mintabie from the air, there was this huge round lake called Swan Lake. And surrounding this beautiful blue water was the red-green of the Sturt Desert Pea. Oh, it was like an Aboriginal picture, painted on the ground. Exquisite. Just exquisite. But it was real frontier territory, I can tell you.

Nelia—Qld

There's not too much you can say about Nelia, really, because
there's not much there. Well there certainly wasn't back in '63,
anyway. I mean, just say you're going from Julia Creek towards
Townsville, what you'd call the township of Nelia was on the left-
hand side and it only consisted of a pub, a little general store,
and a butcher's shop. The railway station was also on the left-
hand side. It was just one of those little flat ones with a covered
area and there always seemed be stacks of kangaroo skins,
waiting for the next train to come along and pick them up. Then
on the other side—on the right-hand side of the road—there was
just a house for the station master and about six or seven fettler's
tents. And that was Nelia. At a pinch there would've only been
about thirty or forty people.

If you stood on the railway station and looked out, you'd see
nothing for miles and miles. Then if you went further down
towards the Flinders River, there was a cattle station called Nhill
Creek. Mrs McDougall owned that. They reckoned that one time
she bloody advertised for a manager-foreman-mechanic who had
a wife who was a cook and the chap and his wife she gave the job
to, well, she promised this and that and everything else. Oh, she
promised him the world. Then, when the chap and his family
arrived on the train, with all their furniture and that, Mrs
McDougall refused to pay the rail fare. So the poor bugger and
his wife and his family and all their furniture was stuck there
and they had no money to pay their way back home and so, in
the end, they had no choice other than to go out and work for her,
just on a regular wage and nothing more.

Actually, my uncle, Arthur Fayers, he was rumoured to have
had a bit of a fling with her. But, to me, he was the kindest and
biggest-hearted person I'd ever met so I don't know anything

about that though, when I went out there to work for old Arthur, in '63, he'd disappear nearly every bloody night, up to the homestead. Then one time he came racing back early. 'What's up?' we said, and he said to us, 'Quick eat this,' and it was about ten pound of this bloody beautiful fillet steak. Apparently the cook from up the homestead had knocked a beast over and, while his back was turned, old Arthur purloined this slab of fillet because, a couple of hours later, the cook come down and he said, 'Hey, you blokes haven't seen a piece'a fillet, have yer?'

'Not on yer life,' we said. But we'd already eaten it by then.

Anyhow, so that's what was on that side of Nelia. Then over the other side of the railway line was a sheep station called Nelia West. Old Charlie, an Aboriginal stockman, looked after the sheep for the owner and he had a white cook who done the cooking for him. This bloody cook would've been well into his eighties, easy. The two of them lived in a little humpy, way up in the bare paddock. Old Charlie was only being paid thirty bob a week while the old white cook was on seventeen pound ten a week. See, that was the basic wage back then so you couldn't pay a white man anything less. But the poor old 'Abo'—this Old Charlie—well, he only got thirty bob a week and yet he was the boss over the old white cook there. Anyhow, I said to Old Charlie one day, I said, 'If you're getting paid so poor, why don't you leave?'

And he said, 'I can't.' He said, 'I come from Palm Island 'n' if I leave there'll be a black mark against me 'n' me family 'n' we'll never be allowed off the island ter work again.' So he must've been indentured or something, ay? So, yeah, that was Old Charlie. As black as the ace of spades, he was. Then, somewhere along the line, one of his sisters must've come to visit him because he told me, 'Noel,' he said, 'your uncle, he's a bad man.'

'Why, what'd he do?' I asked.

'He got one of me sisters inta trouble.'

So I don't know when that happened in the string of things because, as I said, when I was out at Nelia, old Arthur was also rumoured to be having a bit of a fling with Mrs McDougall. Anyway, that was my uncle, old Arthur Fayers. Arthur was my late father's elder brother and they called him 'the Galloping Ghan' because he'd turn up anywhere and everywhere but whenever someone wanted to get hold of him, he was nowhere to be found. And that's how I got out to Nelia. I was only eighteen. I'd just left school. I was living down near Newcastle, in New South Wales and old Arthur asked if I wanted to make some money because, see, out at Nhill Creek, the stockyards were in bad repair and Arthur had gotten the contract to fix them up, so I said, 'Yeah, I'll come along.'

Anyhow, old Arthur owned an old 1938 eight-cylinder Chev. It was a big old dark blue thing where the two back doors opened forward and, in the middle of the back seat, it had a sort of dicky-seat. So you could fit about three or four in the front and about five in the back. But, oh, it was a bugger of a thing. You always had to jump-start it, then, once you got it going, it wouldn't stop. Only Arthur was game enough to stop it. See, what he'd do was that he'd put his fingers on the spark plugs and it'd stop dead. Oh, the shock of it didn't bother old Arthur. He was as tough as they come, maybe even tougher.

And whenever Arthur needed fellers to help him he'd go to the pub and get all these old bar flies. And, oh, they were a wild mob. Real old hardened bushies, you know. So, this time, old Arthur gathered about six or seven of these old bar flies up and me and these blokes, we piled into Arthur's Chev. We were on our way out to Nhill Creek to set up a camp before we got to work on the stockyards. Arthur was going to follow on later in an old truck he'd somehow purloined. Anyhow, he said to me before we left town, 'Look, Noel,' he said, 'I'll be along a bit later with the truck so I want you to go out with these fellers, okay.' Then he said, 'And I want you to keep an eye on these blokes and make sure they don't stop at the Nelia pub.'

I mean, here I am, I'm only eighteen, fresh out of bloody school and I'm supposed to keep an eye on these hardened old bushies. So what do we do? We all pile into Arthur's old '38 Chev—oh, that's right, we had to jump-start the bloody thing first. So we done that, then we said 'Goodbye' to Arthur. Then these fellers, they drove around the corner and they stopped at the Nelia pub and they piled out of the car and in they went. I went too. I mean, I had nowhere else to go. Like, you'd stick out like a sore thumb sitting by yourself in a car like that, out in the middle of nowhere. Anyhow, I didn't drink then and I still don't drink now but I went into the pub and pretty soon these chaps had drunk all their money so then they turned around to me and they said, 'Noel, have you got any money?'

I said, 'No I haven't got any money.'

Then they seen that I had a watch on so they said, 'Well, give us yer watch.'

I said, 'No.'

So then they're into me, trying to take me watch off and that's when Arthur turned up. Boy, didn't I breathe a sigh of relief when I saw him because he didn't look too pleased with what he was seeing. I thought, Gee, he's really gonna get stuck inta these fellers. But he turned around to me and he said, 'Noel, I thought I told yer not ter let these bastards stop at the Nelia pub,' and, you know, here's me, just an eighteen-year-old green-eye, against these old hard bushies.

Now, I can't exactly remember who they all were now but some of the fellers he'd get from time to time was a feller by the name of Bickling and there was bloody Maurie Vittler. Maurie was a real dark closed sort of a feller; real hard to get to know. Another was poor old Adrian Backhouse. He was a gun shearer. He done 250 plus, a day, till he died in a level crossing accident on his way home to Dubbo for Christmas. Then there was bloody Merve Ducker. Actually, it turned out that Merve's brother was my girlfriend's bloody uncle. Small world, ay? Actually, poor old Merve died a few years later on, because Arthur happened to be talking to an old acquaintance and he asked him, 'So how's Merve going these days?'

And this chap said, 'Oh, Merve's dead.'

So Uncle Arthur said, 'Yeah, how did that happen?'

It turned out that Merve went out drinking with some 'Abos' and got drunk and he somehow fell into a bore drain that was right at the head of the bore, where the water comes out steaming

Uncle Arthur and his purloined truck—The Fayers Collection

hot, so when they found him the next morning he was pretty much stewed. So that was Merve Ducker. Then there was another feller, Copper Wire Jack. Copper Wire Jack got his name from when they were putting through the second railway line out to Mount Isa. And when they were putting through this rail line they also decided to put another wire on the telegraph poles. Anyhow, all the linesmen used to wear green overalls and every morning when the boss went out to work he'd see this bloke trailing along a couple of kilometres behind the rest of the linesmen, with these green overalls on. So the boss just assumed that this feller was coming along behind, checking that the other workers were doing a decent enough job of laying the copper line. So the boss'd give him a wave and the bloke'd wave back, nice and friendly. Then it wasn't till about three weeks later they realised that this bloke was taking all the copper wire down and flogging it off almost as fast as they were putting it up. Yeah, so that was Copper Wire Jack and apparently every summer he'd ring up the police and let them know that he was going to break a shop window or something just so he'd get three months inside. I don't know why he done that. Maybe he just wanted to go back inside to spend the summer with some of his mates. I don't know. So they were just some of the fellers old Arthur used to go around and grab out of the pub when he needed some work done.

But like I said, there was nothing around Nelia so there was no decent gidgee for the fence posts and strainers and all that for the stockyards. The nearest gidgee belt was about two or three hours away. So Arthur loaded all these old bar flies into the truck he'd purloined and away we went. Anyhow, when we got near where the gidgee belt was, we stopped and waited till it got dark and then we hit the bush. Dead dark. No lights or nothing and down through the scrub we went. I didn't have a clue where we were going but it took about an hour to get to this place and we set up camp. Of course, old Arthur must've also purloined the tents because they had Queensland Government Railways written on them. Then the next day we started to cut up the timber and each night we'd sneak back out with a load—no lights or nothing—and we'd take it back to Nelia, unload it, then sneak back in through the bush before it got light again.

And that's when I saw my first Min-Min light. Old Arthur and me, we was sneaking back to camp one night and this old truck he'd purloined, it only had a passenger side door. No driver's side. I don't even think it was registered. Anyway, it's dark and I looked out the passenger side and about 300 or 400 yards away, just travelling level with the truck, was this light pink thing, about the size of a round football. It was all crispy and sparkly, with a half-inch fuzz around it and a thin line of a tail behind it. So I watched it for a while then I said, 'What's that, Arthur?'

And he sort of just said in passing, 'Oh, that's a Min-Min light.'

Well, I had hair in them days and, I tell you, it stood up on the back of me neck. Anyhow, like I said, I don't know what was going on with all this driving in and out in the dark. Then when we got to the camp all the blokes are just sitting around doing nothing. So Arthur said, 'Hey, come on, you blokes. How about a bit of a go?'

But, apparently, Arthur was illegally cutting the timber because this other bloke came out from behind a tent and the first thing he said was, 'Yes, I thought it'd be you, Arthur Fayers.'

So Arthur said, 'Gee mate, give us a break, I've only been here a couple'a days.'

And the bloke said, 'You lying bastard, this clearing's about 200 metres wide.' Then he said, 'And what's more, Arthur, what've your blokes been living on?'

Arthur said, 'Kangaroo.'

Then the feller looks around and there's about six sheep skins hanging on a fence so he said, 'Yeah, well they must be pretty woolly bloody kangaroos.'

That was the end of it then and Arthur had to get his gidgee via other means. So we went up to Millungera and old Booker Harrison was the manager there and he must've owed Arthur a favour or two because when Arthur said he wanted some good gidgee timber, old Booker Harrison said, 'Well, yer can take stuff off here but don't tell anyone.' That's because he didn't want the owners to find out.

So there's just some of my memories of Nelia. As I said, really, there was nothing much there. I mean, I heard of five-year-old kids out that way who didn't even know that water came out of the sky in the form of rain. Like, you'd tell them and they'd just sit there with their gobs wide open in wonder because they'd never seen rain before. Yeah, that's true, so they must've got a hell of a shock the day we had a huge storm and it rained fish.

But I guess Nelia just grew out of a fettlers' camp on the rail line between Townsville out to Mount Isa because, like I said, there was only the few fettler's tents, a pub, a little general store, a butcher's shop and the railway station. But what the fettlers done I don't know. As far as I could see, they spent most of their time in the pub. And she used to get pretty rough at times. See, they were all sorts of nationalities and so they'd have a big blow up every now and then. One night they had a big brawl and by the time the police come over from Julia Creek the fight was over and all they found was an ear left laying in the street. Then another time they found this drunk bloke, sitting in the main street at 3 o'clock in the morning, hammering one of those survey pegs into the ground, so they said, 'What the hell are you doing?'

And this drunk feller replies, 'I'm driving a peg inta the arsehole of the world.'

Nhill—Vic

My name is Marjorie Woodhouse. I was born 5 July, 1917, here in Nhill. Prior to getting married my maiden name was Rintoule. It's quite a well-established family name in the area. We even have a street named after us. Nhill's about halfway between Melbourne and Adelaide, in the Wimmera area of western Victoria. When I was young it was more mixed farming but these days they mainly grow wheat. In fact, Nhill's said to have the largest single-bin silo in the Southern Hemisphere.

Now, as far as the history of Nhill goes; the first white men to come to the area were Dugald Macpherson and George Belcher, who were looking for land. That was at the beginning of 1845 and the story goes that they came across a group of local Aborigines who said they were part of the Nyill tribe and the two men thought they said Nhill. Nhill instead of Nyill, which has the meaning of 'mist over calm waters'. So there was a bit of a mix-up there and from that mix-up came the name of Nhill.

Then, as to how the Rintoules came to live here, there's a bit of a story about that, too. See, my great-grandparents, James and Barbara Rintoule, were originally from Scotland and they arrived in Adelaide in 1840 on the Indian-line ship, *Rajasthan*. James and Barbara paid their own way and they arrived with two children, Alexander and Margaret. In the ship's book they spelt the family name as Rentoul. But that was wrong. It's Rintoule, and that was quickly corrected. James and Barbara remained in the Adelaide area until 1862, which was when another child was born—Robert, who was my grandfather. The family then decided to move over to Stawell and, during the trip by bullock wagon, Barbara died and was buried at Spring Hill, at Harrow. I don't know how she died.

Then my grandfather, Robert Rintoule, he later married Elizabeth Sarah Ridgwell in Stawell. Robert was a bullock driver and general carrier who also carted wool and later sleepers for the Stawell to Horsham section of the Melbourne to Adelaide railway line. Then in 1878, when the Victorian government was opening up land in the western districts, Robert was allotted land at Nhill. So they left Stawell and they came over to Nhill to get the farm up and going. At that stage there was only about a hundred people in the town and when they came to Nhill, Robert and Elizabeth Sarah also brought our great-grandfather, James, with them and he later died in 1892.

When they arrived they were rolling the mallee and clearing land and they did the fencing and all that. Then a couple of years later Robert bought the only pub in town for fifty pound. Originally it was just a little wooden shack along the street. Sort of a small weatherboard place. Now I've got a piece out of the local paper here in Nhill, the *Messenger*, dated 18 July, 2001, which has more information about the hotel, and it says, '*Clem Hardingham had his wooden pub moved from Kiata by bullock wagon and re-erected it on the site in Victoria Street, and this was the beginning of the Union Hotel in Nhill.*' And now this bit's interesting. It says: '*Robert Rintoule made his purchase of the Union Hotel during an evening session but did not realise until next morning that he had offered to buy, or that his offer had been accepted. To pay for the Union he had to toil hard both as carrier and selector while his wife, Sara, ran the hotel.*' So that would've been Elizabeth Sarah, Robert's wife. Then it goes on to say that '*when Robert took ill he leased the hotel to Nicholas Rauert Senior for two years but his wife—Nicholas' wife—died after eighteen months and the Rintoule family took possession again.*' It goes on to say: '*The hotel became very popular with farmers who enjoyed its excellent meals prepared by Miss O'Leary. It was always crowded at show time and when horse and cattle sales were held. In 1887, the Presbyterians broke loose from the Dimboola parish and the Rev. William Mathew even held services in the Union Hotel parlour.*'

So that's how it became known as Rintoule's Union Hotel. As you can see, it's had quite a varied history. Apart from being a gathering point for farmers and all the locals, plus its religious connections, it survived a cyclone in 1897 and a fire in 1902. Also in 1902, Grandfather died and so Grandmother, Sarah, carried on with her two eldest sons, Thomas and James junior. Then in 1911—and I've still got all the dockets and everything here—the hotel was rebuilt from the little wooden shack into a two-storey place. Upstairs-downstairs I call it. And, oh, it was a beautiful building. I had a painting done of it, years ago. It says here, in the *Messenger*, *'1911 saw the opening of the new two-storey brick hotel built at a cost of seven thousand and thirty-six pounds, ten and ten pence ... and the appearance is now enhanced by one of the finest, most conveniently designed and handsome hotels in provincial Victoria.'* Then, when Grandmother died in 1916, the boys carried it on and they sold it in 1923. The hotel's still there but these days it needs a good face-lift.

As for myself, I've led a very average life. As a child I lived on the farm with my father and my mother. Those were the days of the old buggy and horse and I remember as a little girl I always used to sit between my parents when we'd go the five miles into Nhill to do the shopping. And I rode Dolly, the white pony, to

Rintoule's Union Hotel—Nhill—The Rintoule Family Collection

school from when I was a six-year-old up until I was eleven. But my parents died in unfortunate circumstances. My father just went out to feed the horses; you know how they did in those days—groomed them at 5 o'clock in the morning—and the horses raced in and they knocked him over at the gates and he never recovered. Then, whether it was too much strain on my mother or not, I don't know, but four-and-a-half months later, she passed away. My father was forty-three and mother was forty-one. So that was rather traumatic because that left just us three orphans: Arthur, myself and the baby, Clem.

But we were very fortunate actually because my brother, Arthur, who was fifteen years old at the time, he stayed on the farm with the help of his uncles and I was cared for by a bachelor uncle and two maiden aunts. Then there was Clem. He was just twenty-two months old and our Uncle Don, and his wife, Aunty Marie, had an understanding from right back when Clem was coming along that, if anything should ever happen, they'd look after him, which they did. So that's the story of the three orphans: Arthur, Marjorie and Clem. We were all blessed in a funny sort of way, really. I always say that I had, not a gold spoon, but a silver spoon in life. So I've had a wonderful life and I was looked after wonderfully well.

But with my grandmother dying a year before I was born I haven't got many clear memories of the hotel other than going in there for family occasions and the like; you know, dinners for birthdays and things like that and having a meal there, occasionally. Even so, in the old days it was rather personal and I was always told that it was 'the family's hotel'. But it was such a long time ago now that I don't have those sorts of feelings for it any more. Anyway, I'm getting a bit old for going out and having meals these days.

Nhulunbuy—NT

I was in Nhulunbuy for a while. That's an interesting place. It's in north-east Arnhem Land, right where the Gulf meets the Arafura Sea. Really pretty country. Amazing coastline. Great fishing. The town was only built in the early 1970s because of the bauxite mine. So it's a strange mix 'cause there's a new town that's just shot up, then about fifteen k out there's this modern mine, then you've got, like, the real traditional Aborigines—the Yolngu—living around the area in their communities and stuff. And they're nice people, that's for sure. They've got a lot of knowledge of the land and everything and, like, every year they have what's called the Garma Festival.

The Garma Festival's just a big get-together, really. It's when all the different clans and tribes come from around Arnhem Land and the desert and they do all the ceremonial stuff. White people also come. Anyone who's interested in learning about Aboriginal culture is allowed to come. Everyone camps out for the week and the whites can go to workshops and, like, you can learn to make a spear or learn about bush medicines with the women. All that sort of stuff. Then in the late arvo, that's when they do a lot of their dancing and at night they have bands playing. Yothu Yindi used to be one of the main bands that played there. It's really a good festival.

But I just went there for a holiday, to visit my cousin. He was working for an Aboriginal community out of Nhulunbuy. They'd started a croc farming project and they had a white guy helping co-ordinate the Aboriginal workforce. Anyway, the white guy, he quit. Chucked it in for some reason. So I got the job and the big thing coming up was the egg collection from the wild—like, going out and stealing eggs from the nests—and it was pretty dangerous 'cause the female crocs are very, very aggressive and protective. So, like, one minute I'm there for a holiday, to have a good time with me cousin and catch a few fish and have a few beers; next minute I'm getting pushed into a helicopter, heading out to collect croc eggs.

Anyway, I had an Aboriginal guy to help me, Stewey. Stewey only had one good eye. His other one was gammy. They gave him a fourteen-foot wooden boat paddle and his job was to keep an eye out and protect me from being attacked by whacking the crocs over the snout with the paddle. They don't really like that too much. But, how we went about it was that we'd get some of their nest material and we'd pack it into a couple of eskies and we'd put the eggs in with the nest material. As far as the nests go, we were after saltwater croc's eggs and the Saltie makes a big mound, anything up to a metre high and three or four metres round and they build them near water; like, around a river or a wetland area.

But it's really hard to see what you're doing 'cause, in that country, there's all this long cane grass and stuff. I mean, you could see the nests from the air okay and the chopper pilot, he'd try and land as close as he could. But, like, because of the trees and all that, more often than not he'd have to land 300–400 metres away and you'd have to hike through the long grass; me with the eskies and Stewey with his one good eye and his gammy eye and the fourteen-foot wooden paddle. And you'd always have to be on the ready 'cause a good-sized nesting female might grow to around three-and-a-half metres. They don't get as big as the males. But they're big enough.

Then, when you'd get near the nest, like, she might just explode out of the water at you. Or maybe she'll be laying hidden in the mud and she'll fly out at you from there. And sometimes you'd get stuck in the mud. So there's Stewey, with his one gummy eye and his one good eye, thrashing away at this croc with this bloody wooden paddle. And quite often, 'cause they're so powerful, they'd shred the paddle like it was nothing; like it's just a bit of foam. So after a couple of weeks the fourteen-foot paddle had gotten chewed down to about six foot. But most of the time we got the eggs. But it was pretty hairy—pretty stressful and nerve-racking—so my beer intake shot up from about six cans a night to about fourteen. But you see some good country. Like, from the chopper there's some really nice views of the wetland areas and that. So that was my first job at the croc farm.

Then by the time I left the farm, like, we had about thirty-five adult crocs that we'd caught. And we had one real big male croc who was over four metres and really, really girthy. Like, he'd probably weigh half a ton. He wasn't with a female and so before I left I wanted everything to be paired off and in good order, 'cause I was pretty conscientious. Anyway, over the couple of years I was there, this big croc had been there and, like, because the concrete in his pen would go all green with slime, about twice a week we'd grab these stiff brooms and we'd get in and scrub his pen and hose the concrete down. And we'd do it all around him and he wouldn't even worry. He'd just lay there. So I thought he had a really quiet, dopey nature. So on my last day, I'd organised these two females to be in another pen and I wanted to catch him and move him in with them.

So I had a bit of PVC pipe, with a noose at the end of it, right. Like, crocs have got that big tooth halfway down their jaw and so you just get the noose behind that and you pull it tight and you've got them. We had a big cage there and we were going to drag him into that, then just lift him over to the other pen and let him go with the females. About ten Aboriginal blokes turned up to help but because of his quiet nature no one was too worried.

So I jumped into his pen. He was half in the water, half out of the water. I was only about two metres from him so I poked him in the guts, right, so he'd open his mouth so I could noose him. Well, he just exploded out of the water. He come at me so quick, I never even seen him. And he would've nailed me for sure but, somehow, he flew straight into the noose and noosed himself, which is really, really lucky. And it's happened, like, at blinding speed and you should've seen these Aboriginal guys. Their eyes just about jumped out of their sockets 'cause they thought I did it. They thought, Shit, did you just see what Phil just did?

Anyhow he was noosed so we pulled him in the cage then we let him go in with the females and, like, after that, I was a legend, ay. Yeah, a true legend. But no one knows the truth of it. I've never told no one the real story. And it was only luck 'cause if he hadn't have noosed himself he would've just got me and flung me around the pen and I would've been dead for sure. So that was a pretty close call, too.

Noccundra—Qld

Considering how the infamous horse thief cum dubious-explorer cum dodgy character Andrew Hume—no relation to Hamilton Hume of Hume and Hovell fame—died of thirst out this way, while he was searching for the missing Ludwig Leichhardt expedition, it's no small wonder that the first building to be erected at Noccundra was the pub. That was in 1882 and it remains the town's only occupied building. And even to this very day, thirst prevention remains an extremely high priority for the few locals and for the tourists that visit the place.

Now, for those that don't know, Noccundra's in the south-western corner of Queensland, in the Cooper Creek–Wilson River area and the story goes that we were flying out to Tibooburra to do a RFDS clinic when we received an urgent request to divert to Noccundra. Someone had been severely burnt. The odd thing was, though, the chap who put through the call couldn't stop laughing. Naturally we thought it mustn't have been too serious, and we said so. But the chap, the one who was laughing, was adamant that the victim was badly burnt, and yes, it was anything but a laughing matter, which he was, if that makes any sense.

Now, as the story unfolded, it'd been a stifling hot, still day and a few of the locals had gravitated to the Noccundra pub attempting to prevent a thirst. The problem being that a large tiger snake was thinking along the same lines. It appeared in the pub, had a look around, but when it saw the accumulated gathering, it decided that it didn't like the company and so it headed off to the next best place it could think of, that being the outside toilet—one of those long-drop types. So out of the pub the tiger snake slithered, down the track a bit, into the outside toilet, and it disappeared down the long-drop, where it was nice and cool.

Noccundra Hotel—The Marsh Collection

I'd better not mention any names so, for the sake of the story, we'll call the chap Joe. Now, Joe saw where the snake had gone and he came up with the bright idea of incinerating it. He downed his drink, put on his hat, went and siphoned a gallon of petrol out of his ute, then wandered back through the pub, down the track a bit, into the outside toilet, and he tossed the fuel down the long-drop, where the snake was. The problem being, after he tossed the petrol down the long-drop, he searched through his pockets and couldn't find his matches.

So he wandered back inside the pub. 'Anyone seen me matches?' he asked.

As I said, it was a very hot, still day. Stinking hot, in fact. So after Joe found his matches, he thought that he may as well have another thirst quencher before he went back outside and sorted out the snake. Meantime the petrol fumes were rising up from out of the long-drop and, with there not being a breath of a breeze to disperse them, the toilet soon become nothing short of a pending, gigantic powder keg.

Anyhow, after Joe had downed his drink, he grabbed his matches and put his hat back on. 'I'll be back in a tick,' he said, then he wandered outside, down the track a bit, in the direction of the toilet and, without having a clue as to what he was in for, he walked into the toilet and took out his matches.

'Goodbye, snake,' he said and struck a match over the long-drop.

Now, there are those from the outlying districts that go so far as to say that they felt the reverberations of the ensuing explosion. I don't know so much about that but one thing's for sure, it certainly put the wind up the blokes in the bar of the Noccundra pub. Such was the instantaneous impact of the blast that they didn't even have the time to down their drinks before they hit the floor. Mind you, that's only a rumour because knowing some of the chaps out that way, no matter what the emergency, they'd always finish their drinks before taking any action, even if it is a reflex action.

Still, you've got to feel sorry for poor old Joe. Left standing over what'd once been the Noccundra pub's long-drop toilet, his clothes smouldering away. Critically burnt he was and he stunk to high-heaven as well. And the shock, poor bloke. Even by the time we arrived he was still standing there, as dazed as a stunned mullet.

Normanton—Qld

To give you some idea, the Carpentaria Shire is as large as Tasmania. So it's pretty big, and there's always been a large Aboriginal population, not only in Normanton itself, but also throughout the entire Gulf region. Then, the first European to navigate the Norman River was William Landsborough. That was in early 1867, and on that trip he chose the site of the township and just a few months later the first settlers arrived, more or less as pastoralists. But Normanton really came into its own as a supply port, when gold was discovered around the Croydon area, a couple of years later. They'd bring the gold here and ship it out, down the fifty-six mile, to the river mouth at Karumba. And so, between Normanton and Croydon is where they have the historic train, The Gulflander. The building of that began in the late 1880s and the original steel sleepers, track, station and goods sheds remain, making it the oldest original rail line in Australia, if not the world, still in use today.

After the gold rush, Normanton settled down, the population dropped, and it returned to being a pretty sleepy sort of place. And that's the way everyone liked it. So, I guess, like so many other small towns, the locals got used of each other's company and newcomers were viewed with a large degree of suspicion until they'd somehow proved themselves. Take Rita Pointon for instance. She turned up here in the early 1950s to take over as Matron at the hospital and no-one wanted to be the first to visit her. Not until she'd proven herself, anyway. So everyone just stayed at home and put up with their illnesses, aches and pains and grumbles. And it wasn't till things were starting to get a bit desperate on the health front that someone turned up at the hospital with a horse—a foal—and said, 'Matron, me horse's crook, can yer do somethin' for it?'

Now, I don't know what was wrong with this foal but, with nothing better to do, Rita took it into her care. Then everyone waited in eager anticipation for the outcome. You know, if it lived or died. Well it did live, and the day after Rita released the now healthy horse from hospital she was met by a waiting room full of people, with all sorts of ailments. And, back in those days, the matron had to do everything. She was the doctor, the nurse, she pulled teeth, stitched people up. She set broken legs, the lot. So I guess you could say that Rita had 'passed muster' and from then on she was accepted. In fact, during her nineteen years as Matron, she become a very much loved person throughout the community. A true legend.

Then they built the new hospital in about 1984. That's where I worked as a Registered Nurse, and that's where this story took place just over twenty years ago. Anyhow, this particular night I was rostered on with a male nurse's aide by the name of Jacko. Jacko was a real character. He'd lived and worked in Normanton for many years so he knew everyone and everyone knew him. There was never a dull moment. He was always full of energy and fun. Staff and patients alike loved him and he could make even the sourest person smile and feel good about themselves. A top nurse's aide. Totally efficient. Great to work with. And he called a spade a spade. There was no beating about the bush with Jacko.

Anyhow, there was only ever two staff on duty for a night shift and around midnight myself and Jacko, we had a call to the front door where we found a drunken woman, doubled up, apparently in severe pain. Now, I don't know which hotel she'd been drinking in because there's three pubs in Normanton. There's what everyone calls the Top Pub, which is the National. Then there's the Middle Pub, which is the Central. Then there's the Bottom Pub, the Albion. Now, as it turned out, Jacko knew the woman from somewhere. Like I said, Jacko knew everyone. Anyhow, we helped her into the hospital and up onto an examination table. We didn't know what was wrong but she was moaning and groaning and going on about how bad the pain was and also that her and her de facto, who was apparently also drunk, they'd had a blue and, as she told us, 'He's gonna get me, good 'n' proper, missus. Says he's gonna kill me.'

By then we had a doctor working at the hospital. The only trouble was that the poor fellow was on call every day and night of the week. If he was lucky he might get four or five days off a month, but that's only if a relieving doctor could be found. And relieving doctors were as scarce as hens' teeth. Anyhow, after taking the usual vital signs and observations, it was still hard to assess this woman's problem, so we decided to call the doctor. He arrived, tired and strung out, and after an initial examination he decided he'd need to examine the patient further. He was a very prim and proper fellow, very committed to his work, even at all times of the day or, in this case, the night. Anyhow, so that he could have a more thorough investigation of the patient, he decided that a rectal examination was necessary. So he said to the patient, 'Excuse me,' he said, 'would you mind turning over on your side so that I can examine you more thoroughly?'

The woman didn't have a clue what he was on about and so she answered with an abrupt and drunken, 'Ay?'

'Well,' said the doctor, 'I need you to turn over on your side, please, because I'd like to do a P.R. examination.'

'A what?'

So the doctor tried to make it clearer by saying, 'Look, I'm afraid that I have to do a rectal examination to more closely assess your condition.'

The woman was still confused so she turned to Jacko. 'Hey, Jacko,' she slurred, 'what's this bastard talkin' about?'

As quick as a flash, Jacko replied, 'Oh, don't worry, he just wants ter stick his finger up yer arse.'

Well, what a miraculous recovery. 'Fuck that,' the woman shouted and she was down and off the table in a flash and she took off down the corridor, screaming out about how she'd be better off dealing with her de facto's threat of killing her than having some stranger stick his finger up her behind.

And as the woman scampered out of the building, the doctor turned to Jacko and said, 'Well, Jacko, you certainly have a wonderful way with words, mate.'

Papunya—NT

This is a little story that had its beginnings out at a place called Papunya, a small Aboriginal settlement in the Northern Territory, about 250 kilometres west-ish of Alice Springs. Now, to give you some idea, it's very much sandy, deserty country. Low shrubs. Flat, as far as the eye can see. Oh, there's one mountain range, there to the south, Haasts Bluff.

Now, in the mid-60s, when I was visiting there, it was a government-run place. This was long before Geoffrey Bardon arrived. Have you heard of Geoffrey Bardon? He was a teacher who came to Papunya in the early 1970s and got the Aboriginal men involved in painting, which was the start of a big art movement based on what's known as the Papunya Tula painting style. But that's another story because this happened well before all that and it's a story about, well, I guess you could call it a one-in-a-trillion chance.

See, around that time they were launching rockets out of Woomera and, because they didn't want to hit some poor unfortunate Aborigine who just happened to be wandering about out there, they were trying to get the last of the tribes out of the desert and into settlements. When I say 'they', I think the organisation was known as the Department of Native Affairs, back then. So Papunya was basically a welfare place. I mean, the men were supposed to work on maintenance and building projects and cleaning up and all that. But not too many did. They just hung around, basically. There was a school, and actually, they were pretty keen on getting the kids educated. Then there was a bit of a hospital. They also had a big kitchen area, where the Aborigines were fed twice a day. So they didn't have to do much of their own cooking. Really, they didn't do too much at all because the whites did most of the running of the place. Oh, and, apart from the whites, it was supposed to be a dry area and I could tell you a few stories about that too. But I won't, just in case I incriminate anyone. It's dangerous territory.

As far as the living conditions went, in many ways it was quite primitive. Some were still living in wurleys and there was government housing. But, what the white fellers hadn't realise was that, if an Aborigine died in a particular area, they'd all move out and they wouldn't return till it'd been cleansed by a thunderstorm. So when someone died, all the houses and that would be deserted, and that could be for some time, seeing how you don't get too many thunderstorms out that way.

Anyhow, they were very big on getting the Aborigines vaccinated against everything because, having lived out in the wilderness, so to speak, they had no immunity to white feller diseases. So we'd go out to missions or to remote cattle stations and we'd jump in a vehicle and drive out to some little Aboriginal camp or other, and the doctors and sisters would jab them. And also they were big on recording their Aboriginal names; like, who their father was and who their mother was. Though that got a bit confusing because too many of them seemed to have had too many of the same fathers and mothers. But that's the Aboriginal way of family.

It was a real eye-opener because, you know, you'd see all sorts of things; like, some of the living conditions were indescribable and the women had legs no thicker than broom handles or sometimes their arms or legs had been broken and had set awkwardly. I was there one day and something must've happened because the kadaitcha man—the witch-doctor—was doing his rounds trying to find out who the bad medicine was. Eventually someone got speared, I think. But the thing was, when the kadaitcha man was around, everyone stayed in their huts and wurleys, which meant that the kids weren't getting fed, so a lot of them ended up suffering from dehydration. Actually, I picked up seventeen on one trip and brought them back into Alice, to put them on drips and hydrate them again. So, by saying it was a bit primitive, that's what I mean. They still held onto a lot of their belief systems. That kind of thing.

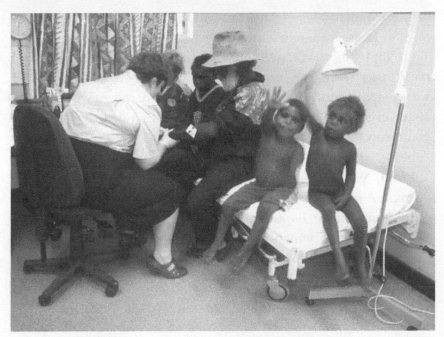

'So they were jabbing the Aborigines and recording their names and so forth'—RFDS Archives

But, anyhow, I've gotten completely off the track here because, as I said, the story I was going to tell was about this one-in-a-trillion chance. See, we were out doing the rounds one time and I was visiting Papunya and one of the nurses there was pregnant. Her name was Marie. So while they were jabbing the Aborigines and recording their names and so forth, I went and had a cup of tea with this Marie. Then, as we were flying back to Alice, I said to the doctor, 'Gee I'm itchy.'

He said, 'Let's have a look.' So he took a look and he said, 'You've got German Measles. We'll have to go back and do the rounds again tomorrow and give an injection of gamma-globulin to all the women you've been socialising with out there. Let's hope you haven't caused any problems.'

So we went back out the next day and, I don't know if you've ever seen it or not but the gamma-globulin needle is this great, big, long needle, which they jab into the rump. It's like a length of no. 8 fencing wire. Anyway, unfortunately, I'm sorry to say that, in Marie's case, she miscarried. She lost the baby.

So, that was that. Then a few years later I got married. Now, I hadn't met any of the in-laws before then and so, at the wedding, we were introduced for the first time. And my newly acquired sister-in-law looked vaguely familiar, so I said, 'Haven't I seen you before?'

'Yeah,' she said, 'I know you from somewhere, too.'

I said, 'What's your name?'

'Marie,' she said, and it turned out that she was the same Marie from out at Papunya, that time, and I'd just married her husband's sister, which made me her brother-in-law. So what's the chances of that happening? About one in a trillion, I'd reckon.

Pindar—WA

Now, this's going to sound like I'm a hardened drinker when I'm not, but Pindar is in the south-west of Western Australia, between Mullewa and Yalgoo; a bit closer to Mullewa. So if you head out from Geraldton you'll get to Mullewa, then there's Pindar. And, well, the story is that, when people moved out into the pastoral areas during the late 1800s and early 1900s, they had some very good seasons and there was so much bloody feed that they overstocked to buggery and, with wool prices being so high, a lot of the stations employed so many people that they became like mini towns, within themselves. But then, along came the drought and a lot of those people started to really struggle. A lot of people had to move away and a lot of the flocks were decimated.

Anyhow, I was working out on a sheep station and before I got there there'd been a few years of drought so they'd sent a lot of their sheep away down south, to near Pindar, on agistment. Then, when the seasons changed, I was sent down in a Commer truck, with three young fellers, who were about eighteen, nineteen and twenty, to muster up these sheep, to be sent back home. Some horses were sent down on a train and they were unloaded at a little siding called Wurarga, which is just east of this Pindar. Anyway, we were down there for quite a while mustering these sheep in this bloody Godforsaken country. Oh, it was horrible. A lot of it was so thick that you couldn't even get through it with a horse and a dog. You virtually had to trap the sheep at the windmills.

So it was really tough going and we were camped right out in the bloody bush. Then one day I decided to take the three young blokes down to Pindar for a bit of a piss-up, to break the monotony. Pindar was stuck out in the middle of nowhere. All it

Outback toilet—The Marsh Collection

consisted of was your typical double-storey pub, with just a few settlers' cottages along the railway line. And that was it. So we arrived at Pindar, thirsty as hell from all this hard work. We front up to the bar. There's another couple of blokes there; probably the balance of the town's population. So we settled in. You know, we weren't downing them one after another but we were drinking nice and steady. Then we'd spent quite a bit of time drinking when the eighteen-year-old who was with me said, with a bit of a slur, 'I need ter go ter the dunny.'

Now, the dunny was one of those long-drop ones that was away down the back of the pub, somewhere. 'Okay', so off he went and we kept on drinking. You know, not downing them but nice and steady. Then, along the line somewhere, I started thinking how the eighteen-year-old, who'd gone off to the toilet, had been gone for quite some time. So I went looking for him, to see if he was alright. I called out. But there was no answer. Stuck my head inside the toilet. He wasn't at the urinal. So I went over and opened the sit-down dunny door and there he was slouched on the can, with his trousers down around his ankles, sound asleep. Dead to the world. So I left him there and I wandered back inside the pub. At least he was safe.

So we continued drinking; just taking it nice and easy. Then I was having a bit of a chat with the publican and the local fellers we'd met in the bar when I heard a bit of a sound to my left-hand side and, when I looked around, I noticed that the nineteen-year-old had started to sort of nod off. Then, it was like in a slow motion film; one second he was standing there and then, as his legs slowly collapsed underneath him, he just sort of slid down from the bar and down onto the floor, where he passed out. Dead to the world.

'This's no good,' I said and so, me and one of the locals, we picked him up by the legs and the arms and we took him out and we shoved him on a bed that was in the hallway of the pub. Then we picked up the bed and we took it out and we put it in the middle of the road, where I wouldn't forget him and he'd be safe. I mean, the chances of getting run over on the road through Pindar were less than the chances of getting struck by lightning on a sunny day. Then, after we'd deposited the boy out there, we went back inside and took up our nice and easy pace and it wasn't long before, lo-'n'-behold, the twenty-year-old passed out as well.

'This's no good.' So me and the locals, we picked him up and we took him outside and ... 'one' ... 'two' ... 'three' ... we heaved him up on the back of the truck and just left him there, dead to the world. Then we went back inside and after we'd had a few more the couple of locals got a bad case of the wobbly-boot and they passed out as well. So had the publican. I can't remember what happened to him. He was there one minute, gone the next.

'This's no good,' I said and, being the sort of bloke who doesn't like to drink by myself—I'm more of a social drinker, you could say—I decided I'd better take these young fellers of mine back out to the camp. The only trouble was, by this stage, there's no one left to help me. So I had to go down to the dunny and wake up the eighteen-year-old, off the can, and get him to come and give me a hand with the nineteen-year-old, who was still dead to the world on the bed, out in the middle of the street, and we managed to toss him up onto the back of the truck, with the twenty-year-old, who was also still dead to the world. Then we carted the bed back into the pub and I bundled the eighteen-year-old up into the truck and I drove them all back out to our camp.

And that's about as much as I can recall about that visit to Pindar, which, mind you, was far more than what the three young fellers did. The next day they couldn't even remember visiting the place. What's more, they couldn't even work out why they felt so crook.

Purlewaugh—NSW

Us kids went to a little school at a place called Purlewaugh, in central-northern New South Wales. It's about twenty mile east of Coonabarabran. It was just a primary school that went from the lowest grade up to sixth class. That's when they had sixth class. Of course, since then the government's closed down a lot of those little schools so the Purlewaugh school's not a school now. As to the population? I'm not real sure but if you put down that there was twenty or so kids going to school and our family provided about half of them, that might give you some sort of idea. I mean, there wasn't ever a pub in Purlewaugh; just a post office, the general store, a hall and two churches. There was a Church of England church and a Catholic church and the Catholics used to think they was better than us 'cause their church was up on the hill. Closer to heaven, maybe.

How we got to school was that, see, we had three horses and so me oldest sister used to get up early and catch them for us. So we'd sort of have our breakfast, then we'd all pile on the horses and off we'd go. I think school started at about nine o'clock, the same as it does now. But we'd be off early, see, 'cause we'd meet up with another girl who rode her pony to school, too, and so we'd wait at the gate for her. Oh, and, geez, if we rode on without her, boy, didn't she get angry.

Originally we come from Victoria but our father did a lot of droving and that and so we moved about a lot. And when we were moving we did our schooling by correspondence. But we didn't get to learn much 'cause, being always on the move, our mother was still around at the time and she was so busy with other things that she never had much time. So when we asked her how to do something—like show us how to write and that—she'd just write it down and we'd copy it out exactly like what she'd done.

You know, it's like someone writing a book and saying to me to copy it out. I could do that but I couldn't write the book. So, you know, that's how I sort of grew up.

Then, when we were in one house, I remember we got burnt out and so we sort of lived in tents from then on. Well, actually, for some reason we got burnt out a couple of times from different places. But I was too young, see. Then, when we came up to Purlewaugh, we lived on a bloke's property and Dad did bits and pieces around the place, but mainly he did the burning off. You know, after they cleared the trees around the property then he came along and burnt them. Other times he'd help move cattle from here to there. But it was mainly burning off he did.

Now, as far as the family went—now let me count—I think there was fourteen of us in the family. That's Mum, Dad and all us kids. But anyway, we didn't have a house, see, so we just lived in our tents. Really, a drover's tents and their covered wagon was their house anyway. They was tarpaulin tents. One was for the girls and one was for the boys. There was about five of us girls but one sister was sort of split up from us when she was younger. Then Mum and Dad had a tent on their own. And we also had a tent to eat in. But we only used that in bad weather 'cause we mainly just sat around the camp fire at night. You know, like what drovers did. Anyhow, our meals were mainly cooked over the fire or in a boiler or in the camp oven and you just sort of dished it all up on tin plates and pannikins and we ate it that way, around the camp fire.

Then for washing and that, see, 'cause we didn't have a proper wash-house or a proper bath, we used to go down to the dam and boil up the water for washing our clothes and after we done our clothes washing we'd get the block of soap and just jump in the dam and have a wash ourselves. But the yabbies didn't worry us. Maybe 'cause there was too many of us. But we used to go yabbying sometimes. You know, we'd make those cage things and we'd catch the yabbies, then we'd feed them to the pigs. We never ate them. Those days you never ate yabbies. Now you do. Actually, these days they say they're a real delicacy. But we didn't know that back then.

So it was in those few years we was at Purlewaugh that quite a few things happened that, you know, I thought might be of some interest. See, being a drover, Dad was a horse man through and through so, when he finally got a vehicle, right, he knew nothing about it. I think it was an old Holden ute, but I'm not sure what sort of Holden ute it was. But it was a ute. Anyway, one day not long after we got this vehicle, Dad loads us kids up to go out hunting pigs and kangaroos. So we had shotguns and .303 rifles and there's all us kids in the back of the ute and there's all the dogs, also in the back of the ute. So we're all packed in and we're driving along and the vehicle got a flat tyre.

So we all piled out; us kids and all the dogs. And, of course, Dad and the boys—me brothers—they get out to change this flat tyre and, not knowing enough about it, after they put the new tyre back on, they didn't screw the wheel nuts on properly. So then we all pile back in the ute—dogs and all—and we're all laughing our heads off in the back of the ute about having this flat tyre. Of course, Dad's not too impressed with all this going on

Off to school—The Penney Collection

'cause, let alone have his mind on what us kids are up to, see, he's also trying to learn how to drive, and so we're going faster and we're going faster like he's forgot where the brakes was. Next thing, there's this almighty 'bang!' and the new wheel—the one they'd just put on—well, it come off, see, and it flew right past the vehicle and it went down the way a bit and then it bounced clean over the fence. Of course, as soon as the dogs see this wheel go past they think it's a pig or something so they're out of the back of the ute in a shot and take off after the running-away tyre. So us kids are laughing our heads off and, anyway, of course, then the vehicle grinds to a halt.

When Dad gets out, he's not too impressed so he starts whacking us kids, left, right and centre, giving us all a good clip over the ears. So we all jump out and take off after the dogs, who are over in the bushes, around this runaway wheel, barking their heads off, wondering what the hell it is 'cause they thought it was a pig or something, when it first took off past the vehicle.

So then, when Dad catches up with us, he gives us all another good clip over the ears, for good measure, and now we're all bawling our eyes out, which only makes things worse. So Dad got the boys to bring the runaway wheel back to the ute and he got them to jack the ute up with two pieces of wood. The only trouble was that we'd lost all the wheel nuts, so Dad gets us to go back along the track looking for them. And luckily we found a few of the wheel nuts so we brung them back to the ute and they put the wheel back on. So then we had a rough ride back home over the bumpy old road, with all the dogs and all us kids, packed in the back of the ute, with the dogs still barking their heads off and us too scared to say 'boo' 'cause Dad was in such a really foul mood about everything.

So yes, I thought that might be of interest. But, no, there wasn't ever a pub in Purlewaugh. It was too small for that. So I think the ones that had vehicles used to go into Coonabarabran to get on the tar. That's where the nearest pub was 'cause there was one bloke, when he'd come back home to Purlewaugh he'd drive all over the road. And, actually, one day he got out of his car and he cursed us kids for riding our ponies along the road and I said, 'If you weren't flamin' drunk you wouldn't have ter worry about us kids.'

And he shouted back, 'What would you know about a man being drunk!'

But, oh, it was a fantastic sort of life, even with all us kids and all the dogs and all of us living in tents, like we did. Just wonderful, it was. So there, there's a bit of a story for you and you can use my name if you like: it's Covey Penney. Me original name was Mayall; you know, like as in 'May all your troubles be little ones'.

Rabbit Flat—NT

I was wondering if you've heard the story about Rabbit Flat? Back in the mid-1970s it was in all the newspapers and magazines as well as being on television and radio. Of course, you know where Rabbit Flat is, don't you? Oh, well, it's in the Northern Territory, out on the Tanami Track, on the way to Halls Creek, roughly 600 kilometres north-west from Alice Springs and about 150 kilometres shy of the Western Australian border. It's typical desert country, flattish, just spinifex. Actually, come to think of it, there's not a lot out there apart from the roadhouse that's privately owned by the Farrands, Bruce and Jackie. It's one of those places where a weary traveller can get just about anything, from fuel and food to camping gear to a cold beer.

Anyhow, Rabbit Flat had a population of two and, at the time this incident occurred, Jackie was about six weeks away from giving birth. Actually, I can give you the precise date; it was the 6th of August 1975. Anyhow, the night before, on the 5th, I got a call from my boss asking me to fly out early the following morning to arrive over Rabbit Flat just on first light. Apparently, the Flying Doctor Service Base had received a radio message via either Perth or Darwin or somewhere and it looked like Jackie had gone into labour. Bruce couldn't get in direct contact with Alice Springs himself because of the poor atmospheric conditions. Then just after the message had arrived the conditions turned so bad that radio contact was cut completely and they couldn't get anymore information about Jackie's situation.

So we took off before sunrise and we flew out to Rabbit Flat. There was just myself and a nursing sister, Maureen Eason. I can't remember exactly but it took us something like an hour and a half and we arrived just after first light at Rabbit Flat. We circled over the roadhouse to let Bruce know we'd arrived then,

'We took off before sunrise'—RFDS

when we landed, he came out in his vehicle to pick us up.

The first thing Maureen said to Bruce was something along the lines of, 'Has anything happened yet? Is Jackie okay?'

'Oh sure,' said Bruce. 'She's already given birth.'

Maureen was quite surprised at that news so she said, 'Oh, so how's Jackie and how's the baby?'

'Well,' Bruce replied, 'the first baby's fine.' Then he said, 'And so is the second one.'

So there were two of the little buggers. Twins; both boys. And no one knew. Not even Jackie's doctor. Anyway, the babies were fine. Bruce had them wrapped up in cotton wool, in a washing basket. So Bruce and I had a cuppa tea while Maureen attended to Jackie and got her ready to be transported back into Alice Springs. We'd taken a humidicrib with us, so Maureen put the baby boys in the humidicrib and we put Jackie on the stretcher. Then just before we hopped into the aircraft, Bruce said to me, 'Oh, this'll be good publicity for Rabbit Flat, ay.'

'Oh yeah, okay,' I said, and I took off.

Well, it was a bit strange for Bruce to say something like that; you know, about wanting publicity for Rabbit Flat, because he was such a quiet sort of bloke. A bit of a loner, really. You'd have to be to even contemplate going out to live in a place like Rabbit Flat, wouldn't you?

But anyway, on the way back into the Alice I began thinking that he really must be keen on seeking some sort of publicity. So after I landed and my services were no longer required, I raced over and there was a phone in the corner of our hanger, and I rang the local ABC Radio in Alice Springs. A male voice answered the phone—I don't know who it was—and I said, 'Do you want a good story?'

He said, 'Yeah.'

'Well,' I said, 'the population of Rabbit Flat doubled last night.'

Now, the last thing I expected was to be quoted verbatim. But the next thing I know, it actually started hitting the headlines as a human interest story. I'm pretty sure it was on the front page of *The Australian*. If you go back and look on the 7 August, 1975 issue you'd probably find it in the paper, there somewhere. It even made the *Women's Weekly*, and I think it probably went into *Pix* or *Post* and most of those magazines.

It was also actually written up in some publication or other over in England. So it was a big story and it even went international because Bruce got phone calls from everywhere, all over the world. So then it became a bit of a stampede out to Rabbit Flat, there for a while. But it got a bit too much for Bruce because he was left out there to deal with it all by himself till Jackie and the babies, Daniel and Glen, were ready to go back home.

Then, I think it was *A Big Country*, well, they went out there and did a television program on Bruce and Jackie and the boys and their lives in Rabbit Flat. In fact, a while back, they approached Bruce again because they were rerunning some of their old stories and I think they wanted to do something along the lines of *A Big Country, Twenty Years On*. So they rang Bruce about doing a follow-up program. But Bruce's a bit shy of publicity these days. In fact, he's not real keen on it at all. He reckons he had enough of it back in '75 to last him a lifetime.

Ravensthorpe—WA

I remember when I was in Ravensthorpe, down on the south coast of WA, between Albany and Esperance. The main street just drags through town and there's this huge hill and at the top of the hill there's a wonderful pub—the Ravensthorpe Hotel. It was your typical country hotel. Corrugated iron, brick with great timber floors. A very solid building. Posts outside, and it had a magnificent cellar—a cool area underneath—that stretched out, right under the main road, almost across to the other side.

The publican was a lovely bloke. We all got on well with him. His only down side was that he was a bit slow. You know, he'd just shuffle around the bar or wherever, taking all the time in the world to do whatever it was that he was supposed to be doing. As slow as a wet week he was. Naturally, this was a little frustrating to us patrons who'd have to queue up and wait and wait till he got around to serving you. Anyhow, there'd be comments flying left, right and centre like, 'Come on, yer old bugger. Get a bloody move on or a man'll die of thirst.' Things like that.

But he'd sort of ignore all that and just laugh back and continue on at his own pace—snail's pace. Of course, this got us guys thinking about how we could get him to speed up a bit. But everything we tried, the old bugger would not have a bar of it. It seemed like nothing could ever faze him. Then, one day, one of the guys was travelling along the road, coming back to Ravensthorpe, and he ran over this big snake. Huge it was. It might've even been a tiger snake. He killed it, anyway. So then he thinks, Oh, I'll chuck it in the car. So he put this huge, dead tiger snake in the car and he continued on his journey. When he got back to Ravensthorpe, he came into the pub and he pulled us guys aside and said, 'This'll get the old bugger moving.' At that stage the publican was ferreting away behind the bar, wiping up

'It was your typical country hotel'—The Hansford Collection

beer glasses; you know, wipe, wipe, with the tea towel, then he'd hold the glass up to inspect it and, if it wasn't to his satisfaction, he'd go back to wiping it again: wipe, wipe, nice and slow. Of course, while he's doing this, there's guys queueing up for a drink. So he's completely oblivious to all this.

So the guy who's got the snake in his car goes back outside and, when everything's set, he kicks the door of the pub open and he bursts in, wrestling with this snake. 'God, almighty,' he's calling, 'look, a bloody tiger snake.' Then he hurled this snake over, into the bar area, where the publican's wiping up a beer glass. The snake hits the floor. There's dead silence. Everyone's just looking, waiting in expectation for the publican to react in some sort of way. But, no, the old bugger, he just kept on wiping the beer glass, nice and slow, wipe, wipe with the tea towel. Didn't miss a beat. Then, as he held the glass up to inspect it, he said in that drawling, laconic voice of his, 'Whoever threw that bloody thing in 'ere come 'n' pick it up 'n' get it outta the pub.' Yeah, he never missed a beat; wipe, wipe. So that was the publican at the Ravensthorpe Hotel, and he was a real character.

But in the town itself, I'd say there was probably only about 200 people. It used to be a mining town—copper mining. I can't remember what company started mining there but Ravensthorpe had a German background. So when the war started, a lot of the Germans who were already living throughout those parts of Western Australia, they were interned in the Ravensthorpe area. That's where the strong German influence came from and so, naturally, they got involved in the mining and they built some quite large and beautiful buildings.

Then, when the mine closed down, the population dropped away, and they opened up for farming and a lot of people from the eastern states came over on what was called 'conditional purchase blocks'. A block'd have a shearing shed, a sort of a hut, which was their house, and around about 3000–5000 acres of property that'd already been 40–50 per cent cleared by running a chain between two tractors to pull down the mallee. Then behind the two tractors they ran another tractor, which had seed boxes, and they seeded straight into the ground to get it ready for pasture. But a lot of the mallee just sprang straight back up again. So it wasn't a success and, of course, they also opened up some marginal areas that should've never been opened up. So there was a lot of hardship. Then, after that failed, the Western Australian government stepped in and took it over and they did it properly and so many farmers have done very well out of it and now I hear that the area's booming again.

But there was always a great sporting rivalry between the farmers and the workers. And with Ravensthorpe being a two-football town in a four-team competition, a few of us played in the team that sided with the workers, which didn't make us too popular with some in the town. And so, during the footy season our pub was the Hopetoun Hotel, which was forty kilometres down the road, on the coast, east of Bremer Bay. So the team'd go down there quite a lot and we'd drink and talk and all that. Now, I won't say who was running the Hopetoun pub but often of an evening, on a weekend, he'd be tired or whatever and so he'd leave his wife in charge. Of course, we'd still be going on till pretty late and so she'd say, 'Look, I've had my lot,' then she'd just give us the keys and say, 'Look, boys, just make sure you tidy up before you leave.'

'Okay,' we'd say and we'd continue on drinking through till sun-up or whenever. Everything was on an honour system. No one fudged. It was all legitimate. But the thing was that the publican at Ravensthorpe—the old bugger who was as slow as a wet week—he knew we were going down to Hopetoun and drinking at the pub there and one time he said to me, 'I don't know why you guys go down ter Hopetoun.' He said, 'Hopetoun's the arsehole of the world.'

And I looked at him and I said, 'Mate, if Hopetoun's the arsehole of the world, then Ravensthorpe must be forty kilometres up it.'

Roebourne—WA

Hey, do they do police checks on these stories? Because I've got one here that could well land a mate of mine into a bit of hot water if they found out. See, back in me twenties, me and a couple of mates was doing the old 'around Australia trip'. We'd already crossed the Nullarbor to Perth and we were pretty skint and we'd heard there was work in Broome, so we're heading north and we came across a little town called Roebourne. Roebourne's on the road to Port Hedland. I can't remember too much about the place now other than there were a lot of Aboriginals living there; you know, around the streets and that, which was pretty typical in them sort of places.

Anyhow, it was around lunchtime and we decided to drop into the pub for a bite to eat and a beer or two. Good idea. So in we go. There were already a few locals in there—white fellers—and, even by that time of the day, they were pretty well on the way. Like, they'd had a few. It might've even been a weekend. Anyhow, we got talking to these fellers and somewhere along the line, one of me mates came across an idea. I mean, it sort of started out innocent enough, I guess, but I'll change the mate's name, just in case. Let's call him 'Bill', for argument's sake.

See, Bill was a fanatic punter. He used to punt like there was no tomorrow. He'd bet on two flies going up a wall if you gave him the right odds. He was that sort of feller. Anyhow, before we got to Roebourne we'd been staying a few hundred k's back down the track at Carnarvon and while we were there they'd run the English Derby; at Ascot, I think it was. There might've even been an Australian horse running in it or something. I don't know. But, see, seeing how the English Derby was run during our Australian night-time, Bill had recorded it all on his big, new, fandangle radio-tape recorder so he could listen to it more closely the next day, when he was sober.

So we're drinking with these Roebourne fellers and Bill takes a sudden look at his watch and said, 'Geez, the English Derby's on in a tick. I might go 'n' have a listen to it on me portable radio.'

Now, as I said, these blokes were pretty well gone so I don't know if they even twigged that the English Derby had already been run or not and, if they did, they'd forgot. But, whatever the caper, they said, all excited like, 'Oh, bring yer radio in 'ere so we can all 'ave a listen.'

So Bill went out to the car and he got his radio-tape player and he put in the tape of the English Derby and he brought it back into the pub and set it up on the bar and there's all these blokes gathered around, primed up, ready to listen to this race. So Bill pretends to turn the radio on, but instead he starts the tape going and the Pommy race caller comes on and he's going through the horse's names and giving out their starting prices and that. Now, I'm not sure whether Bill'd actually planned all this out or not but, when a few of the Roebourne boys started reckoning to each other what horse would win, Bill piped up and said, 'Who wants ter lay a bet?'

'Me. Me. Me,' all these fellers said.

The Derby hat—The Hansford Collection

'I'll take the odds, then,' says Bill, and when the race caller gave out the final starting-price fluctuations—you know, which horse's odds were shortening and which horse's odds were lengthening—Bill got to work, making sure that whenever someone wanted to place a bet on the winner-to-be, he halved its starting price.

Anyhow, when the race started, there's all these Roebourne fellers—pissed as newts—around this radio-tape player, all yelling and hooting and going on, trying to bring home the horse they'd put their money on. And, actually, Bill ended up making a tidy sum out of that little caper and that's about all I can tell you about Roebourne because we buggered off out of there pretty soon after that.

Silverton—NSW

In fact, back in the 1880s Silverton was the largest town in the west of New South Wales. True. It had a population of over 3000, and all because of the mining. Mind you, this was before the much larger amounts of silver, lead and zinc were discovered, just south-east, at Broken Hill.

But to give you some idea, Silverton even had its own railway company, the Silverton Tramway Company. And why a tramway and not a railway? It was all to do with the unbelievably negative attitude of the New South Wales government. For starters, they wouldn't allow the South Australians to build a rail line the short distance from the SA–NSW border to Silverton. And they also refused to build a track any further west than Dubbo. The upshot there was that all the ore from Silverton had to be loaded onto bullock wagons and carted over into South Australia where it was loaded onto trains and taken down to Port Pirie, to be shipped out. Of course, the locals soon said, 'Blow you', and they decided to build their own railway line into South Australia. And the New South Wales government even tried to stop them doing that. 'You can't call it a railway company,' they said, so the locals called it a 'tramway company', and they built it themselves.

That's all in the story 'The Silverton Tramway Company', which is in your book, *Great Australian Railway Stories*. But, the point is, that's what the people out here are like. If they decide to do something, nothing or no one's going to stop them. That's why the place is full of a history that's not only had a huge impact on Australia but all over the world. For instance, the trade union movement, called the Barrier Ranges Miners' Association, was first started in Silverton. It was all aimed at looking after workers' rights, under the slogan of 'United we stand, divided we fall'. Then it's little known that Broken Hill Proprietary Company

Limited, or BHP Billiton as it's known these days, was formed in the old Silverton Hotel, back in the mid-1880s.

Anyhow, as I said, after silver, lead and zinc were discovered in much larger quantities at Broken Hill there was a huge shift from Silverton into the Hill. Now there's less than sixty people living in Silverton. Not that that's lessened the great attraction of the place because not only have many of our local artists, such as the late Pro Hart, Jack Absalom and their mates—the brushmen of the bush—been inspired by the landscape, but also artists from all over the world go out there to paint. Then the Silverton Hotel and the nearby Mundi Mundi Plains have been used as locations for more films and television series than you can poke a stick at. To name a few, there's *Mission Impossible*, *The Adventures of Priscilla—Queen of the Desert*, *Wake in Fright*, *As Time Goes By*, in which I played a small part, as I also did in *The Craic*. Then as far as television goes there was the series of the Royal Flying Doctor Service and the mini-series of *A Town Like Alice*, where I also played a small part. Plus there's been a raft of advertisements shot up and around Silverton, in which I've also been involved. Mind you, many were just walk-on-walk-off parts. But none the less. So, anyhow, that's Silverton for you. It's worth the visit.

Even when I was a young kid, living in Broken Hill, I remember how they used to hold a Zinc Mine Picnic day, out at Silverton. I've actually got a story about that because my Uncle Bruce used to work on the Broken Hill mines. He worked hard. He trucked underground for a while, meaning he pushed an ore truck, like I went on to do. He had a lovely wife and, at about this time, he had two daughters, one about ten, the other about eight.

But he did like a beer, did my Uncle Bruce. See, when you worked hard on the mines—and I try to explain this to people, especially visitors, all about the term of 'taking up sweat'. Do you know what taking up sweat means? Well, when you're working underground, where there's not much breeze, it can get terribly hot and you lose a lot of body fluid. So after work, when you get down to the pub, your first six middies are just taking up that lost sweat; replacing body fluids. Then once you've done that, and you've taken up the sweat, you can settle down and relax and have another half a dozen or so and have a bit of a chin-wag with your mates.

Anyhow, Uncle Bruce not only loved a beer but he also loved a pie. Just loved his pies. Now, at Silverton there's a park known as Penrose Park. It's on a creek and that's where they held the Zinc Mine Picnic. And what the mines corporation did was that they'd get about thirty or forty ore trucks, sweep them out, put blocks in them, lay some planks over the blocks. Then they'd get little ladders so that you could get up into the ore trucks and they'd hook them up to a train and everyone'd jump in and they'd take 3000–4000 people out along the original Silverton tramway line, out to Silverton. Have you been to Silverton? Well, that little building, just before you get there, was a railway station, and so we'd arrive and I can remember just being a toddler and I'd be first out of the train and I'd run flat out down to the creek, armed with a basket and a rug, and spread it out under the shade of a gum tree. And that was our spot for the day.

But those days were absolutely fantastic, especially if you were a kid. You know, there'd be all the raspberry you could drink, all the ice cream and cakes you could eat. All the tucker you could eat. Then they'd always hold a pie eating competition for the men. The pies were hot. They had a warmer there. And I just loved to watch it because my Uncle Bruce was the champion. Now, I'm not talking about those piddly little pies you get these days. We're talking about the real fair-dinkum 'man-sized' pies you used to get back when a pie was a pie was a pie. But don't get me wrong, this wasn't a race. It was judged on the number of pies you could eat. The last man standing, you could say. The idea was that, if you ate a pie, you could also drink a glass of beer. And you never had stubbies in those days. You had big glasses of beer. Of course, this suited Uncle Bruce down to the ground because he not only loved his beer and he not only loved his pies but it was all free; free pie, free beer.

'There's been a raft of advertisements shot up and around Silverton in which I've been involved.'—The Hansford Collection

So all the contestants would line up on this platform thing. There'd be about twelve or fifteen men, and they'd say, 'Right. Ready. Set. Go,' and I'd just sit there watching Uncle Bruce. Oh, he was a joy to watch. Poetry in motion. While all the other contestants were going flat out, Uncle Bruce, he'd just eat a pie, nice and quiet, then he'd drink his beer, nice and steady. By about half an hour, after they'd eaten about seven or eight pies each and they'd downed seven or eight glasses of beer, a couple of them would drop out. After an hour they'd be on their twelfth pie and their twelfth glass of beer and there'd only be about six fellers remaining. By the hour-and-a-half mark they'd be onto their fifteenth pie and their fifteenth glass of beer. By this stage there'd only be a couple left. Uncle Bruce and another contestant.

'Come on, Uncle Bruce. Come on, Uncle Bruce,' I'd be calling.

Anyway, eventually the last contender, apart from Uncle Bruce, that is, he'd say, 'No, no, I've had enough. I've had enough.'

So then the judge, he'd jump up on the platform and grab hold of Uncle Bruce's arm and he'd thrust it up into the air and call out, 'And here's the winner!'

But, no, Uncle Bruce wouldn't have a bar of it. He'd pull his arm out of the judge's grip and say, 'Hang on. Hang on. I haven't finished yet,' and so they'd have to keep feeding him free pies and free beer till he was satisfied.

You don't believe me, do you? Well, here's the piece out of the paper if you like, and I quote how Uncle Bruce won *'the Musician's Club Pie Eating Championship on Sunday night December 7. "Just an appetiser," commented the champion. "When's supper?" And when supper arrived our champion was first in and ate as heartily as other members.'*

Simpson Desert—SA

Have you ever heard the expression 'Twice around the head in a sock gets the beer cold enough to drink'? No? Well if you're writing about outback drinking spots, I'd reckon that this would be right up there because it took place in one of Australia's most isolated areas where, by default, I'd lay claim to being the first publican of the Simpson Desert.

It all started back in 1963, when we carved a road through the Simpson for the seismic survey mob Compagnie Generale de Geophysique (CGG). Now, how I got a job was that I'd just lobbed into Brisbane and so I went around to the unemployment office to see what's going and they said, 'Oh, go along to CGG in south Brisbane. They're hiring blokes.'

Mind you, it's the Friday afternoon, nearly four o'clock. 'Okay,' I says and they gave me the address and so off I go to south Brisbane.

I get there and the girl says, 'There's no jobs. We're all filled.'

I said, 'Well, I can do the radio and I can do accounts.'

And just then a bloke's voice booms from the side office. 'You do accounts?' He said, 'Would you be ready to start on Monday morning?'

'Oh yeah,' I said. 'I guess so.'

'Consider yourself hired, then. See you out at Eagle Farm airport, Sunday morning at six am.'

So I lobbed out at Eagle Farm on the Sunday morning and this same feller—I didn't even know his name—he came up to me and he said, 'Here, take this tin,' and so I put the tin under my arm. Then he said, 'Take this.' It was a cash book. So he armed me with that.

I mean, he doesn't know me from a bar of soap. So there I am with this tin under my arm and a cash book in my hand and one of the blokes who'd also been employed came up and said, 'Can yer give me twenty quid?' His wife was short of money or something. So I opened up the tin and, blow me down, there inside was 2000 quid. Yes, 2000 pound. And, as I said, the feller who'd given it to me didn't know me from Adam. So I gave this bloke twenty quid and I wrote out an IOU in the cash book and he signed it. So there, I did my first financial transaction at Eagle Farm airport.

But, here's the thing, see: even at that stage I did not have a clue where we were going. Not a clue. So we get on the charter plane; a DC 3. We take off and we head west, stopping at all the station properties along the way, and we arrived in Birdsville late that afternoon. Then from Birdsville we took off again and as we're flying out over all this desert country, I said, 'Does anybody know where we're going?'

Anyhow, a couple of the blokes who'd previously been working for CGG said, 'Well, we were working in South Australia before, so I suppose that's where we're headed.'

And that was confirmed when we arrived at Mount Dare. It was nightfall when we got in. No food. Nothing, and the camp consisted of just five caravans. That's it. Five solitary caravans. So we slept on the floors, and in the morning I woke up and went outside and, as did many of the others, I saw my first ever spinifex and my first ever sand dune and my first ever claypan. And that was to be my home for the next year or so.

Now, not to have a clue where you're going or what you're going to do when you got there, and to suddenly find yourself standing out in a desert, was what the word 'isolation' is all about. I mean, even the Aborigines had enough sense not to live in the Simpson. Yes, they passed through but they never actually lived there. And it still gets to me at times when I think about it because, when you see absolute desolation for the first time, you never forget it. It engulfs you totally. So there we were, at the start of the Simpson Desert, and we hadn't even been told that we were going to build a road right across it.

There were forty-five of us in the group and we stayed out there for three months straight on that first mission. And here I was in my little office. I've got an Olympia typewriter and I've got an old Olivetti adding machine and I'm doing the payroll and I've got a two-way radio that was connected, first, to Ceduna, in South Australia, then further into the desert I had to change to Alice Springs and, when we got on the Channel Country side of the Simpson, we'd call up Charleville then Birdsville.

But once we got going it all began to come together and aircraft started bumping down on makeshift claypan airstrips near our various campsites and trucks began to roll in with fuel and explosives and stores and, of course, the most important was the grog dump. Now, in the camp, one of the caravans was aptly named Café de Blitz. Café de Blitz was the only one with refrigeration so it was the dining room cum cook house and, of course, the pub. So another duty was added to my list, that of 'publican'. We had brine fridges, similar in design to the Coolgardie safe where, in this case, the brine gets pumped around and dribbles back down the edges again. Mind you, it didn't freeze anything. It even struggled to cool down the allotted four beers per day for the forty men, which didn't leave much space for fresh food. Not that we ate much fresh food. We virtually lived on canned everything so no wonder we ended up with scurvy.

The only fresh food we got was when we were at either side of the desert and close enough to a station to go and get a bullock. I'd go over and we'd kill this thing then stick it in the back of the Land Rover and pack as much foliage as we could around it to protect it from the heat, the flies and the dust, and I'd bring it back to camp. And that's what we'd eat night after night till, at some stage of the game, all the cook had left was the hooves and the horns and he'd probably call it 'sirloin'. But the most important thing was that the beer was kept, sort of, cool and, after dinner, the tables were cleared and the area was magically transformed into a bar. It was a cash-free camp so, with me being both the pay clerk and the publican, I kept a tab and on payday, at month's end, the appropriate deductions were made.

So, yes, away out there, within that amazing isolation, we managed to maintain a few of life's simple comforts. And, actually, some of my fondest memories are from back then; like the nights we'd crank up the old record player and settle down outside Café de Blitz and have a few beers with the honeyed tones of Joan Baez wafting across the desert. That's right! The tune that comes to mind was 'What have they done to the rain?' Ironical, ay. But, I mean, just getting the grog out there was a huge problem. Sometimes we'd even have to fly it in. I remember, one time, we were flying back out with a load of stores and grog and the pilot, Kron Nicholas, was looking a bit worried so I said, 'What's up?'

He said, 'We're a bit too heavy. We won't make it out to the camp. I'll have to drop you off with some of the load.'

So he landed the plane out on this claypan, away out in the middle of absolutely nowhere, and he dropped me off, along with twenty-five cases of beer. And after he'd taken off, it struck me, Well, if he crashes, what'll happen to me? I mean, I've got no radio, nothing. There's just me and these twenty-five cases of beer. But, anyway, he did come back and he somehow managed to dodge the saltbush and we reloaded the twenty-five cases of beer—minus what I'd drunk—and away we went. Then when we got further north, up into the channel country, I'd take the Land Rover into the nearest pub and pick up fifty cases of beer at a time. It was all in steel cans back then and so I'd struggle back to camp with this huge load of grog.

But, anyhow, with this expression, 'Twice around the head in a sock gets the beer cold enough to drink'. That came about when we'd run out of grog one time. Then, finally, a semi-trailer turns up with 200 cases of beer, plus supplies and all that. It's fifty-five degrees centigrade in the shade and the blokes are there. But they're not worried about unloading the supplies. It's more like, 'Geez, I haven't had a beer for a while.'

'No, me neither. But how can we get it cold?'

Of course, in life, if you believe in something hard enough, it happens doesn't it, even if it's only in the mind, right? And the assumption was that, if you put a can of beer in a sock and swing it around your head then, like with the canvas waterbags, the air cools the water down a bit. Now, whether it worked or not, it didn't really matter. But that's just how desperate they were. It was 'Twice around the head in a sock gets the beer cold enough to drink'.

South Stirling—WA

Look, you might be able to make something of this. This happened in a very small community called South Stirling, which is about seventy kilometres north-east of Albany, in southern Western Australia. I was the principal at the three-teacher school there. There was no pub, nothing; just the school building, the Principal's house, then down the back of our house was a shack where one of the other teachers lived and a third teacher always seemed to be found from the wife of one of the local farmers. Other than the school buildings there was just a town hall and a church. Interestingly enough, the school, the teacher's housing, the hall and the church were all run off the school's power plant; an old diesel 4KVA generator—4000 watts. So if something like the electric kettle was turned on in the house, while there was a church service going on, everything in the church went black. And if my wife tried to put the iron on while we were running the projector at school, 'pfff', the fuses blew. So that's where I was teaching and everything came in by truck—beer, food, the lot—or else you made the trip down to Albany yourself.

But, to make a bit of extra money, on weekends I'd go out and work on various farms. I did all sorts of jobs really, from tractor driving to root raking, seeding to mulesing. And, I can tell you, I was a very poor muleser. And, of course, seeing how my background was teaching, all the local farmers looked upon my farming abilities with a certain degree of suspicion. Yes, they fully accepted and respected me as a teacher but, as to my farming abilities, they had grave doubts.

Anyhow, one particular Friday I got a call from Keith, one of these local farmers. 'Look,' he said, 'I've just got an urgent call to go to Perth and I've still got a whole lot of sheep to get ready to be trucked to the saleyards this Saturday, would you be able to

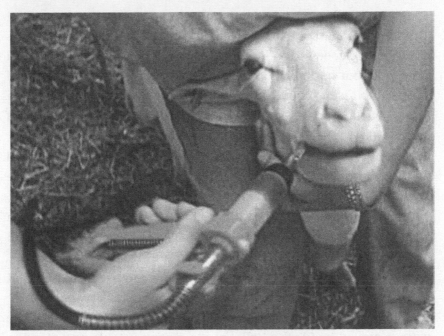

Where do you stick the drench gun?—The Hansford Collection

do the job for me? The truck's booked and everything.'

'That'll be fine,' I said. 'What do you want me to do?'

He said, 'Well, first you find the dog, then you go and find the old ex-army Jeep.' He explained how to start it. 'Then once you've got the Jeep going, you and the dog go and round up the sheep, take them to the yards'—he told me where—'then you drench them and get them on the truck.'

These were things I was very capable of doing so I said, 'Yes.'

Keith's property was about ten kilometres south of the school house where my wife and I lived so I went out there on the Saturday morning and I did exactly what Keith had told me to do—I found the dog, found the old Jeep, got it going and then me and the dog rounded up the sheep. There was about 250 of them, and we got them back into the yard where they were to be loaded. So then I drenched the sheep, the truck arrived, we loaded the mob and off they went to the saleyards. Job done. It took about three, three-and-a-half hours.

Now I must explain about drenching. To some, the word 'drenching' might mean a good downpour of rain. Not in this case. In this case I was drenching these sheep for worms, which was a job that had to be done before they went off to market. And the way you went about drenching the sheep was that you had a liquid backpack, which was filled from a 20-litre drum of chemical drench. This backpack had a tube coming out of it and, at the end of the tube, there was a gun sort of thing, which had a curved nozzle at the front. I'd say that the curved nozzle would've been about eight inches long and, what you did was, you slid the nozzle into the side of the sheep's mouth and, when you pressed the trigger, the right dosage of chemical went down the sheep's throat. So that's what I did and it all went well.

It just so happened that there was a dance in the local hall that night, which my wife and I went to. It was in between dance brackets and, as what happened back in those days, while the women stayed inside the hall, the men went outside and stood in circles, sharing a bottle of beer and telling all sorts of stories. Oh, that's right; and with these bottles of beer—Brownies, I think they were called—the men had different ways of opening them. If you didn't happen to have a proper bottle opener, some fellows could rip the bottle top off with their teeth. Then there were some who could flip the bottle top off with the bottom end of an old tobacco tin or, if they weren't a smoker and didn't want to lose their teeth, other fellows could get two bottles together and flip the two bottle tops against each other and off came one of the tops. Anyway, the thing was that, once the bottle was opened it'd be passed around.

So I was in this group of about five or six fellows who were telling stories about all their farming bits and pieces. By this stage Keith had arrived back from Perth and he'd joined our little circle. It got to be my turn to tell a story so I just said to the fellows, 'Oh, you know, Keith here had me do a bit of work for him, out on his farm, this morning.'

'Oh, yeah,' came the reply, and you could just about feel that hint of doubt I told you about, you know, 'What would a school teacher know about farming?'. To them, it was like getting a boy out to do a man's job.

'What'd you do?' one of the farmers asked.

'Oh, nothing much really,' I said. 'Keith was away in Perth so I just found the dog, found the Jeep, got it started, then, me and the dog, we rounded up the sheep, put them in the yard and then I drenched them ...' and I sort of paused at that moment. You could say it was a dramatic pause to gain full effect, because then I looked over at Keith as if I had a slight concern about something and I said, 'Oh, and by the way, Keith, you do stick the drench gun up their bum, don't you?'

And, oh, you should've seen the look on these farmers' faces. Flabbergasted. Their jaws dropped and there was dead silence. Dead silence.

Tablelands Highway—NT

We live in Traralgon, Victoria, but back a while, my wife, Bronwyn, and I had four months' long service leave owing. So, with our trusty 4-wheel drive and a brand new caravan, we packed up our goods and chattels and our two girls, Madeleine, ten, and Annabelle, twelve, and we set sail on the great Australian outback adventure.

From Traralgon we headed up to Mildura then over to Port Augusta, then up the centre to Darwin, before coming back home down along the east coast. But, when we left Darwin, to head east, we thought, Oh well, instead of going straight down the Stuart Highway to the Threeways then across the Barkly Highway into Queensland, what we'll do is go part-way down the Stuart, to Daly Waters, then head east, out along the Carpentaria Highway, to Cape Crawford, then turn down the Tablelands Highway and drive down to Barkly Roadhouse, where we'd meet up with the Barkly Highway, and then we'd head over into Queensland.

Anyhow, that's what we did and we got to Cape Crawford, then headed south, down the Tablelands Highway. We weren't in any great hurry so each afternoon at about three-thirty we'd start to look out for some side track or other, with the aim of getting settled and having the fire going by five. By dawdling like that it took us two days to go about 200 kilometres, which was okay by me because, in my opinion, camping out's the best part, especially if there's a cold beer available at the end of the day. So then, I'd say, it was at about 9 o'clock on a Sunday morning, we were driving along, when we came across a deserted main roads camp. It was a pretty ramshackle affair with earth-moving equipment and road-making machinery scattered about the place. Then there were the usual caravans, where the workers stayed, with a couple of those transportable loos—toilets—

246

conveniently placed over near the caravans. You know, all the usual for a roadwork's gang.

So that was the layout. Then, just down the road a bit, there was a ROAD CLOSED barricade across the highway and lying up against it was the STOP/SLOW sign. No one was holding it. It was just lying there, semi-propped up against the ROAD CLOSED barricade with the STOP part of the sign facing us. This's a bit odd, we thought; you know, with it being a Sunday and all. Anyhow, we stopped. Like I said, there was no one around so we sat in the car and waited.

Five minutes passed and no one appeared. 'Geez,' I said, 'this's a bit odd.'

'Perhaps they went to Cape Crawford or down to Barkly Roadhouse for a weekend on the booze and they forgot to take the barricade and sign down,' Bronwyn suggested.

She might've had a point there. I mean, these roadworks fellers are pretty well noted for their love of a beer or two or three. Anyhow, we sat for a while longer and still no one turned up. In the end, I got out and checked either side of the road to see if there was any way I could negotiate our vehicle and the caravan around it. But, no, it was impassable on either side. So I got back in the car, and it was while we were sitting there that Madeleine said, 'Perhaps some aliens have taken them.'

I mean, you can't beat kids, can you? Of course, she was only joking, or so I think. But then the longer we sat there, confronted by this ROAD CLOSED barricade, away out in the middle of all this nowhere, in dead silence, with an eerily deserted road maintenance camp just over the way, these type of half-joking scenarios can start to take on some vague sort of reality.

'Maybe,' I said.

Then, 'Dad, did you hear that!' called Annabelle.

'What?'

'It was like someone crying out.'

I tried to laugh that one off, too. But then I heard something. So did the kids. A faint groan coming from over where the workers' caravans were. That got me thinking all sorts of possibilities, and all of them not too good. I mean, you hear some terrible stories, these days, don't you?

'Perhaps you should go over and see if anyone's there,' Bronwyn said.

'Not on your life,' I said. 'I'm not going anywhere near that camp.'

In actual fact I'd started thinking that the best thing for us to do was to turn around and go back up to Cape Crawford. It'd only taken us two days to get this far and, if we went over to the east coast the other way, it'd only add another week or so onto our trip and we'd just have to make up some sort of excuse as to why we'd overstayed our long service leave. I mean, as the saying goes: 'It's always better to be safe than sorry'. Anyway, I'd heard along the way that both the petrol and the beer down at Barkly Roadhouse were the most expensive in Australia.

Then came another strange noise from over at the caravans.

'It's creepy; let's get out of here, Dad.'

'Okay,' I said.

Then, just as I was about to start up the car, the door of one of the transportable loos opens. And out came a bloke. He stood there for a moment taking in the scenery. For the life of me, he looked exactly like that cartoon character 'Norm' from those old television ads. Remember the really overweight feller, with the huge belly, who spent all his time sitting in front of the television, drinking beer? And all this bloke had on was an old pair of boxer shorts. I'm not even sure if he was wearing work boots or not; maybe just an old pair of thongs.

And after he'd had a sniff and a scratch, he ambled over to the barricade as if he had all the time in the world and, when he finally arrived, he grabbed part of the ROAD CLOSED barricade and he dragged it sideways. Then he picked up his STOP/SLOW sign. He had another bit of a scratch. Looked down the road to the south. Looked up the road to the north. Had a bit of yet another scratch. Then, when he'd checked all was clear, he turned his sign around to SLOW and we crawled through the opening, and down the road we headed, with the girls in stitches of laughter and me and Bronwyn shaking our heads: 'Only in Australia'.

Thargomindah—Qld

If you're looking, you'll find Thargomindah, out in the far south-west of Queensland, a couple of hundred kilometres west of Cunnamulla and about 1000 k's west of Brisbane. It's on the Bulloo River. As far the name goes, it's my understanding that Thargomindah comes from an Aboriginal word meaning 'dust storm' or 'cloud of dust', and we do get some pretty decent dust storms out this way, especially with the drought. At present we've got a population of around 180. Most of those work out on properties or for the council, on road projects, you know, where they go away for ten to fifteen days at a time. That sort of thing.

But as far-flung as we may be, we're certainly rich in history. Burke and Wills passed through the area not long before our earliest white settlement. So, basically, we started off as a town that provided goods and services to people coming out this way to open up new country. And some pretty big-name families were involved in that too; families like the Leahy family. Then there was the Durack family. You know the Duracks. They arrived in Australia in the mid-1880s and they spread out all across this area and eventually up into the Top End. There's that famous book that's written by the granddaughter, Mary Durack, called *Kings in Grass Castles*. That's all about the Duracks' pioneering days. So part of that family were amongst our earliest settlers. Kidman even owned property here at one stage.

Then, once the station properties got established, Thargomindah also became a stopover point for travellers on Cobb & Co. plus all the drovers that were passing through. Also there were the bullockers who were carting wool down to Bourke, where it was loaded onto the paddle steamers to go down the Darling River. So the sheep industry was very big. So big in fact that, at one time, there was a lot of pressure placed on the

Thargomindah Bore—The Marsh Collection

Queensland government to build a railway all the way out to Thargomindah. But it only got as far as Cunnamulla. It never got here, and so we're still waiting.

Still, in its heyday, around the late-1890s and early-1900s, Thargomindah was a thriving place. In fact, I think there was even ten pubs here at one stage where, these days, there's only the one, the Bullo River Hotel or, as its known locally, the Thargo. And that's where the murder happened. Well, it was a long time ago now, long before the current owners, Duck and Daisy, got the pub. This was back, say, about twenty years ago, maybe longer, when you used to be able to come into the pub with firearms. Anyhow, there was a certain lady living in town and these two young men both fancied her. On this particular day, some men were sitting in the bar of the Thargo and in that group was one of the guys who fancied this particular lady. Then, all of a sudden, the other guy who fancied her, he bumped into the bar, took out his rife, and—'bang!'—shot the other guy dead. That's the gist of that story, and the bullet hole can still be seen in the pub.

But I don't want to paint Thargomindah in a poor light by harping on murders and the like because Thargo's got far more going for it than that, though there was another one just out on the Hungerford road, here, back in the '30s or '40s. See, there were two miners, a boss guy and his worker. They'd worked together for years, drilling holes and whatever. But things started to go wrong and the employer—the boss guy—fell behind in his wage payments. Then one night it all came to a head around the campfire, which led to the murder of the employee and his body being tossed down a mine shaft they'd just drilled.

Anyway, many months later the employee's family went to the police all concerned that they hadn't heard from him for such a long time. And when the police dug around a bit, they became highly suspicious because the boss guy had a lot of overdue bills. So they came out to investigate. They caught up with the boss guy, who still happened to be camped near the mine shaft where he'd dumped the body, and they started asking all sorts of questions. 'Whatever-his-name has gone missing and his family are worried. Have you seen him?'

'No, he just disappeared one day.'

'We see by his bank accounts that you hadn't paid him for quite some time.'

'Well, things were a bit tight but that didn't mean I killed him.'

Oops, so the boss guy had really put his foot in it then. 'Who said anything about him being killed?' the police said.

'Well, I thought that's why you came out to investigate.'

So they pretty much had him on toast then and so in the end the boss guy confessed and told them where the body had been dumped and the police nabbed the guy and he got punished.

But like I said, I don't want to make a big thing of any of that because Thargomindah's far better known throughout Australia—even the world—than for just a couple of murders because Thargomindah was the first town in Australia to have hydro-electric power. True. See, back in the 1890s they were drilling for water in the artesian basin and when they struck it, it shot to the surface with so much pressure that some of the more enterprising locals came up with the idea of using the pressure of the bore water to drive a generator which, in turn, would supply the town with electricity.

So that's what they did, and, in fact, the first place in the world to have electric street lighting was London, England. The second was Paris, France. Then just a day after the electric street lights were turned on in Paris, the street lights were turned on in Thargomindah. And that's fair dinkum. Only a day after Paris. Yes, away out here in far-flung south-western Queensland. So that's our little claim to fame, and it's a big one at that.

Three Springs and Arrino Siding—WA

Three Springs: if you look on your map, it's a couple of hundred miles north of Perth, along the Midlands Road. It's a wheat and sheep area. The nearest large town would be Geraldton. When I first got there, Three Springs, I'd say, had less than 500 people but by the time I'd married Mick and we left in '76, to come down to Tassie, it was getting bigger because Western Mining had found rutile close by and so they'd moved in, in a big way, and they'd put in bitumen roads and they'd air-conditioned the school and there was a couple of butchers' shops and a Wesfarmers store that sold everything and there was also another grocery store.

There was also a pub, of course: the Commercial. That was always a hive of activity. I forget what year it was now but when they won the grand final, it was for the first time in ages and so I didn't see Mick for two days because he'd gone off celebrating and I later heard that he had the lawnmower going in the bar. Oh, apparently it was some sort of dare so he had the bloody lawn mower going full throttle up and down the front bar. See, when we lived there, Mick was still a young feller and he was a little bit wild and he had lots of mates and that. But he's sort of settled down now, just a little bit.

Anyhow, so, yes, Three Springs was quite a thriving little place, there for a while, with a post office and all that. But I think it's quite small again now because Western Mining's moved out and a lot of the shops have closed down. I don't think there's even a butcher's shop there now. The hospital, where I worked, it's still there but, because there's a lot of elderly, it's got a nursing home attached to it. I don't think they even do surgery anymore. It's more like a holding place for people if they have to be transferred to a bigger hospital or if they're recuperating from an operation.

And, also, the population's fallen because, see, Three Springs is about eighty miles inland and now that they've built the Brand Highway, more or less right along the coastline, most people use that because it cuts miles off the trip to the well-known seaside resort of Dongara.

But Three Springs was a great place to live and even though it was only small there was a lot of young people there, so it was quite a vibrant town. And it certainly had some characters. Actually, Mick and I were laughing about this one just last night. See, we had a mechanic chap in Three Springs called Jack Broadhurst. Jack was known to all and sundry as 'Ripper'. I mean, if you were talking about Jack you never called him Jack, you just called him Ripper. I suppose it came from 'Jack the Ripper'. That's the connection and so everyone in the town called him Ripper for short and, of course, that's what he answered to. Now, Ripper used to work for a bloke called Don Hosken and Don's little boy was called David, and, you know, kids being kids, young David was always around the back part of the garage, in the mechanics shed, where Ripper fixed all the cars and that. So David knew Ripper very well and they spent many an hour together.

Then one Christmas, Ripper got landed the job as Santa. So he dressed up as Santa and, of course, as what happens in just about all these little community halls, the place is all decorated out for the occasion, with Santa sitting on a big chair up on stage and around him were the presents for all the kids. Then, as each child's name was called out, the kid'd climb up the stairs, onto the stage, and they'd go over and sit on Santa's knee and Santa would ask them if they'd been good this year and what they wanted for Christmas, then Santa would give them their present. So, of course, Ripper's up on stage, dressed as Santa, with a big white beard, red coat and pants, boots, and all the gear and he's saying to the children as they sat on his knee, 'Ho, ho, ho 'n' have you been good this year?'

'Yes,' would come a whisper of guilty innocence.

''N' what would yer like fer Christmas?'

Then the child said whatever it was they wanted and so Ripper would hand their present over and the kid'd jump down off Santa's knee and go outside to open it. So eventually the name was called out, 'David Hosken', and so little David climbs the steps and he goes over and sits on Santa's knee and Santa says to David, 'Ho, ho, ho have yer been a good boy this year?' And little kids, they're very astute, aren't they, because before David answered he gave Santa a good looking over, then he says, 'Hey, you're not Santa.'

'Ho, ho, ho yes I am,' Ripper said. 'So what would yer like fer Christmas?'

And David said, 'Well, if you're Santa, how come yer got Ripper's watch on. What? Did yer nick it off 'im or somethin'?'

So that's one story that happened. But before Mick and I got together I was working in the local district hospital and there was this old Aboriginal bloke called Kenny Binder. A real identity he was. He actually came from a place just out of Three Springs

Apparently Mick had the lawnmower going full throttle up and down the front bar—The Hansford Collection

called Arrino Siding, which was where Mick was living at the time. But seeing there wasn't a pub in Arrino Springs, Kenny spent a lot of time in Three Springs. Kenny was married with about ten kids and, oh, he was real character; always getting into mischief.

Anyhow, I was working at the hospital this time and Kenny had gotten into a bit of trouble after a football match. See, they take their footy very seriously up there. Now, I'm not sure what but apparently, Kenny'd had a few too many down at the Commercial and he was creating a bit of noise and, you know, fighting with a couple of people. So he'd been arrested. How they treated situations like that back then was that the police'd take them to the station and they'd just let them stay in the lockup overnight to sleep it off and cool their heels, then they'd let them out the next morning. But this time Kenny'd thrown a few punches and, unfortunately, he'd also received a few punches. So he was arrested and he had to come into the hospital to have some sutures in his cheek and I think his knuckles were a bit swollen also.

This was around, oh gosh, when did I marry Mick? From memory, we were married in '69 so this would've been in, probably, about 1968. I'd already met Mick by then, and I know we were going out together because Kenny couldn't ever remember my name so he'd call me 'Mrs Mick'. You know, it was, 'How yer goin' Mrs Mick?', 'Nice day, Mrs Mick, ay?' and all that. Anyhow, Kenny was brought in to have these wounds taken care of. But, because he was under arrest, a policeman had to stay with him. Now, our matron was Dot Barrett. Dot was a lovely lady, a very down to earth sort of woman. And being married with three children of her own, a lot of her treatment was dealt with in a very practical way. So the policeman was there sitting beside Kenny's bed and I was in the room taking temperatures or whatever and Dot came in and she said to the policeman, 'How're you going?'

'Good thanks, Dot.'

She said, 'You know you're wasting your time sitting here, don't you?'

'Well,' he replied, 'I've gotta stay with him 'cause he's under arrest.'

'Look,' Dot said, 'Kenny's not going anywhere.' She said, 'He's got a comfortable bed 'n' he's getting three good meals in his belly a day, so why on earth would he want to escape?' She said, 'You just go 'n' find something else to do with your police work. Kenny's happy enough here. There's no need for you to be hanging around him.'

And here's this Kenny, he's sitting there in the bed, grinning away, and he's nodding away and agreeing with everything Dot's saying. 'Yeah, too right, missus. I'm stayin' 'ere. Life's too good in 'ere, missus.'

So then the policeman up and off and went about his other duties leaving Kenny, as happy as Larry, tucked up in a nice comfortable bed, being waited on hand and foot and with a decent meal at hand. Oh, he was such a loveable character, was Kenny. But there were some beautiful Aboriginal people in that town, you know. When you think about the problems they have these days, it just wasn't like that back then. A lot of them worked for local cockies so they had something to do and some sort of income and there was no animosity whatsoever. So, yes, they were just wonderful people.

Which reminds me of another story about Kenny: as I said, before we got married, Mick lived at a little place called Arrino Siding. Arrino Siding was only ten miles out of Three Springs. Apart from the huge silos, there wasn't much there really, just a few houses. Mick lived in one little weatherboard cottage, then there was a bit of bush, then the next cottage was where Kenny lived with his wife and his tribe of kids. There were no shops or anything, not even a post office. It was simply on the map because of the huge silos and also the cockies ran a few sheep.

Anyhow, Kenny was known to be a bit light-fingered at times and he used to work as a farmhand on a property doing all sorts of odd jobs. Actually, the cocky that owned the property was related to Mary Durack. But every now and then one of this cocky's sheep or whatever would go missing and the owner knew it was Kenny because Kenny had all these kids to feed. So it was never a big issue. But one day Mick was over there shearing at this cocky's shed and Kenny was helping out and the boss said to Kenny, 'Geez, a lot of my chooks' eggs have gone missing lately, Kenny. You wouldn't know anything about it, would yer?'

Kenny said, 'Oh, no, not me, boss.' He said, 'I wouldn't take any of dem eggs off'a yer, boss. No, never, boss.'

'Oh, well, that's good, then,' the boss said, 'and just as well because I laced the last lot with strychnine.'

And the eyes just about popped out of Kenny's head. 'Oh, boss,' he said, 'what'a yer tryin' ter do? Kill all me kids?'

Tibooburra—NSW

I've got a story here from up the far north-west of New South Wales, at a place called Tibooburra. It was told to me by a mate of mine, R. Paul Brady, and it comes from a book he wrote called *Silver, Lead and Saltbush*. It's a good read too, if you can get hold of a copy.

Now the name of Tibooburra comes from the Aboriginal word for 'heaps of rocks', which might give you some idea what the first white fellers came across; fellers like Charles Sturt who passed by in the mid-1840s, looking for the inland sea, then Burke and Wills, fifteen or so years later. So there wasn't too much to enthuse anyone until gold was discovered in the late 1880s. Of course, with the whiff of gold in the air, thousands of hopefuls soon arrived and so the town grew out of that.

But, when the gold days passed, the place lost its appeal, what with nine out of ten years being in drought, stinking hot summers, freezing cold winters and the winds, both summer and winter, so bad that you had to make sure the dunny door was shut or you'd lose it. Even into the 50s, when this story took place, Tibooburra still didn't have electricity or gas. So you had to be made of pretty stern stuff to live out there, which most people aren't and so, if you would've fired a shotgun down the main street, the chances of hitting someone would've been next to none.

Anyhow, there was this bloke in Tibooburra, see. A small, fat bloke. A bootmaker by trade. From Greece he was. His name was Peter Christapoulas or just Pete to his mates though, mind you, he didn't have too many mates because whenever he got a bit of coin he'd be off to the pub, where he'd get on the turps and try to pick a fight. Pete lived out on the Dead Horse Creek side of town in an old lean-to made from rusted corrugated iron and flattened old kerosene tins. Of course, being made from corrugated iron and kerosene tins, he was more or less open to the elements; like, if it was hot, he sweltered, if it was cold he froze. So that's where Pete lived and he lived on the smell of an oily rag, with just a mattress on the dirt floor, a bit of a stove, cupboards made out of fruit boxes.

But there was one event held in Tibooburra that attracted people from all over. It was the annual weekend race meeting, and even though it was on when the first chill of winter blew in, they'd still come from everywhere—Broken Hill, Menindee, Wilcannia; some even from as far as Quilpie and Thargomindah. And so, when this race meeting was on, all the station owners, ringers, shearers, bookies, bludgers and what-have-you, who came to town, took the opportunity to get their boots mended. So Pete'd be flat out with his tack hammer, raking in the dough.

Now there were two watering holes still standing from the olden days; one was Barney's Pub and the other was Tibooburra Hotel and so, after the race meeting was over, Pete'd be cashed up and he'd go on a binge. First port of call was Barney's but, after he'd had a few, sure enough, he'd try to pick a fight with some poor unsuspecting bugger and it wouldn't be long before Barney'd boot Pete out of his pub. 'Bugger off, Pete,' he'd say and out Pete'd stagger, out of Barney's, abusing everyone in Greek and he'd stumble over to Tibooburra Hotel, where he'd have a few more and try to pick a fight there. Loved a stoush he did. So it'd be, 'Bugger off, Pete,' and Pete'd stagger out of the Tibooburra, into the biting wind, and stumble home to his corrugated iron and flattened kerosene lean-to. That was his pattern after race weekend, night after night, till all the money was gone.

Anyhow, just after this particular race weekend, the local copper, Sergeant Bill Holmes, checked his wood heap and seeing that it was getting low he got in touch with the local odd-job bloke and organised a load. The only trouble was that, when the wood arrived, it arrived in an uncut state. Worse still, it was a mix of gidgee and mulga which, as you might know, are about the hardest woods to cut. Now, Sergeant Holmes had an aversion to physical activity so it was, 'Bugger it'. Then, just as he was thinking that he'd have to chop the lot himself, he heard a ruckus over at the Tibooburra Hotel. 'Here's a go,' he said and he strode over to the pub.

Of course, it's Pete, pissed as usual and throwing a few at some stockman or other who'd drifted in from Naryilco.

'What the bloody hell's goin' on here?' says the Sarg.

Pete says, 'This bastard won't pay me fer fixin' his boots.'

'Friggin' well did, Sarg,' says the stockman, 'but he's too pissed ter rememb'a.'

'Okay,' says Sergeant Holmes, 'I'll sort this out.' So the Sarg said to Pete, 'Pete, piss off home 'n' meet me at the station tomorra mornin'. I've got a little job fer yer.'

Nobody argued with Sergeant Holmes. Nobody. Not even Pete. And so it was, 'Okay, Sarg,' and Pete staggered out into another freezing night and headed back to his corrugated iron and kerosene tin lean-to.

Then the Sarg said to the stockman, ''N' you bugger off tomorra as well.'

'Okay,' said the stockman, and he staggered out the back, crawled into his swag and he pissed off at first light, swearing that he'd never come back to Tibooburra—for two reasons, Pete and the bitter cold.

Anyhow, next morning, there's Pete. He's at the police station. There'd been a black frost. He's shivering. The Sarg gives him an axe and a wheelbarrow and points him to the pile of wood. 'There yer go, Pete, chop that lot 'n' stack it nice 'n' neat over b' the house. It'll soon warm yer up.'

'But, Sarg?'

'No buts about it, 'n' I want it all done b' the time I get back from me rounds.' His rounds took in places like White Cliffs, Wanaaring and Milparinka. That's most of the day.

'Yeah, okay, Sarg.'

So the Sarg jumped in his truck and off he went and Pete gets stuck into the wood.

Pete was a bootmaker by trade—The Hansford Collection

Anyhow, it was a long day. As I said, you'd hardly get tougher timber than gidgee and mulga. But when the Sarg returned from his rounds, that evening, there was Pete finishing off the last of the wood and stacking it in a neat pile over by the house. The Sarg, he inspects the woodheap. 'Geez,' he says, 'I thought there would'a been more wood than that?'

'Well,' says Pete, 'what yer've gotta realise, Sarg, is that I cut it up so neat 'n' I packed it in so tight that it looks like there's less than what there is.'

'Yeah, suppose so,' says the Sarg. 'Well, off yer go 'n' fer Christ's sake, Pete, go easy on the piss or yer'll be back ter do another load.'

'Yes, Sarg,' says Pete, and off he went back home. Then when he got there, he knocked the top off a beer, dragged a chair over near the stove, put his feet up onto a nice pile of freshly cut gidgee and mulga and said, 'Here's ter you, Sarg.'

Tocumwal—NSW

If you're heading south, down the Newell Highway, then Tocumwal's the last town you'll get to in New South Wales, before you go over the Murray River into Victoria. From what I can gather the name comes from an Aboriginal word meaning something like 'deep waterhole', and according to legend a giant Murray cod lived in a waterhole there and it used to eat any children who fell in. That's what they say, anyway, and that's why there's a giant fibreglass Murray cod in the town square; you know, not to eat kids but because of this giant cod legend.

Then as far as European settlement goes, the area was first opened up round the mid-1800s and a feller called Hillson soon bought land along the river there and it's on that land the town was built. But it wasn't till ten years later that a punt arrived and, with that, like so many pre-Federation townships along state borders, a customs depot sprang up and the place began to kick along. Then a bridge was built in the late-1890s and the railway was connected to the New South Wales system at the beginning of World War I.

But the real heyday of Tocumwal was during World War II when the Yanks built the largest aerodrome in the southern hemisphere there. The project was classified and so the fact that I am about to tell you is not well known: the aerodrome facility spread over twenty-five square miles. It had something like four runways, each around two-and-a-half miles long, and they reckon there was anywhere up to 5500 men housed on the base. So she was a pretty big deal, ay?

So that's a brief rundown on the place, and like many of these small towns they've all had their fair share of famous people. For starters old Yabby Jeans, the renowned Australian Rules coach of St Kilda, he came from Tocumwal. And I believe that the brother of the ex-Footscray VFL footballer, the late-and-great Teddy Whitten, once owned a pub there. That's Don Whitten. Don also played a few games with Footscray before going bush and coaching and playing for Tocumwal. There's four pubs in the town so I'm not a hundred percent sure which one Don owned but it could well have been the Terminus Hotel—affectionately known by the locals as the 'Swinging Tit'.

Now, talking about well-known locals, of course, there's Whacker Day. Have you ever heard of him? Well, here's a yarn about Whacker. One of many. It basically goes like this: see, Whacker'd been drinking at the Swinging Tit and when he came home he found a note from his wife, on the kitchen table, explaining just where he could stick the now cold sausages, spuds, peas, carrots and gravy she'd spent hours cooking for him and, what's more, she'd gone to bed and didn't want to be disturbed.

Now, being the sort of bloke that always tried to obey his wife's every word, Whacker stuck his dinner in the rubbish bin then went out on the side verandah to try and make himself comfortable on the old couch. But, as it turned out, the bitch next door was in season—that's the dog, not the woman—and try as he might, he couldn't get to sleep because the racket that all the local male dogs were making was annoying the piss out of him. In the end, he got up, snuck outside, put the bitch in his ute and, with a string of dogs in tow, drove her ten mile out of town, dropped her off and said, 'Sort out yer own problems. I've got enough of me own.'

But, unfortunately, on his return journey, Whacker was pulled over by the new copper in town, a young constable. 'You've been drinking, sir,' says the constable.

'Yeah, but give us a break. I'm nearly home, mate,' says Whacker.

'Doesn't matter,' says the constable. 'I'm taking you down to the station.'

So the constable put Whacker in the back of the police car, took him to the police station, got him to empty out his pockets and commenced to book him for DUI (Driving Under the Influence). So Whacker's mid-way through being done for DUI when his best mate, the local Sergeant, arrived at the station, and when the Sergeant saw that Whacker was being booked, he pulled the young constable aside and explained that, when you're a copper in the bush, there are a few unwritten rules—like, never book your boss's best mate. In the end Whacker received a caution and the constable was ordered to chauffeur him back home.

'See yer later,' said the embarrassed constable, ''n' sorry for that.'

'Yeah, see yer,' Whacker mumbled. 'Thanks fer nothin'.'

Anyhow, after Whacker had waved the constable goodbye he went to grab the house keys out of his pocket only to discover that they were still back at the police station, along with his car keys and his wallet. Any rate, with Whacker realising just how much his wife needed her beauty sleep, the last thing he wanted to do was to go banging on the front door and disturbing her. So there he was, having a pee in the gutter, waiting for inspiration to strike, and it did. 'Geez,' said Whacker, 'there's a stepladder round the back. I'll just get in the verandah door and try and go back to sleep on the old couch.'

Now, why he needed a ladder to get in the verandah door was also a bit of a moot point around the Day household. See, Whacker's house was one of those that's built on stumps and while he'd eventually got the concrete pathway poured right up to the verandah door he was still yet to organise any steps from ground level up to the door. Things moved pretty slow in Whacker's life. Anyhow, there wasn't much he could do about it just now so Whacker decided to play fireman. He went around the back, got the stepladder, then he brought it around to the side of the house and he put it up against the verandah door, with the aim of climbing up, putting his hand through one of the broken louvres—another job she had on the list—and undo the lock on the inside of the door.

But, unfortunately, as he climbed the stepladder, he somehow missed his footing on the third and final rung. Down he came with an almighty thump, right onto the concrete footpath and knocked himself clean out, and breaking his arm in the process. So there he was, stone-cold out to it, and as Whacker tells it, 'When I come to there's the bloody bitch from next door, lickin' me face. She'd somehow found her way home and, what's more, she'd brung about fifty of her male mates with her.'

So that's a little story about Whacker, and he used to drink at the Swinging Tit, or the Terminus Hotel if you're a non-local. It's just a double-storey place, typical of most towns. It's directly across from the railway station, which reminds me of another story.

See, with Tocumwal being on the Newell Highway a lot of truckies passed through and, as it happened, the wife of the publican became a little too friendly with one of the fellers who carted wool to Melbourne. Anyhow, what he'd do was, he'd park his truck right next to the curb, outside the pub, and he'd get out of the cab and climb up on top of the stacked wool bales and over the balcony he'd go. Then he'd sneak across the verandah and through the open window, into one of the hotel rooms, where he'd meet up with the publican's wife. So they were having a fling.

The publican didn't have a clue that all this was going on and neither did anyone else, apart from a few of us regulars who soon put two and two together and came up with a dirty, stinking rat. Of course, no one allows this sort of thing to happen to a mate, especially when that mate's your publican. So whenever we saw the truck parked outside and the publican's wife having excused herself from bar duties, due to 'a bad headache', we'd casually remark to the publican, 'Geez, mate, there's a strange noise comin' from upstairs, yer'd better go 'n' investigate.'

The only trouble was that the staircase was very old and rickety and it made a lot of noise. So, as soon as the truckie and the publican's wife heard any noise, the truckie'd grab his clothes, slip out the window, onto the verandah, vault over the balcony and drop down onto his load of wool bales, then into his cab, start her up and away he'd go.

Now, it could well have even been Whacker—the master of the stable relationship—that came up with the idea in the first place.

But during one of these visits between the truck driver and the publican's wife, he and a couple of mates got together and they towed the truckie's truck forty feet or so further on down the street. After they'd done that they came back into the pub and said to the publican, 'Geez, mate, there's a strange noise comin' from upstairs, yer'd better go 'n' investigate.'

So off up the stairs trudges the publican. Meanwhile, the truckie hears these footsteps coming up the stairs. As quick as a flash, he grabs his clothes, shoots out of bed, through the open window, out onto the verandah, and it was only when he was halfway over the balcony that he noticed his truck wasn't where it should've been. 'Splat!'

'Serves the bastard right,' announced Whacker, before he headed off home to spend another night out on the side verandah, cuddled up with the bitch next door.

Tyringham—NSW

My name's Birdy Fahey. I'm nearly seventy but when I was about fifteen, I went out jackarooing on properties, then I took up shearing and went all over the place. Even went to New Zealand. Ended up back here, at Tyringham, where I come from, and managed a couple of places and ended up a fencing contractor. Got a bit of land. Just a few cattle and stock horses. I bred the stock horses. Oh, and I was at the Sydney Olympics opening ceremony, doing whip cracking.

Tyringham? Well, Dorrigo's twenty mile east, on top of the range, where it rains all the time, then Ebor's a bit further south. These days, there's only the shop and two houses and there's three or four houses close by. That's our little village. A few farms. Then there's an old sawmill and the hippy commune. But it's a good little spot. The history mainly surrounds the timber industry; sawmilling, logging and that. A lot of it's a nature reserve now. Mount Hyland Nature Reserve to be exact. Apparently there's lot of rare types of trees and that up in the bush there.

There used to be a 'plonk shop' here, as they called it, where you could buy wine. You could say it was a 'wine saloon'. The lady that owned it was Janet McLennan and her husband was Leon. They had both the plonk shop and the grocery shop, where you could also get some petrol. But, back a while now, the wine saloon burnt down. So then, with the bigger grocery shop being only about eighty metres down the road, Janet moved them both in together. So it's all combined: the store, the house and the plonk shop. And, when she moved it all in together, they got a licence to sell beer. So you can get any sort of alcohol there while you're doing your grocery shopping and you can fill up with petrol as well.

But Janet died about three years ago now and Leon died sort of six months after. You wouldn't believe it because both of them were that tough you couldn't have killed them with an axe. But, see, Janet had emphysema and, there one time, she couldn't get to her medication and so she choked to death. And Leon, well, he'd been knocked down by a cow a few weeks before and he got a tumour—like a little blood clot—and he just died from that. The grandson runs it now. But everyone still says they're going down to 'Janet's' for a drink.

Beer's never been on tap. It's just bottled beer and bottled wine. The licence says that you're supposed to take it away, see, but, what we normally do is that, when we all sit around having a few, you just go into the bar part and help yourself, then leave your bottle tops there and, when you've finished, say, you've got eight bottle tops, you just pay for them. That's because they don't have a licence like a pub does. So if anything happens—like if the coppers turn up or that—then you can tell them you're just sitting around having a drink as a house guest. And you are, more or less, because you haven't actually paid for anything, not until you leave the place you don't, and then it's too late. But nobody worries too much. So there's always ways of getting around things, ay.

I mean, even Russell Crowe comes up here on the odd occasion. He's got property down on the coast and, one time, back when Janet was alive, he and Tom Cruise come up the mountain, around through Tyringham on their motorbikes. Anyhow, they pulled up outside the shop and got a couple of drinks and all the hippies were down there talking to them and when they left someone said to Janet, 'You know who those two fellers were?'

Janet used to swear like bloody hell. 'Nah,' she said, 'who the fuckin' hell were they?'

'Tom Cruise and Russell Crowe.'

She says, 'Who the fuckin' hell's Tom Cruise 'n' Russell Crowe?

'They're big film stars.'

'Oh, I don't have time to watch bloody TV. I don't know any film stars.'

Then about two months later Russell Crowe come back with a few mates and they're having a drink and Janet's busy inside and so they're having a chat to some of the hippies and one of the hippy fellers yells out, 'Janet, Russell Crowe's out here 'n' he wants some petrol in his motorbike', and Janet yells out, 'Well, tell him he can get his own fuckin' petrol, just like anyone else, 'n' make sure the bastard doesn't piss off without payin' fer it.'

So that's just one little yarn. But the one I was involved in was when Leon had this toothache. This happened before he died and, see, I'd been out fencing and I'd just called in for a drink and, well, I've got a brother who's a dentist and so, somehow, Leon must've concluded that, just because I had a brother who was a dentist, I knew all about dentistry. Anyway, Leon says, 'Pull me tooth, Birdy.' By then he'd had a few rums to try and anaesthetise himself. Leon liked his rum, he did.

I said, 'Not on yer life.'

'No,' he said, 'you're my dentist. You do it.'

So he's sitting in the lounge chair, in the kitchen. Everybody's watching, and like I said, I'd just come in from fencing and so I had my fencing pliers with me. Well, fencing pliers are bigger than normal pliers. They'd be about nine inches long, with thick jaws on them. Like, they'd only fit in your mouth just as long as you had your gob stretched open, real wide. It was one of his molars, right up near the back.

Anyhow, I got the fencing pliers and I gave the molar a few roosts but the pliers kept slipping off the tooth. I just couldn't get a decent hold of it. See, I didn't have any cloth or nothing over the grips of the pliers and so they kept slipping. By then Leon's pretty well tranquillised himself with all the rum he's been drinking. Any excuse, ay? But, anyhow, I finally got a good grip and I latched onto it and I gave it one hell of a yank and out she come, eventually. But, geez, it hurt him alright; too right it did, even after all the rum he'd drunk.

So that was the first tooth I pulled. Then about twelve months later he had another one. I comes around there and this time he's all prepared. He's there waiting for me with a pair of his own pliers and a bit of cloth. 'Here, use these,' he says.

But I didn't like the look of it. See, his face was real swollen because there was an abscess there. 'Not on yer life,' I said. 'Go 'n' get a proper dentist ter pull it out.'

But he just wouldn't have a bar of it. He said, 'No, Birdy, you're my dentist. Come on, get stuck into it.'

There was about ten of us there then, some even sticking their heads through the window, having a look. One girl even took a photo. And so I grabbed hold of the tooth but, as soon as I touch it, it was that sore, he shot his head back with the pain of it all and, lo 'n' behold, it just came out. 'Pop!'

I said, 'Leon, you'd better get some disinfectant, like some mouthwash sort'a stuff, 'n' give it a bit of rinse or else it could become infected.'

He said, 'Bugger that, I'll just gargle a six-pack,' so he had another couple of rums and then he got stuck into a six-pack.

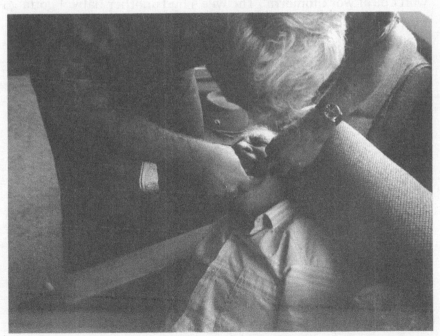

I got the fencing pliers and I gave the molar a few roosts—The Fahey Collection

Then I hadn't been down to Janet's for a few days and the next thing I hear is, he's in hospital, on a drip. But he got over that all right. So that was my go at a bit of dentistry, yeah.

But, oh, we've got some great old characters around here. One feller, his missus had left him. He's had a few beers and he's feeling pretty maudlin about it all and he says, 'Bugger it, I'm gonna jump off the Ebor Falls.' See, the Ebor Falls are just down the road a bit. 'I'm gonna end it all,' he says. 'I got nothin' ter live for, now.'

So he took off, then he turns up again a while later and someone says, 'What, did yer change yer mind?'

He says, 'Yeah.' He said, 'I looked over the side of the falls 'n' it looked too dangerous.'

Then there was another feller who worked in the sawmill. Jack was his name. I forget his last name. Jack was in his mid-forties and he was having a kid just about every year—well, his wife was. So he turns up at work one day and he says to the manager, 'I won't be at work tomorra'. The wife's had another baby. I gotta go inta town 'n' pick her up.'

The manager said, 'God almighty, how many have yer got now? That must be at least twelve, is it Jack?'

Jack says, 'Oh, I don't know about twelve.' He says, 'I think I've only got eleven, but that's not countin' the new one.'

Yeah, so there's always something going on here.

Windorah—Qld

Perhaps this is a bit of an odd one but I've always sort of wondered how someone could hang on to something for so long and for so little reason. I don't know. But it all happened at Windorah, a little place on Cooper Creek, in the south-west of Queensland. Windorah comes from the Aboriginal, meaning 'a place of large fish', and I can assure you there's some pretty good fishing to be had out there, too.

But that whole region, right through the south-west, is what's called 'the channel country'. It's great cattle and sheep area—cattle in particular. Now, I don't know what you know about the channel country but, when the flood waters come down, it's like nature's way of flood irrigation. Just south of Windorah I've seen the Cooper seventy miles wide. When that happens, the grass—mainly Mitchell grass—can grow taller than the cattle. True. And, when it dries out, the grass dries like hay and it retains all its goodness and the cattle just thrive on it. So, even though it mightn't have rained for two or three years, the stock remain in good condition. So that's what's called the channel country. Then added to that, around Windorah, you also get a blending of what they call the 'desert country', which is ridgy sort of sandy soil—huge, red sand hills—and everything that grows on those sandy ridges is sweet. So Windorah's a prime spot. In fact, the heaviest bullock ever to go through Cannon Hill bullock yards, near Brisbane, came from Mayfield Station, at Windorah.

So it's got the lot; top quality cattle, great fishing and the yabbies are pretty tasty as well. Actually, in more recent times, Windorah's gained a reputation for its annual International Yabby Races or 'the running of the yabbies' as I prefer to call it. That's held in early September and it's a hoot of a weekend.

Anyhow, I suppose it would've been around 1964. I was a First Officer with TAA. We were flying with a crew of four; Captain, First Officer, Hostess and Loader and we had a night stay-over out at Windorah. We arrived in the morning and, along with our passengers, we booked ourselves into the Western Star Hotel. Then, with not having to fly out till the following day, a few of us decided to spend the afternoon fishing, out on the Cooper. A feller who lived on the edge of town offered us a loan of his Land Rover, which was pretty normal practice, back then.

'She's not in the best'a shape so take her nice 'n' easy,' the feller said.

The Cooper was only about five k's out of town so we weren't going that far, anyway. 'Just as long as she gets us out there 'n' back,' we said.

'Yeah, she should do that.'

Now, a compulsory part of fishing on the Cooper is that you have to take a well-stacked esky along with you. And that's what we did. We loaded up the Land Rover and off we went to this spot of fishing. Then, during the afternoon, one of the station people came down and we had a barbecue. Beautiful. So by the time it came to head back into town we were in a pretty relaxed mood. Like, we weren't drunk or anything, just nice and mellow. I wasn't driving. The Loader was driving. Anyhow, we arrived back in town and we swung into the car park at the pub. But when the Loader put his foot on the brakes of this old Land Rover, nothing happened. No brakes. Straight through the front fence we went. 'Bang!' Down it went. I wouldn't say we decimated it but we gave it a pretty fair old whack.

So that was a bit of a shock. But what really shook us up even more was the attitude of the publican. Oh boy, didn't she take a dim view of the accident. She was ropeable. It was almost as if she thought we'd driven through her front fence on purpose. She went right off her scone. Nothing would placate her. We tried to apologise. We tried to offer to pay for the damage. We tried to sympathise with her. We tried to offer to get the fence fixed. We did everything to try and calm her down but, no, she wouldn't have a bar of it. She just went completely off her rocker. 'Out,' she said, "n' I never wanta see yer ugly faces in this establishment ever again', or words to that effect. So we were booted out of the pub. I forget where we ended up staying that night but it wasn't too much of a hassle and we flew out the following morning. And that was that, and I just passed it off that she must've had a real bad day and so she took it all out on us.

Then about two years later we were flying back from Birdsville. I had the same Loader with me; the same feller who'd driven through the fence. We landed okay at Windorah but then, on take-off, we had an engine failure so we had to take the passengers back into Windorah to stay overnight, while we had a spare engine flown out from Brisbane. When we rocked up at the pub, the front fence hadn't been fixed. This's odd, I thought. Because, like I said, we'd offered to pay for the damage and everything, all of which she'd refused. So we wandered inside. Then, the instant the publican saw me and my mate, she shouted, 'You two, I told yers before, yer not ter show yer ugly dials in here! Yer not welcome. Git! Both'a yers, git!'

Like, this's two years after the accident and she's going on like it'd just happened. Talk about someone harbouring a grudge, ay? Oh, the passengers, they were allowed to stay, alright, just not me or my mate. There was no way she was going to let us stay in her pub. 'Git,' she shouted, 'yer not welcome 'ere.'

Anyway, we ended up out at Mayfield Homestead, the same place that the heaviest bullock to ever go through Cannon Hill bullock yards came from. But, for the life of me, I don't know what was going on there, with the publican, and, what's more, when I passed through Windorah some forty years later, the fence still hadn't been fixed.

Winton—Qld

So we arrived in Winton, which is known as being the 'home of Australian bush poetry'. Winton's sort of out in the middle of Queensland, on the Landsborough Highway between Cloncurry and Longreach. It's got heaps of history. It was originally named Pelican Waterhole, back in the mid-1860s. Then, a few years later, when the postmaster arrived, the story goes, he got so sick and tired of having to write such a long name as Pelican Waterhole that he renamed it as Winton; the place in England where he was born.

It's actually a big cattle and sheep area. But, really, you'd have to say that its greatest claim to fame is that it's the place where Banjo Paterson wrote 'Waltzing Matilda', back in the late-1800s. I think he was visiting Dagworth Station at the time. Now, they say that, after he'd written the song, he gave it its first public airing in the North Gregory Hotel, at Winton. Well, to be honest, it's not the exact same hotel. The original hotel, the one where Banjo Paterson first performed 'Waltzing Matilda', was just an old bark and corrugated iron place. So it'd been burnt down and rebuilt a few times before Bob and I stayed there, along with lots of grey nomads. Of course, Bob and I are a long way off being grey nomads.

But, oh, it's such a gorgeous hotel. Though, mind you, I really don't think anybody out there seemed to fully appreciate the wonderful art deco of the place. Like, they had this beautiful dining room and that, but that was underused. Lovely art deco furniture. The bar area. You know, it was all there for people to appreciate though I'm not sure if too many did. Like, if the North Gregory was in a city, it'd be the place to go. But not out there. Out there, people are more into corrugated iron and bushy things like swaggies. And, oh my God, if ever I see another stuffed swaggie I'll just die. You know how you get stuffed scarecrows well, out there they've got all these stuffed swagmen. Oh, they're everywhere. It's like the high art of the outback to have a stuffed swaggie, stuck on a chair, you know, sitting out on your verandah, looking out over the street, waving hello. Oh, my God.

So it was a beautiful hotel. Then out on the grassed median strip, along the main drag, there were, say, six or so allotments of sculptures depicting the story of 'Waltzing Matilda'. Like, one might've been an installation of pistols, then another was of the horses and so forth, until you got to the very end of the street, where there was a billabong sort of thing, with some cast bronze pelicans around it, which was supposed to represent the billabong where the swagman drowned himself. And that was the story.

So, anyhow, Bob and I were staying at the North Gregory with all these oldies and, you know, we just wanted to mix with some people of our own age for a while. Now there's lots of pubs in Winton but there was one just across from the North Gregory that had a disco on a Friday night. It was, like, known as the 'young people's pub'. So it's Friday night and everyone's come into town to let their hair down. This place's packed out with a hundred or so young people. Not too many women. Mostly they were young guys who looked like they'd come in from off the outlying cattle stations. You know, the big hats, the jeans, the shirts, the cowboy boots. All that sort of gear. And, well, this disco bar, it didn't even have a mirror ball. All it consisted of was a couple of red, green, yellow and blue lights, flashing on and off, and an old juke box, blaring out songs from a decade or more ago.

So we were there and I was dancing by myself because Bob had wandered off to the toilet or somewhere. You know, you had to walk out the back of the pub, then down the side. So he was outside and this complete stranger—like, I hadn't even been talking with him or anything—well, he came up while I was dancing and he gave me a can of Dark 'n' Stormy. It's some sort of pre-mixed drink, like a rum and coke. I don't drink those sort of drinks but, anyhow, to be nice I said, 'Thanks' and I just put it down, thinking that Bob might drink it when he came back inside.

The original North Gregory Hotel was where Banjo Paterson first performed 'Waltzing Matilda'—The Hansford Collection

So I'm dancing away with myself, not taking too much notice of things, when another guy comes along. He's seen this can of Dark 'n' Stormy, just sitting there. He picks it up. It's full. It's nice and cold. He thinks he's scored a free drink and so he starts drinking it. I mean, I didn't care. But, anyway, the guy who'd given me the can in the first place, he certainly cared. It's like, to buy a woman a drink was some kind of ownership sort of thing. You know, 'What the fuck do yer think yer doin', knockin' off me bird's drink,' or something like that. So he's, like, up and he's into this other poor guy. Then, before I know it, there's about twenty or so guys going at it like it was the most excitement they'd had for weeks. So now I'm, inadvertently, the cause of this almighty punch-up.

Anyhow, the disco bar had about four French doors, which led out onto the main drag. You know, those doors that open up like a concertina, to let the air in when it gets too stuffy. Anyway, as soon as the fight started the bar staff started to shut them up. It was like it was a well drilled manoeuvre. So I'm guessing that Friday night free-for-alls were pretty much the norm and so they'd shut these French doors, as quick as possible, just in case the cops saw what was going on and closed the pub down. But it was like, 'boom, boom, boom' and the doors were closing. Now, there was no way I was going to stay in there with this fight going on so I managed to scoot out the last door just before it was shut.

Of course, Bob didn't have a clue that any of this was going on. He's still down the back somewhere, contentedly checking out the stars or whatever. So I just went and sat on a chair out on the median strip, where all the sculptures were. But then, after a while, I started to freak out. You know, like, Where's Bob? God, what if he goes back inside and gets involved in the fight. So I went around the back of the pub in the hopes of finding him. But we were like ships in the night, you know. While I'd been out on the median strip he'd come back into the disco, to find this hell of a brawl going on. Then, when I'd gone around the back of the pub, he'd somehow found his way out onto the median strip, looking for me. You know, we were just following each other around. Anyhow, in the end, I just thought, Blow this, and so I scooted back outside again and I found Bob sitting out on the median strip, and we scurried back to the safety of the North Gregory.

Then, in the morning, because our room was, like, directly across the road, we were woken by the tinkle, tinkle, tinkle of glass. And when we had a look they were sweeping heaps of broken glass out of the pub and shovelling it up.

So that's my memory of Winton; a pretty wild sort of place.

Wittenoom—WA

If there's any town in Australia that's gotten a bad name it's Wittenoom, in the Pilbara region of Western Australia, about 300 k's south of Port Hedland and around 1500 k's north of Perth. I mean, really, you'd have to have been living on Mars not to have heard about the problems with the asbestos mining, there. Just look on the net and you'll see Wittenoom described as being the 'home of Australia's greatest industrial disaster' and the 'valley of death'. Stuff like that.

Originally, it'd been a pastoral area. Then in the 1930s they started mining and eventually Wittenoom was built as a 'company town' for the miners and their families. And, from the early 1950s right through till the early 1960s, it supplied the asbestos for the building industry, for paper, for textiles. Asbestos was even used in brake linings for vehicles. But then it was discovered that the fibres could cause fatal diseases like mesothelioma, asbestosis and lung cancer. And that was about it, then.

How I got to Wittenoom was that my brother was running tours through the Wittenoom and Yampire Gorges and I went to visit him and then, you know, I ended up staying there for eleven years. And oh, it was just great. Oh, we had some good times— boozy times—wonderful people. A great community. I was living in an old convent. See, by that stage, people had started suing the government for mesothelioma and all that and so they were trying to shut the place down and, well, the convent belonged to the Catholic Church and they were going to sell it to the government who was then going to knock it down. But then a group of people got together and they bought the Convent with the idea of it being used for tourist accommodation. So after they did it up they needed somebody to run it. That was me, and I'd take my brother's overflow of mostly backpackers.

Oh, I did lots of things. I also drove the ambulance and I worked in the takeaway because, see, when I first arrived, there wasn't a fuel stop along the road between Newman and Port Hedland and so, if you needed fuel, you had to come into Wittenoom. So there were still enough visitors to keep a few of the businesses going. But then they decided to put an end to that as well and they built a roadhouse out on the main road. But we were still living out there at Wittenoom. We had the air testers and all that. But there was nothing. I mean, there were people who'd lived there far longer than me—you know, people that smoked and drunk, like most of us did—and there was nothing wrong with them. It was pure air. A lot better than Perth, most of the time.

I think that all that bad stuff mainly affected those who'd worked in the mines for years or the kids who'd grown up there. Because, see, they used to dump all the asbestos tailings on the

Apparently there are even signs telling you to pay careful attention to the warning signs—
The Hansford Collection

hillside and, of course, kids being kids, they'd get sheets of tin and they'd slide down these mountains of tailings, like they were on a ski slope. And at that stage no one knew any better so they'd also use the asbestos in their gardens and around the schools, on the roads, at the race track, even out at the airport.

These days I hear there's less than fifty people living there. It's virtually a ghost town. The shops are boarded up. There were two schools. They're now closed, of course. The cinema's gone. Everything that had, at one time, been part of a busy mining town, like the pub and all that, well, they've long gone. Now I've been told there's danger signs everywhere, you know, warning people not to go near the asbestos tailings and how they cause cancer and so on. Apparently there's even signs telling you to pay careful attention to the warning signs.

But it was such a beautiful spot—absolutely beautiful, especially up through the gorges. Anyhow, I ended up managing the caravan park and I remember this old fellow; his father had been a mine manager at Wittenoom. So he'd gone to school there then, when he was a teenager, he helped bag the asbestos. So he was in the thick of it, really. But he and his wife, they lived in Sydney and he was having chest problems and the doctors told him that he was dying and they advised him that, if he wanted to prolong his life, he should get out of the city and go to a dryer climate. So he came back to Wittenoom, thirty years after he'd left. He and his wife were on this nostalgic trip. And we got talking and, you know, just like me, he was saying how his time in Wittenoom had been the happiest years of his life.

So, you know, Wittenoom, it was the most beautiful place on earth, and yet, on the other hand, it was also the most tragic.

Yantanabie—SA

Well, I'm at Streaky Bay these days, sitting down getting bloody lazier and lazier, but it was at a place called Yantanabie where I spent most of me life. Yantanabie's also over here on the west coast of South Australia.

There was nine of us kids in the family; five girls and four boys. Dad first bought the block of 3300 acres at Yantanabie, back in 1941, and we went there to live in about '47 or '48. It was a wheat- and sheep-farming property and the town itself was a railway place—a fettler's camp—between Port Lincoln and Ceduna. I'd say there would've been about twenty-five or thirty people. There would've been about six or seven blokes who worked on the railway gang and their wives and kids. It had a school, with just the one teacher. He was generally a married bloke and so he and his wife might've had a kid or two in tow and there was a nice dance hall and a store and a post office and a few other odds and sods. But, see, there wasn't a pub ... and I'll get to that. But, oh, she was a real goer of a place, just like a lot of them towns were, in those early horse-and-cart days. But then, with the invention of motor cars and better roads, a lot of them little places went by the board.

So the town's all gone now. All gone. And just on this pub business; a feller said to me, one time, he said, 'John,' he said, 'the only place that'll survive is a place where there's a silo.' But he was wrong, in my opinion, because the only place that'll survive is a place where there's a pub. True; because I know plenty of places that's got a silo and bugger all else. But where there's a pub, there's always something, even if it's just a house or two. You can just about guarantee it.

Any rate, the rail went through Yantanabie in 1924 and I was born in '26 so I don't remember much about that early part. But it was all steam trains in them days and there was a big underground tank to catch the surface water and there was also a big shed that covered two and a quarter acres, with a big galvanised roof, and they caught the water off that to use for the trains.

So then, when my niece rang the other night to say that you were going to ring and ask me some questions about Yantanabie, you know, I'd forgot who she was. Then it struck me; it was Pam, and I thought, Well, bugger me. So that alerted me and yesterday afternoon I started writing down some stories related to Yantanabie. Look, is there any remuneration in this? Nothing? Geez, that's a bit stiff because my eldest daughter, she wrote a story related to living in a dug-out and she sent it off to the *Grassroots* magazine and weeks and weeks went by and, eventually, they wrote back to her and they sent her a cheque for seventy dollars. So she was tickled pink.

Anyway, after the daughter got paid from the magazine, she said I should write a story related to a fox whistle. So I done a bit

*The rail went through Yantanabie in 1924—*The Carter Collection

of research related to it and, you know, there's bugger all ever been written about a fox whistle. See, a fox whistle's like a decoy, like a duck whistle. You blow this whistle and it imitates the squeal of a rabbit in distress and it brings the fox. You know, as if that's caught in a trap or it's been caught by a dingo. Anyhow, I sent the story into the *Grassroots* people but I don't know what they've done with it. But, oh, I've also got reams and reams of stuff here related to horseracing on the west coast. I've been writing that down and gathering it up and getting it together for a bloody good while now, hoping to get it into a book form. But I can't type and this's supposed to be all typed up, you see.

Yantanabie? Oh, that's right; well I haven't finished writing that down yet. Like, I don't even know how the place got its name. But there was a well of water there, in the early days, before the trains, and that was the only good water within thirty mile. Oh, it was wild old country back then, and my mother was born in 1900 and she lived most of her life around the area and this well, it had a windmill and it went down 190 feet and they used the water out of that well back when she was a kid. Then, apparently, away back, even before then, there was also another well at Yantanabie, but my mother couldn't ever remember that second well ever being in production.

Any rate, my old grandfather, he was a boundary rider and a shearer and a bushman and, see, he'd be away for weeks at a time and he had a pretty good vegetable garden there on the flat by the well. Oh, he just loved his garden, he did. It was the good water, you see, so he could just about grow anything. Anyhow, the rabbit plague was on and he'd put this big rabbit-proof fence all around his garden so none of the rabbits could get in and eat the vegetables. Then, one time, my grandmother called all the kids in for tea and they didn't come home. So down goes Grandfather and he caught one of his sons, Bob—Bob was only about ten or eleven at the time—well, he caught him and he give him a bloody good hiding for not coming home when he was told to. And so Bob runs back to the camp and as he goes he grabs this big yellow rabbit and he stuffs it up his shirt. Then, when he got home, he dropped it over the bloody rabbit-proof fence and he said, 'I hope he eats all the bloody old man's cabbages.' So, yes, Grandfather went to a lot of trouble to fence all the rabbits out but then Bob dropped one in there and it got stuck into all the veggies. And wasn't Grandfather crooked about that.

But it was a great life. We made our own fun and we did a lot of things that kids haven't got time to do now. We'd go out and kick a football and play a bit of cricket, go kangarooing, set a few rabbit traps. All that sort of thing. These days life's gotten too fast, in my opinion. Then, later on, I was about five years with the rodeos. Oh, I went all the way from Rockhampton, in Queensland, to Perth, in Western Australia. I even won the South Australian Buckjumping Championships back in '53, I think it was. Actually, we were on the bus going to Perth, one time, and a bloke and his son were in the seat in front of us and there was a woman in the seat behind us and this woman—the one in the seat behind—she and I got talking and when we got along the Eyre Highway a bit, to a little place to have some afternoon tea, this guy, the one who was sitting in front of me, he said, 'Are you gonna write a book?'

I said, 'What?'

He said, 'What you 'n' that woman have been talking about is what the kids are gonna be wanting to read about in twenty years time,' and he come from Tumut, up in the snowy country. So I've been at it ever since, writing down bits and pieces and now I need it all to be typed out. But have you read the Streaky Bay book? We all wrote various stories for that and I wrote a story about the early days of the blacks—the Aboriginals—and we got a feller to compile it and I was in the council one time and this compiler feller, he said, 'Are you the guy who wrote the story related to Corroboree Lake?'

I said, 'Yes.'

He said, 'That's a bloody good story.'

So I've got all these bits and pieces here but I need someone to type them in. Any rate, good to have a yarn to you, and I'll finish this story off about Yantanabie and I'll send it over. So, sorry I haven't got anything I can tell you about. But when you go travelling, you just have a good look around the place and I'll guarantee you that you'll come across plenty of little places that's got a silo but bugger all else. But where there's a pub, I'll guarantee you that there'll always be something; you know, at least a house or two.

Youanmi and Sandstone—WA

Well, Youanmi and Sandstone are two remote towns out in Western Australia's Murchison Goldfields area. Their heyday was the 1890s into the early-1900s. But, as a teacher in Perth, I took students out that way several times in the mid-to-late 1970s, out on camping safaris into the outback.

We'd sometimes have lunch at the settlement of Youanmi. Gold was first found there back in 1896. The place name comes from an Aboriginal word 'Youani' which some say was a type of mulga tree from around there, while others say it related to what the Aborigines called a bob-tailed goanna. Youanmi had long been a ghost town. While we did manage to find the cemetery, no buildings remained. The sports ground was overgrown with mulga scrub but there was still the cracked concrete cricket pitch, plus the remains of a brushwood shade house and the timber framed scoreboard. We even found some of those old tin numbers that were hung on the scoreboard to display the score.

But the main legacy of Youanmi was the huge open rubbish tip. Nothing had been added to it for years. Even the crows had abandoned the place. So it proved a wonderful history lesson about the lives, trials and lifestyles of our early goldfields pioneers; one that no classroom could match. Mostly, the things we found were made of metal, glass, china, stoneware—no plastics, of course—and there were also curled up, cracked, leather straps and footwear. And, because it doesn't rain much up that way, a lot of the metal stuff hadn't rusted much so we'd find old hurricane lamps and those little enamel 'Wee Willie Winkie' candle holders. Remember them? There were horseshoes and the metal buckles plus other pieces from bridles and saddlery. There were wash tubs, coiled wire springs, lengths of wire cable, chipped enamel mugs and plates, old cutlery, tobacco tins. We even found bent or crushed metal toys. At one stage the kids couldn't work out what the 'very small horseshoes' they found were used for until I explained how they were from the heels of men's leather-soled work boots.

Also, there were thousands of food cans, still with the solder seals in their lids. We found sardine-tin keys, vestas tins, bottles of all shapes and sizes; like old ink bottles, pickles bottles, olive oil bottles, medicine bottles, cool drink and cordial bottles, beer, port and spirits bottles and such. We also found sauce and other condiments bottles with their glass stoppers and lots of bulbous brown Bovril bottles. Of course, a lot of the glass was broken and some of the clear glass had taken on a mauve or purple hue, which apparently happens when the salt in the glass reacts to years of strong sunlight. And, rest assured, there's plenty of sunlight at Youanmi.

We even came across a couple of those heavy, cast-iron, cylindrical weights, out of window sashes, plus old latches, locks and keys, iron brackets and hinges, even bits from horse-drawn carts, early bicycles, motor cars and trucks. And I can tell you, those rusty oval-shaped dashboards looked ghostly with their empty instrument sockets. There were also lots of those black carbon rods out of batteries. In one spot there was a stack of old dunny pans—the backyard thunder boxes, as they were called back in those days. Even the insides of some were still coated with a thick layer of black tar.

But time was always against us and we'd have to move on. So we'd all jump back into our convoy of vehicles then head north-east for another ninety kilometres to Sandstone. Sandstone was still a town, but only just. I'd say, by the late '70s, the population would've been down to less than twenty. In its heyday Sandstone had several pubs and a population of, perhaps, several thousand, mostly living under canvas; tents and that. But, when we were there, there was just the one pub standing, in the extra wide street. Then there was the general store, the shire office and yard and just a handful of weatherboard and iron cottages and an old golf course.

The pub was the only solid masonry building. The general store had the old-style petrol bowser; the type where you had to hand-pump the petrol up into the top glass cylinder. Then inside the store, one wall had rows of Mills and Wares biscuit tins that'd been labelled with the name of the sheep station for which mail and orders were held. Actually, the Shire of Sandstone claimed to be the largest local government area in Australia, and maybe it still is. There'd even been a railway out to Sandstone but that'd long since been abandoned though the old tank stand, that supplied water for the steam engines, still stood, stark against the skyline of the flat desert landscape.

The few old cottages had seen better days. Most of the gardens had long been abandoned and their fences and gates were sagging, broken or missing altogether. Just a few bedraggled feral cactus plants showed a little green here and there. The golf course still had a bit of a shed and the 'putting greens' were oiled, black sand. And on each 'green' there was a piece of pipe fixed to a handle that would've been used to smooth the black sand surface for putting. Actually, there was still a water tank there because we used to camp there overnight so everyone could have a shower.

The Sandstone Shire office had an interesting collection of photos from the boom-time. One photo even showed the huge crowd greeting the arrival of the first train. That was in the early 1900s. We were also told about the schools out that way and how, as the gold ran out, they'd lose numbers and have to be closed down. Then, apparently, the shire grader driver had something like five kids and whenever the Inspector of Schools was due to arrive and assess the viability of, say, a little one-teacher school, somewhere south, the shire would send the grader driver off to grade the roads down that way. The logic there was that he'd take his family and the addition of his five children to the ailing school would deem it a viable proposition and it'd be allowed to struggle on for another year or two. So he was a well-travelled grader driver.

Another place we visited was called London Bridge. That was at the end of a bush track just south-east of the town. London

Bridge was an unusual rock formation, set in some breakaway country. It had a great arch or bridge of rock. In the shire office I saw a grainy photo which showed a horse and buggy on the top of it. Then nearby London Bridge there was a cave which had a crudely cemented floor. That's where they brewed their local drop in the early days, before refrigeration. Of course, the cave was an ideal spot because it was the coolest place to store the all important beer stocks.

But what most intrigued me was the electricity generator that was still supplying power for the shire office, the pub, the shop and the odd cottage or two. See, when we arrived we heard an old diesel engine tonking away. So we followed a straggly line of poles and wires to an old iron shed, which had a blackened exhaust pipe chuffing diesel smoke into the sky. Now this generator was strategically positioned just far enough out in the bush so that the noise wasn't too intrusive in town, yet it was still close enough for whoever had the job of having to wander out there to turn the generator off at night and then refuel and restart the thing each morning; which meant that Sandstone only had power from whenever the engine was started each morning till ten o'clock each evening, when it was shut off.

But what caught my eye in that shed, with its oily red dust, was the ingenious way they'd set up the engine so it'd stop itself at around ten o'clock every night. Clearly someone had got sick of having to walk out into the bush to turn the thing on and off, especially when the cold desert nights got down to zero degrees. Plus, I guess, there was the chance of stumbling across a snake or whatever. Anyway, to save the poor person this unfortunate trial, what they'd done was, they'd crudely fixed an old wind-up alarm clock onto the top of the diesel engine. It was one of those round-faced, bedside clocks. Now this particular clock had long lost the bell and hammer. The glass was also long gone from the clock face. The minute hand was gone, too. But the hour hand was still there and, here's the thing; the hour hand had a length of cord tied to it. Then the other end of the cord was tied to the fuel cut-out mechanism on the engine. And this length of the cord was so carefully adjusted that, when the hour hand reached ten o'clock, the taut cord pulled the fuel cut-out and the engine stopped for the night. Automatic! I mean, it's just amazing how ingenious we can get when it comes to looking after our own creature comforts, isn't it?

Yunta—SA

This was told to me by an old mate of ours, 'Sooty', who, unfortunately, is no longer with us. Sooty worked in the film industry and, one time, he was in his truck, heading up the Barrier Highway from Adelaide to Broken Hill for a job. He might've been taking his generator up there for a television commercial or a film. Something like that. Anyhow, he arrived at a place called Yunta, which is a bit over halfway along the journey.

This's back in the late 1980s and there wasn't too much left at Yunta by then. Its glory days had past. I mean, it'd never been that big but it had some sort of history. Like, back in the 1880s, it'd been a watering point along the stock route, from Cockburn, on the New South Wales border, down to the railhead at Terowie. Then later on, it'd been a railway service town—though it was no longer. So, by now, the population would've only been, say, fifty or seventy. There were a couple of service stations to cater for the passing traffic, a small primary school, basic emergency services, a pub, a bit of a post office. But that's about it.

Anyhow, Sooty was a real pub aficionado so, having never visited the Yunta Hotel, he decided not to let the chance pass. He stopped his truck, got out and in he went. The pub was a pretty bleak sort of place. You know, the usual outback single-storey type that'd weathered its fair share of good times, bad times and the lack of a local painter and decorator. Only a couple of people were in the bar; the publican, who seemed surprised to see a customer drift in, and an old bloke at the bar, who looked like he was part of the furniture. Sooty described him as being a weather-beaten sort of character, wearing a battered Akubra hat and clothes in need of a good washing machine. A cigarette dangled from his lips and half a schooner of beer was sitting in front of him. Anyhow, after Sooty ordered a beer, he got talking to this old bloke about this and that and about how hot, dry and dusty it was and when it last rained in Yunta.

'Rain? Christ, what's that?'

'So, what do yer do?' Sooty asked.

The bloke said, 'Nothin' much, not since the railways left town.'

"N' what did yer do on the railways?'

The old feller said, 'Fettlin'. Fifty miles up the rail line this way 'n' fifty miles down the rail line that way.'

Sooty said, 'Oh, yeah, 'n' what keeps yer occupied these days?'

The feller looked into his glass of beer, shook his head and said, 'Nothin' much, not since the wife left me. Just hang around the pub.'

'Oh yeah, 'n' when did yer wife leave yer?'

And the old feller he sort of looked out into nowhere, like he's, you know, like he's counting back the years to pinpoint the precise date his wife had left him. Not even a prime-mover blowing past the pub disturbed his concentration. Then, finally, he took a drag on his cigarette, a sip of his beer and said, 'I'm not exactly sure what year it was she left me but I know she was on'ter her second bottle'a Angostura bitters.'

The Ending—Derby—WA

One of the great pleasures about writing books like these is that I occasionally get to travel and to sit and talk to the people who are telling me their stories. I remember when I was working on *More Great Australian Flying Doctor Stories* and we took a trip up into the Kimberley region of Western Australia, where the small town of Derby has a RFDS Base. From Adelaide we flew across the Nullarbor to Perth, where I met up with Jan and Penny Ende, who'd worked as a pilot and a flight nurse with the RFDS. Then from Perth we flew up to Broome where we hired a car to undertake the last leg of our journey.

We didn't stick around Broome that long. See, I prefer to settle in a bit and get the feel of a community and the chances of being able to do that in a place like Broome is pretty slim. I mean, it was packed with tourists and their four-wheel drives and their caravans and their loud shirts and their loud voices and their hustle and bustle. Then there were the manicured resorts and expensive holiday-housing developments.

So, no, not for us and we headed north to Derby the following day. Derby's the focal point for so much of the Kimberley. The Royal Flying Doctor Service works out of Derby. School of the Air once spread the word of education throughout the area from its Derby base. The local hospital services the region. Though, mind you, Derby wouldn't be for everyone. Derby's a rusty-dusty, boab environment, with wide streets and buildings in various states of repair and/or disrepair. There's no flash resorts or sandy foreshore, just vast mudflats where signs warn of lurking crocodiles. The mangrove swamps appear and disappear in the yo-yo of ten metre tides. Yes, ten metre tides. And there's the ever-present Aboriginal population, where many keep up their nomadic traditions by spending their days wandering down to one end of the town—say, the jetty end—only to turn around and wander back to the other end of town, timing their arrival at the grog shop to just before it shuts.

And Derby's a 'barra' town. Just about everywhere we went and everything we did, barramundi was either top of the menu or at the heart of the conversation. We went to a mud-footy match where all the various fundraising organisations had set up their barbecues and were cooking barramundi in just about every way imaginable; barra-burgers, baked-barra, barra-fillet, barra-cutlets and so on. Out at the jetty, the restaurant's prize dish was a seafood platter, which consisted of a few oysters, a few prawns, a few calamari rings, smothered in a mountain of barra-wings. The bloke at the fishing shop reckoned he could take us 'to a hundred spots where the barra just about leapt into the boat. Guaranteed. The biggest. The best. The tastiest.' If someone in the street had shouted, 'Barra!', I reckon everyone would've stopped and pricked their ears in expectant excitement.

And we liked Derby. It's the type of town where you could stop someone in the street and, more often than not, they'd take time to have a yarn and tell their stories; like the bloke, Baitsie, who we met on the dirt road, out to the cemetery. Baitsie was riding his gopher, with a respirator attached and tubes up his nose. He had emphysema so he could only talk in part sentences. Yet, he gave us his time. We chatted. He said he'd just been out visiting his son's grave. Apparently there'd been some sort of a medical bungle—nothing to do with the RFDS. He pointed and said, 'You'll find ... his grave ... over there' then he choofed off, back home, the whirring sound of the electric gopher being punctuated by sharp shots of air from his respirator. Then, when we got to the spot in the cemetery, we came across a small cracked-concrete grave and gouged into a piece of tin were the words 'my loving son—murdered by two doctors'.

People like that; people who were prepared to share their tragedies as well as their joys. Actually, now I'm thinking about it, that attitude seemed to have also rubbed off on the tourists. These were mainly grey nomads who, in the evenings, would gather out along the jetty, with their barra dinners, and a simple, 'G'day' could turn into a long chat about anything from friends, family, retirement, superannuation, road conditions and the best and worst spots to visit. And, all the while, below the jetty, the turgid-muddy water tried to rip itself apart and above, a spectacular sunset cushioned itself into the horizon.

So, in our short time, we met and I interviewed as many people as possible and we joined in as many activities as we could. We visited the Leprosarium. We went to the outdoor picture show and it didn't matter that the film was one of the worst we'd ever seen because our attentions were more focused on the canopy of stars. So we played a game of counting the shooting stars.

We also went to an auction of local Aboriginal art. It was, seemingly, a whites-only show, held in the local Sportsman's Club. I'm not sure why there were only white people there. I don't know. But, the thing is, see, I'd never been to an art auction. I'd only caught glimpses on TV, you know, of places like Christies and Sotheby's where everything's so calm, intense and well

Having a chat to Baitsie—The Marsh Collection

mannered. This was different. The set up here was that—if you can imagine—there was a larger space, presumably where dances and that could be held. This was where all the art was displayed on tables, so that you could have a look before the auction began. Then, to the side of that area, there was a small bar in an alcove. Out the back of the bar was a busy kitchen. Anyhow, as the art auction unfolded, most of the locals crowded into the alcove-bar area and got stuck into the grog while the buyers, some from as far as Melbourne and Sydney, sat on plastic chairs, in a section of the larger area, sipping champagne.

The auctioneer was the co-ordinator from one of the local Aboriginal communities. His aim was to sell the art to the punters and the money would be shared amongst the artists and their community. He stood at a lectern. The poor bugger didn't have a microphone so he battled to be heard above the din coming from the alcove-bar. But he must've been seasoned at this because, to keep everyone's focus on the auction, he'd coerced four female teenagers to help him out. They were at that awkward age between innocence and awareness and were dressed up to the nines, in hot-pants and revealing tops. Then, when the bidding was about to start, they'd grab the artwork and parade it around like the bikini-clad women do in a boxing ring, with the numbered placards, in-between rounds.

So, yes, Derby may not be for everybody. But Derby is Derby, and that's what we liked about it; its contradictions. Simple yet complex. Tranquil yet tragic. Just like the night of the art auction where high-brow art dealers mingled with down-to-earth locals, shy beauties paraded themselves to drunken cat-calls, whistles and rude remarks, while a white feller struggled to do his best for his black community. And, amid the chaos of all this, a voice from the kitchen would occasionally blurt out over the public address system, 'Number twenty-six, yer barra 'n' chips is ready!'

More Great Australian
FLYING
DOCTOR
STORIES

Bill 'Swampy' Marsh

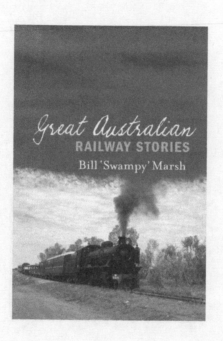

Great Australian
FLYING DOCTOR
STORIES

Bill 'Swampy' Marsh

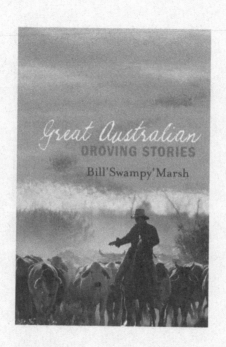

Great Australian
DROVING STORIES

Bill 'Swampy' Marsh

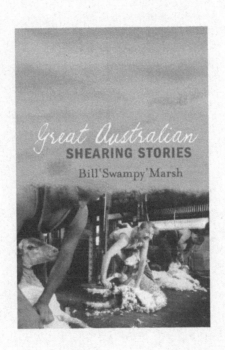

Great Australian
SHEARING STORIES
Bill 'Swampy' Marsh